S0-BDT-619

FORTUNATE SON

The unlikely rise of Keith Urban

JEFF APTER

MASSANUTTEN REGIONAL LIBRARY
DISCARD
Harrisonburg, VA 22801

WILLIAM HEINEMANN: AUSTRALIA

For Diana

A William Heinemann book
Published by Random House Australia Pty Ltd
Level 3, 100 Pacific Highway, North Sydney NSW 2060
www.randomhouse.com.au

First published by William Heinemann in 2009

Copyright © Jeff Apter 2009

The moral right of the author has been asserted.

All rights reserved. No part of this book may be reproduced or transmitted by any person or entity, including internet search engines or retailers, in any form or by any means, electronic or mechanical, including photocopying (except under the statutory exceptions provisions of the *Australian Copyright Act 1968*), recording, scanning or by any information storage and retrieval system without the prior written permission of Random House Australia.

Addresses for companies within the Random House Group can be found at www.randomhouse.com.au/offices.

National Library of Australia
Cataloguing-in-Publication Entry

Apter, Jeff, 1961–.
Fortunate son: the unlikely rise of Keith Urban.

ISBN 978 1 74166 808 7 (pbk).

Urban, Keith.
Country musicians – Australia Biography.

781.642092

Cover images courtesy Getty Images
Cover design by Darian Causby/www.highway51.com.au
Internal design by Midland Typesetters, Australia
Typeset by Midland Typesetters, Australia
Printed and bound by The SOS Print + Media Group

Random House Australia uses papers that are natural, renewable and recyclable products and made from wood grown in sustainable forests. The logging and manufacturing processes are expected to conform to the environmental regulations of the country of origin.

10 9 8 7 6 5 4 3 2

CONTENTS

ACKNOWLEDGEMENTS

Firstly, a heartfelt thanks to Pippa Masson, Meredith Curnow, Brandon VanOver and Nikki Christer, without whom this book would not exist.

My thanks also go out to the following people, who in their many and varied roles – guru, adviser, confessor, insider, *even host* – also played their part in helping this book come together:

Bob Allen; James Blundell; Peter Blyton; Leisa Bye; Cheryl Byrnes; Jeff Chandler ('Galveston' will never be the same); Peter Clarke; Jewel and Barry Coburn; Cameron Daddo; Dan Daley (the Nashville connection); John Elliott; Marius Els; Tommy Emmanuel; Nick Erby; Rob Fisher; Radney Foster; Brian Harris; Kevin Harris; Marlon Holden; Todd Hunter; Fiona Kernaghan; Kris Katsanis; Rod Laing; Narelle Lightfoot; Kirk Lorange; Ged Malone; Angie Marquis; Joy McKean; Kirsty Meares; Gina Mendello; Mark Moffatt; Glen Muirhead; Mark O'Shea; Joanne Petersen; Nik Phillips; Jeremy Potts; Rob Potts; Rick Price; Bob Regan; Sherry Rich Plant (www.sherryrich.com / www.themudcakes.com); Neil Richards; Bob Saporiti (aka Reckless Johnny Wales); Mike Smith; Rhianne Smith; Craig Spann; Deb Suckling; Cat Swinton; Paul Urbahn;

Jeff Walker; Rob Walker (the host with the most); Tom Wall; Biff Watson; Tim Wedde; Tutti Westbrook; Neil Wickham; Jon Wolfe.

A special nod goes out to Chrissie Camp, a true believer who offered sage advice at various stages of the project. Her help and generosity brought some real clarity to this book, while her dog brought a smile to my daughter's face.

And, of course, my hat goes off to Keith Urban, a man who's stared down more than his share of demons to fulfil what he always considered to be his destiny. The world could use a few more dreamers like him.

Prologue

METRO THEATRE, SYDNEY, 21 MARCH 2007

Keith Urban has good reason to look satisfied. The New Zealand-born singer and guitar-slinger is on stage at Sydney's cosy Metro Theatre, a 900-odd-capacity venue that's more likely to host indie rock acts than your everyday, 21st century country-pop superstar. And the Metro is positively Lilliputian in comparison with the concrete super-bunkers Urban's been packing with bottom-line-pleasing regularity over the past half dozen years, right across the country music heartland (America, that is, not Tamworth). But Urban doesn't seem to mind this temporary downsizing. In fact, he seems pleased that, just for once, he can actually see the people as he gazes out from behind his trademark floppy fringe, rather than merely glimpsing them somewhere off in the distance, their mobile phones held aloft, blinking in the night.

The event is a 'secret' showcase gig – a preview of his latest album of slickly crafted, listener-friendly twang-pop, *Love, Pain & the Whole Crazy Thing*. In the crowd is a collection of hardcore true believers who've scored much-sought-after tickets for the show, alongside the usual music biz players who are nursing free beers and whispering bad jokes about how Urban, recently sprung from rehab, looks like he could use a drink. Urban, quite frankly, doesn't care about the makeup of the crowd or the bitchiness of the local media. He's just happy to be back on a stage, with his guitar, playing for the faithful. He's emerged from a year that has put a whole new spin on the term 'emotional rollercoaster', and this wildly received show – 'We Love You Keith' banners and all – is just the sort of homecoming the guy could use. Soon enough, of course, he'll be back for big-ticket shows at Sydney's Acer Arena, but for now, this will do.

Tonight, Urban is flanked by a six-piece band, each member a musical all-rounder, all of whom seem just as thrilled to be back in a world they understand: playing live, rather than sitting at home worrying about their boss's health. Among the band members is bassist Jerry Flowers who, admittedly, is a hard guy to miss. Tall enough to pass for a basketballer, but built like a brick outhouse, Flowers's head is shaved so cleanly that the stage lights occasionally reflect straight off his sweat-drenched skull. This is a guy with way more stage presence than your average Nashville sideman. In fact, he looks more suited to a gig as some big-screen bad guy. Flowers has been there for a good part of Urban's now lengthy career, from early days in America with country-rock contenders The Ranch, through his gradual rise to the top and now as part of the band backing a guy who currently rules the roost. Sidekick and confidant, Flowers has seen, from close proximity, Urban's struggle to deal with addictions and the machinations of the music industry, and has kept right on playing (and not talking). If you could hope for one guy to be watching your back, it would be Flowers.

As clichéd as the album title may be, *Love, Pain & the Whole Crazy Thing* neatly sums up Urban's past year. It started with the high-profile, paparazzi-heavy Sydney wedding, on 25 June 2006, to Australia's current queen of Hollywood, Nicole Kidman, after a relatively swift romance and the usual round of denials. Of course, this wasn't the first coupling of country music star and big-screen starlet: Julia Roberts and Lyle Lovett, and Renée Zellweger and Kenny Chesney, had beaten Urban and Kidman to the altar. But that didn't make their union any less unlikely: she the former Mrs Cruise, he a star in America but still relatively unknown at home – *and what was with that stubble?*

But the confetti had barely been swept off the steps of the stately Cardinal Cerretti Chapel when word started circulating that there was trouble in paradise. Urban, ensconced in the studio, working on the album that was intended to firmly establish his multi-platinum stardom and extend his empire beyond Middle America, had fallen off the wagon with a sickening thud. In fact, he didn't so much fall as stumble off the wagon, bottle in hand, which resulted in a one-way ride all the way back to rehab. (Urban had done an earlier stretch in rehab, for cocaine use and abuse back in 1998, and had allegedly relapsed in 2001.) Naturally enough, Urban downplayed his readmission, insisting there was no 'cataclysmic event' that drew him back to rehab, just a series of 'warning signs'. But there were enough 'warning signs' to have him extend his proposed 30-day stay to three months, a sure sign that some key part of his psyche needed serious realignment.

A member of his management team had inadvertently hinted at Urban's dilemma only a few days before the story broke, when I sent an email requesting an interview. 'Fact is,' the message read, 'that we're in the middle of an album launch tour *etc* at this time, which is taking up all of our time. In the course of the next 12–18 months there is going to be a lot of Keith activity.' The next day, 19 October 2006, Urban checked himself into California's Betty Ford Center, which might explain the back-story to that cryptic 'etc' in the email. 'I deeply regret the hurt this has caused Nicole and the ones who love and support me,' Urban said, in a hastily prepared press release. 'One can never let one's guard down on recovery, and I'm afraid that I have.' Three months would pass before he got the chance to promote his sixth studio LP, which would eventually reach the top spot in the US country charts – his second successive album to hit number one. In a madly conservative sector of the music biz, in an equally right-leaning country, the deeply flawed Urban had somehow managed to stay at the top. It was no small achievement.

As I watched Urban work his spell at the Metro, my mind kept flashing back to my first close encounter with him on a sticky-hot Tennessee afternoon, mid-summer 1998. It was the time of Nashville's annual Fan Fair, a larger-than-life week-long celebration of all things country, where Music City's newest and shiniest stars gather at a speedway track to play infotainment-length sets to their gushing devotees. Thousands of fans, cameras in hand, are shuttled along in front of the stage by security, where they're allowed to stop briefly and take their prized snaps before the steady arm of security swiftly moves them back in the direction of their seats. It's the pedal-and-steel, big-belt-buckled trailer park equivalent of a pilgrimage to Lourdes. After their set, each act retires to a series of huge farm sheds – more like saunas, actually – to sign everything that's flung their way, all the while pushing their latest product. Country king Garth Brooks, an early Urban booster, once spent 24 hours in a Fan Fair shed signing, signing, signing, leaving only when his arms went numb. No wonder he sold so many records: the guy truly knew how to connect with regular Joes and Joannes.

Yet on this Fan Fair day in 1998 Urban was neither playing,

nor signing autographs. He'd been in the States since 1992 but was still without a footing or a true believer in the industry (with the exception of Greg Shaw, his Australian manager). His band, The Ranch, who had released their first LP the year before, had recently folded under not-entirely-pleasant circumstances. There was a gathering of Aussies backstage, who'd come to watch earnest sets from the likes of Troy Cassar-Daley, Gina Jeffreys and Shanley Del, good enough singers who everyone knew didn't stand a snowball's chance in hell of making it in the wildly competitive US market. As if to drive home the point, the Australian showcase, like that of their Canadian counterparts, had been given the dead spot on the bill, kicking off just as the searing midday sun turned the speedway into a concrete-and-bitumen hell. No 'serious' act played Fan Fair before late afternoon, at the earliest.

Urban looked on, shaking a few hands, not giving too much away, pretty much keeping his own company. We spoke briefly and then he said he had to leave. 'Keith's done it tough,' one of the Australian contingent whispered to me as we watched him walk away. I had more to say to Urban – I was hoping he'd agree to speak for a story I was writing – but didn't get the chance. As I soon learned, maybe Urban was 'doing it tough', but he also knew what was required to truly succeed in the USA: you had to stick around, for one thing, and not just fly in for a week's schmoozing. He'd been in the USA for six hard years and was learning how to play the game. He also genuinely believed that Nashville was where he was meant to be – it was his calling.

As Urban once explained, 'I always wanted to go to Nashville to see what it's really like. I'd read about it in all of my liner notes and all the records I had. It was a fictitious place to me and I wanted to see what it was like because to me it was the long-term view. It was the goal that I was working toward.' A close friend of Urban's told me about a phone conversation they had as his star finally began to rise. 'It must feel great to be living your dream,' the friend said. 'It's not my dream,' Urban replied, '*it's my destiny.*'

Back at the Metro, nine years down the line from Fan Fair, Urban was having the last and the loudest laugh. Sure, he'd lived through some dark days, coming to grips with a dangerous cocaine addiction and this recent battle with the bottle. Shaw and many of Urban's other early supporters had been removed from Team Urban and replaced by Nashville-based industry heavyweights. But the cashed-up faithful hadn't deserted him; if anything, as this show proved, they treated him with even more reverence than before – his every 'thanks, guys' and 'wow' were treated as though he was uttering words direct from the country music sermon on the mount. Urban was a survivor, without doubt, who'd given up plenty – a life in Australia, maybe even his musical credibility – to climb to the top of the pile.

Urban had every reason to be pleased: he was hitched to a smart, beautiful woman; and he had buckets of cash in the bank, a stunning Nashville spread and the unconditional devotion of millions of fans. At the end of another song, he stopped, savoured the moment, smiled his signature grin and got back to work. Tomorrow would bring another showcase, some more hands to shake and a new round of temptations to avoid. Rural Caboolture, where he'd begun his wild ride some 30-odd years back, seemed like a million miles away. Maybe it was another lifetime altogether.

One

THE LOST H

Keith looked pretty much the same as he does now,
except with a more pronounced mullet, tight jeans and a
fierce love of Dire Straits and Iron Maiden.

Caboolture High friend, Sherry Rich

Keith Urban once co-wrote a song entitled 'Who Wouldn't Wanna Be Me', and from the outside looking in, it's not hard to understand what he was getting at. Multi-platinum sales, sold-out arena shows, a Grammy, even an Oscar-winning Hollywood star for a wife – it all seems to have come just a little too easily for the man from Caboolture. The standard Urban media profile runs something like this: guitar-slinging country music lover is raised in rural Queensland, learns to ply his trade in various dingy dives, sets his sights on the country music heartland of Nashville, Tennessee, and then shifts Stateside to achieve his goal. Along the way he learns to cope with such inconveniences as a drug and alcohol addiction, failed relationships and the usual vicissitudes of the music industry – fairly typical prices to be paid for the success he has achieved. But the truth, as is so often the case, is a little more complicated than that sketch would suggest. In the Keith Urban story there are more players than in *Ben-Hur*. Ex-manager Greg Shaw, a true believer, deserves an Oscar for his staying power alone, let alone the cash he poured into Urban's career.

Urban didn't choose an easy career path. He targeted possibly the most insular and impenetrable music city on the planet, totally convinced that it was his 'destiny' – more than once he has stated how his career was preordained; simply *meant to be*. Nashville isn't Los Angeles, London or New York – and it's definitely not Tamworth. In those cities, talented outsiders are often welcome and the rules of engagement are relatively straightforward: write great songs and make enough noise to be heard above the din and there's every chance you'll succeed. Although similar in sheer numbers and dollars, Urban's success is quite different to the international acclaim scored by Kylie Minogue, Silverchair or INXS, and more recently, Jet and Wolfmother. Urban targeted Nashville – effectively a big country town, a place more clannish than Amish Penn-sylvania, where an established system has been in place for the past 60 years. As writer Dan Daley pointed out in *Nashville's Unwritten Rules*, his cogent study of the country music epi-centre, rule number one is pretty damned simple: 'Thou Shalt Live Here'. (Although Urban opted to do just that, the unspoken part of this rule is that if you don't come from these parts, boy, then don't even bother trying.) Authenticity – or at least the appearance of same – is part of the country music manifesto. The very notion that an outsider – let alone someone from a place as far-flung as Australia – could get anywhere in the town known as 'Music City USA' rates with sightings of the Loch Ness monster: rare doesn't even begin to describe it.

Of course, Urban wasn't the first Australian with a twang to look Stateside. Many others have tried and failed to gain a foothold there over the years, including James Blundell, Lee Kernaghan, Slim Dusty and, more recently, songbirds Kasey Chambers, Melinda Schneider and Catherine Britt. And yet somehow Urban has broken through without even donning a Stetson, the standard headwear for Nashville's many 'hunks in hats'. So what's his secret? Clearly, Urban had many things working in his favour. He has raggedy-assed good looks complete with designer stubble, blond highlights and the whiff of 'bad boy', hinted at by his earrings and inkwork – even before he opened his mouth to sing he was a publicity department's wet dream, especially in these highly visual times. But this cat can also play: he possesses slick guitar-picking skills and a crooner's way with syrupy ballads, plus an encyclopaedic knowledge of American musical history and its vast back catalogue. He's a crowd-pleaser, too, with the ability to cover everything and everyone from Hank Williams to James Taylor and Tom Petty, while few post-gig autograph hunters go home empty-handed. If Urban had a dollar for every fan's cheek that he's kissed over the years, he'd be an even wealthier man. 'At the end of the day,' said Rob Potts, Urban's close friend and Australian agent, responsible for booking his shows from 1989 until early 2008, 'he's one of the greatest artists this country has ever produced. International success, 10 million-plus records, redefining an American music genre – huge achievements.'

Urban sings it like he means it, too. His songs often possess an old-fashioned, somewhat fawning attitude towards the object of his desire – he either wants to be 'their everything', is dazzled by how they 'look good in my shirt', devotes his time to 'making memories of us' or considers them 'his better half' – so it would be fair to say that searing insight into modern love isn't his specialist area. But he can make pure dross sound

more meaningful than Shakespearean sonnets. And by opting
for full disclosure with his addictions, Urban has created a
public persona – not so much by design, it should be said – that
suggests he's a straight shooter, a no-bullshit kind of guy. Urban
is very willing to play the game, unlike many of his edgier
contemporaries, talking crap with DJs and VJs and 'celebrity
reporters', all of whom he refers to by Christian name, and
smiling on demand.

Revered singer/songwriter Rosanne Cash spoke of this
conundrum in an interview with *The Tennessean* newspaper. 'I
didn't realise there was this game to play [in Nashville],' she
admitted, '[that there was] a line to toe and you were on the
road this many days a year and treated your fans like this and
you dress like this and you showed up at this and that. I just
didn't get it.'[1] Yet Urban understands completely: he didn't
just have a deep and thorough understanding of the music that
emerged from this Mecca called Nashville – he learned to
understand the business. And while Urban may shy away from
discussions of religion, preferring instead to talk up his spiri-
tuality, God is duly and effusively thanked whenever the
opportunity presents itself. That's another positive in the God-
fearing, Bible-thumping South where his core audience resides
and where he spends most of his time. Nashville itself is sometimes known as the 'Buckle of the Bible Belt', and for good
reason.

Even though Urban's fondness for booze and coke doesn't
quite fit the square-jawed, straight-edged country stereotype,
most of his other qualities are essential in 21st century/CMT-
driven Nashville. Urban has immersed himself in a world
where an act is often judged as much by the sexiness of their
video, and their ability to fill a pair of skin-tight 501s while
charming their way through a sensitive heart-to-heart with
Oprah or Ellen, as the heartstring-tugging quality of their

songs. He also understands timing, because he shifted to Nashville just before country music's mid-1990s peak, a time when something like 200-plus twangy acts were signed to major music labels and Music City was generating its fair chunk of the US record industry's annual turnover of several billion dollars. By 1993, a year after Urban permanently re-located to the States, 'country' had become the predominant radio format in the USA, with more than 2500 stations reaching 20 million more listeners than its nearest rival, 'adult contemporary'. And country wasn't a Nashville-only phenom-enon; it was the top-rated format in cities such as Baltimore, San Diego, Buffalo and Seattle (much to the chagrin of one Kurt Cobain). In 1995, country album sales surpassed US$2 billion annually. Who wouldn't want to be Keith Urban, indeed?

But to his credit, Urban has also put in. His current position very close to the top rung of the Nashville ladder reflects the time and energy he's been willing to dedicate to the music biz grind, years that have been filled with seemingly never-ending gigs in shitty dives. It's a testament to an ongoing battle to master the country-pop songwriter's craft, an elusively simple form sometimes referred to as 'three chords and the truth'. He's spent long, frustrating stretches looking on from the sidelines as others' careers flickered and burned out – and he has also watched the supernova rise of such country heroes as Garth Brooks, the Dixie Chicks, Alan Jackson and Brooks & Dunn, from very close quarters. (He was a guitar-slinger for the former two, a video extra for Jackson and an opening act for Brooks & Dunn.) And, of course, Urban has also had to contend with those occasional dark nights of the soul, times when nothing seemed to matter more than his next line and/or shot. More than once he has sought comfort in the arms of some willing backstage stranger.

In order to succeed, Urban has had to sacrifice many things and people along the way; numerous key people have been ditched, especially in the past few years. He once sacked his entire US backing band, possibly as a way of distancing himself from people who reminded him of a more dissolute past. His former manager, Greg Shaw, a man who spotted Urban by chance and nurtured him from the age of 16, has been ruthlessly cast aside, as have other Australian-based supporters. An Urban insider told me, '[Shaw's] the biggest player in the entire story.' 'Absolutely immeasurable,' said another, when I asked of Shaw's contribution to Urban's eventual success. '"Shawree" put up with everything, as did Keith's mother and Angie [Marquis, an early girlfriend and musical partner].' More than one person close to the scene told me that Shaw and Urban had a handshake agreement whereby Shaw would receive US$1 million for his efforts when he stopped managing Urban's career, ideally at the point where he had his first US number one hit. So far, that payback has not been forthcoming. Nor did Shaw receive any 'points' on Urban's US-recorded albums, which could have made Shaw rich even without the 'handshake' money. While managing Urban, Shaw's marriage ended and he was forced to explain to his two young sons why he chose life in America with Urban over his family. At one low point, Shaw borrowed thousands of dollars from his wealthy mother to keep Team Urban afloat, tapping into his family inheritance. Apparently Shaw now lives 'hand to mouth' back in Brisbane, still hoping for his long-overdue cheque. His refusal to speak to me for this book strongly suggests that he believes he and Urban may still reconcile.

'Keith will remove you from his career in a heartbeat if he feels that's what he needs to do,' said Rob Potts, the former head of Allied Artists, the premier country music agency in Australia.

Greg's line was: 'As soon as I get Keith to number one I'm going home.' But Keith had made it very clear to Greg that he wasn't cutting it. They were living in each other's pockets, out cutting grass for cash; it was way too close a relationship to be successful in a place like Nashville. But I think with Greg, he legitimately put his own life into Keith's career. His marriage fell apart, he lost his house, whatever reasonable inheritance he had would have gone into Keith's career. He was totally committed; it was an amazing thing.

I had days in my early relationship with Keith where I was a total believer, and then I would question it. I don't think Greg ever gave up. Imagine doing the day-to-day business and constantly coming up against: 'Who the fuck's Keith Urban?' or having Michael Gudinski, when I tried to get Keith to open for Jimmy Barnes, saying: 'I'm not having no fucking honky country act open for my artist.' Now Gudinski's got his publishing.

At least two long-suffering girlfriends have also been left in Urban's wake, one of whom, Nashville local Laura Sigler, appears to have nothing but ill feeling towards her former beau. She even sent out a public warning to Urban's wife, Nicole Kidman, just before their very high-profile wedding, stating that Urban was not cut out for the long loving haul. 'She adored him,' I was told, 'but Laura was also a very smart woman and knew what would be the inevitable outcome.'

Urban's also had to water down his obvious gifts as a musician in order to make inroads at Nashville. 'Keith could play the industry game that I couldn't,' said James Blundell, who tried and failed to break through in Nashville. 'He had the good sense to work out who was who, while I'd alienated all of them by telling them, "Fuck it, I'm not changing." ' And Urban, frankly, has yet to totally deliver as a songwriter: his albums are littered with awkward co-writes and covers, mandatory steps along the path to Nashville's yellow brick road. But

Urban's success cannot be denied: his market worth reached a new high in 2004, when *Be Here*, his third solo release in the US, shifted a handy four million copies. In the process it scaled the top of Billboard's Country chart and even reached number three in Billboard's Top 200, a mainstream chart that brings together sales from every part of the world's biggest music market, including R&B and rock, the heaviest sellers of all. During its breakout first week of release, the only records to out-sell *Be Here* were new releases from pop-punks Green Day and hip-hopper Nelly. At the time of writing, his four solo recordings have racked up sales above and beyond 10 million units, while he's delivered 16 US Top 10 Country hits. He was also the first Australian country singer since Olivia Newton-John to claim a Grammy. Not bad for a guy who once sported a dodgy mullet and began his career cranking out covers to disinterested drinkers in suburban beer barns, alongside some guy called Rocky.

It would be a massive stretch for the 50,000 or so citizens of New Zealand's Whangarei (pronounced 'Fong-a-ray') to claim that their town was some country music ground zero. The most far-flung city on the country's North Island, whose temperate yet soggy climate has led locals to christen the area 'the winterless north', it does have its share of famous prodigals: various well-known hockey players, funny man Billy T. James, and political agitator and parliamentary front-bencher, Winston Peters, are all locals. But apart from a couple of members of the little-known rock band Steriogram, not many players and pickers can call this place home. To be totally frank, the area is better known these days for its large indigenous population and equally prominent crime and unemployment problems than for being a hub of musical creativity.

Yet it was in Whangarei that Keith Lionel Urbahn entered the world, kicking and screaming, on 26 October 1967. He was the second and final child of Bob and Marienne Urbahn; their first boy, Shane, had been born two years earlier. Keith was named after iconic Kiwi race caller Keith Haub, a larger-than-life man of the track, known for his razor-sharp wit and 'colourful' personality. Haub is Keith's godfather. (His middle name, Lionel, was taken from one of his mother's brothers.) During the 1950s, while still in their teens, Haub and Bob Urbahn played in a covers band, pounding out a setlist that encompassed pretty much everything that was big in the day, including the songs of Buddy Holly, Elvis Presley and Bill Haley and the Comets. 'As the 1960s rolled around,' Urban recalled, 'my dad went more the country route than the rock and roll route, and has remained a fan ever since.'[2] When asked about Haub, Urban once said: 'My godfather is New Zealand's best race caller – and he'd kill you if he heard you say that.' They remain close some 40-odd years down the line.[3]

Urban would also joke about how his father played the drums until 'he had to get a real job'. With the exception of watching his bandmates mow a few lawns in Nashville during the 1990s, and some time spent with a lighting company, this was a burden that was never imposed on Keith Urban.

Interestingly, those of the family who stayed behind in the Shaky Isles, such as Bob's brothers, Brian and Paul, have hung onto the original spelling of the Urbahn name, but Keith shed that bothersome 'h' on the road somewhere between Caboolture, Tamworth and Nashville. He and his family weren't long for Whangarei, anyway, leaving and settling in Brisbane, Australia in 1969.

While much of the Western world was in the midst of an LSD- and Woodstock-fuelled revolution by the time the Urbans reached Australia, the same couldn't really be said for

Brisbane. It was essentially a large country town ruled, like the entire state, by an influential peanut farmer, also a New Zealand expat. Country music, sometimes called the 'white man's blues', seemed a natural fit for a state as pale-faced and conservative as Queensland. Despite the unlikely success of indigenous country crooner Jimmy Little (and Charley Pride, in the USA), country was essentially a safe, listener-friendly genre made by Caucasians for Caucasians, and it had no more logical heartland than Queensland, especially under the tight-fisted rule of Joh Bjelke-Petersen.

As recently as 2001, Keith Urban passed judgement on his adopted hometown's nature, saying: 'It still feels like a country town and I love that about Brisbane.'[4] Urban also gives Brisbane due credit for his relatively unaffected, bullshit-free demeanour, and it should be said that despite the 'star-making machinery' that now surrounds him, there's still a hint of Brisvegas hanging about the guy. This may also account for his apolitical nature; rather than offend anyone, Urban, unlike peers and friends the Dixie Chicks, has opted to offend nobody at all. When Urban was growing up in Queensland it was best not to make any kind of political statement, apart from ticking the box next to Joh's name on the ballot. Some of Urban's few close friends, including his straight-talking groomsman Marlon Holden, still live north of the Tweed.

But what Brisbane did have working in its favour was a number of broad-based radio stations including 4BC, 4BH and 4IP, all pumping out hits of the day, many of which appealed to Urban's music-loving father Bob. While another Brisbane station 4KQ shifted to a strictly country-only format in the late 1970s, none of the aforementioned stations played musical favourites: in 1969 there wasn't the same 'compartmentalising' of music, and radio, as there is today. You could hear pop, rock, soul and country back-to-back on such stations as 4BC and 4BH, and no one would complain. So in 1969, as the Urbans settled into Queensland life, they were as likely to tune into hits from the Box Tops, Neil Diamond and Creedence Clearwater Revival as they were to hear such country-pop stalwarts as Kenny Rogers (whose 'Reuben James' was huge in 1969), Glen Campbell – an early hero of Keith Urban, who topped the charts that year with 'Try a Little Kindness' – and Roy Orbison. This musical mix explains a lot about Urban's crossover appeal today; even as a kid, he was exposed to a broad array of quality mainstream music. Over time he would distil the best bits of what he heard into his own repertoire.

Years later Urban chewed this over and cited the AM radio he heard while growing up in Queensland as a key component of his musical apprenticeship. 'The great thing about AM radio at the time,' he told a reporter, 'was the diversity. You would have Johnny Cash and then the Beatles and then Glen Campbell and then the Rolling Stones. It was a great mix.'[5] A glance at a pop chart from the time drives his point home; you would find Joe South's mournful, rootsy 'Don't It Make You Want to Come Home' sharing chart space with such homegrown hit-makers as one-time Queenslanders the Bee Gees, as well as one-offs like Oliver's 'Jean' and Bobbie Gentry's 'I'll Never Fall in Love Again'. Urban was right – diversity truly ruled.

As for his father, Bob, country really was his genre of choice. Like his pal and former bandmate Keith Haub, Bob would become something of a colourful local figure, given to sporting large moustaches and equally large cowboy hats, and driving anything gas-guzzling and American, ideally a Pontiac. (His moustache still droops proudly today, even though it's sprinkled liberally with grey. Worn with his ever-present Greek fisherman's cap, it gives the Urban patriarch the appearance of an ageing sea captain. He cruises around the Sunshine Coast on a Harley, a gift from his cashed-up son.)

There was a lot of music to be heard in the Urbans' Brisbane HQ: Bob was mad for Dolly Parton, Charley Pride and Don Williams – who he'd first fallen for when Williams was a member of the Pozo Seco Singers – while Marienne, the 'rock' of the Urban household, favoured the smoother sounds of Neil Diamond and the Everly Brothers. 'My folks' record collection has been the main influence on what I've done musically,' Urban admitted in 2000.[6] 'You can't help being influenced by your surroundings.'[7] But equally important to their second son was Bob's all-encompassing love of American culture, something which seeped into Keith's subconscious. 'I inherited this kind of love for the American dream,' Urban has admitted. 'I fell in love with the music, the cars' – and, crucially – 'the whole idea of America.'[8] Marienne Urban, who'd met Bob as a teenager, also had a deep fondness for all things American.

While in Brisbane, the Urbans ran various mixed businesses and corner shops, but nothing that was especially successful. Keith's older brother, Shane, began school at Toowong, while Keith enrolled at the now heritage-listed East Brisbane primary school. Bob and Marienne remained keen gig-goers, often dragging their barely school-age sons along to shows. They'd sometimes leave Keith to snooze beneath the table while they took in the show, and this musical baptism remains one of Urban's fondest and most vivid early memories. 'I would curl up under a table and go to sleep,' he recalled in 2004, 'with the bass drum and the bass guitar pulsing through the carpet. In hindsight, it was terrific training for me – great rhythmic influences.'[9] 'A lot of Keith's talent came from Bob,' said Rob Potts.

He was a drummer and Keith's sense of rhythm is what gives him his musical base, and what makes him such an amazing guitar player. But their relationship, as with his brother, was very tested and testy for a long time. Bob doesn't say a lot, but I have an immense amount of time for him. I think he's a genuinely kind soul.

The first concert that Urban could actually recall, or at least the first gig where it seems as though he stayed awake, was a set from American Tom T. Hall – best known for his syrupy hit, 'Old Dogs, Children & Watermelon Wine' – in Brisbane in 1972. But soon after, Urban had a quasi-mystical revelation when he attended another Festival Hall show with his father. The Beatles may have rocked this very stage in 1964, but that meant little to Urban. On this night he had a close encounter with The Man In Black, Johnny Cash, who was currently experiencing a career rebirth on the back of his revenge fantasy, 'A Boy Named Sue' and the subsequent smash, 'What Is Truth'. At one point in Cash's set, Urban looked up and noticed a spotlight beam, just above his head, cutting through the smoke – and then the light hit Cash's guitar like a thunderbolt. The image struck Urban with the force of a religious awakening. 'It was at that moment,' he recalled with due pathos, and more than a little embellishment, 'that I realised my own destiny.'[10] The charismatic Cash, a man whose craggy face wouldn't have been out of place on Mount Rushmore, could have that effect, even on someone as young as Urban.

It was only natural that Urban's nascent love of music would lead to him trying out an instrument. But his first weapon of choice was hardly the stuff of musical legend: at the age of four he fooled around with a ukulele, a gift from his parents. It didn't really fill any holes in his soul, although his folks did notice how quickly he learned to strum in time to what he was hearing on the radio. The stars he idolised all wielded 'real' guitars, so he dreamed of doing likewise. Then one day, in another incident that seems to have been lifted straight from the lyric of a country song, a woman named Sue McCarthy (now Sue Crealey and still a family friend) walked into the Urbans' East Brisbane store, asking if she could place a handwritten ad in their window, advertising guitar lessons. 'How much would it cost to do that?' she asked the Urbans. They opted for a contra deal, the caveat being this: 'Can you teach our son how to play?' She baulked, at least at first, when they said that Keith was six years old, but reluctantly agreed to at least check out his playing and see if he was teachable. She was won over when she found that the boy was already playing rudimentary rhythms, which he'd learned directly from his father's vinyl albums and the radio. 'OK, sure,' Crealey agreed, little realising that she had just secured a bit part in 21st century country music history.

Years later, when asked about Urban's nascent guitar skills, Crealey said that the kid was a natural. 'He just had it in him,' she said in 2005. 'It was a like a focus, even back then. [Playing music] was all Keith ever wanted to do.'[11] She taught him the basics over the next year or so, until she moved overseas, but admits that after some months the student had clearly out-grown his teacher. One day, Crealey approached Urban's mother, Marienne, with a confession: 'I just can't teach him any more – I only know the basics.'[12] (The same happened with his next guitar teacher.) The first song that Urban learned to play in its entirety was the grim blues standard, 'The House of the Rising Sun', as reworked by Eric Burdon and the Animals. Within a year of his first lesson with Crealey he made his humble public debut, performing Dolly Parton's homespun 'Apple Jack'. (In 1976, Urban performed another Parton chestnut, 'Coat of Many Colours', on TV's *Pot of Gold* and managed to escape the wrath of the show's arch judge, Bernard King. Urban scored 6 out of a possible 10. He appeared again on the show in 1978, and fronted on the *Have a Go* show in 1980 and *Reg Lindsay's Country Homestead* in 1981.)

While Urban was hardly an overnight sensation, his musical acumen was evident from the get-go. When asked about that period, he admits to being connected to his guitar in the same way the *Peanuts* character Linus was attached to his security blanket. Urban even named one of his early Fender Telecaster guitars Clarence, in honour of the character in the film, *It's a Wonderful Life*, a personal favourite. At the age of five, Urban got his first taste of the Tamworth Country Music Festival. It was 1973, the initial year that the awards – whose central focus was the distribution of Golden Guitars – were presented. (Proving just how humble the event's origins were, the organisers were only able to broadcast it on local stations 2TM and 2MO when Tamworth company Insulwool Insulations coughed up the necessary $45.) Slim Dusty's immortal 'Lights on the Hill', written by his wife Joy McKean, won the very first Golden Guitar ever handed out, for Best Song. Many years later, Urban and Dusty would become friends.

In 1973, a starry-eyed young Urban did a little busking and a lot of listening and learning as he walked up and down Tamworth's Peel Street. But his musical education came more from the vinyl albums that his father treasured: records from such American country-pop stars as Johnny Cash, Don Williams and Glen Campbell – especially Glen Campbell. Not only did Campbell's crossover classics 'Galveston' and 'Wichita Lineman' seep into Urban's subconscious, but he also noticed that Campbell was the real deal: he actually sang *and* played guitar. 'As a kid, *I wanted to be Glen Campbell*,' Urban has admitted. 'I really admired him.'[13]

He admired him so much, in fact, that when Campbell toured Australia in late 1974, Urban somehow managed to swing a few minutes backstage with the handsome Arkansas-born picker and singer. 'I play guitar, too, Mr Campbell,' the cocksure seven-year-old told the startled singer. Campbell –

who at the time was carrying around a cassette containing a demo of the song 'Rhinestone Cowboy', a down-and-out ballad that would soon revive his flat-lining recording career – was duly impressed when the kid with mousy blond hair picked up a six-string. 'He could play the guitar better than I could when I was his age.' This was no small rap, coming from a guy who was a legendary studio picker well before he donned the rhinestone. You can hear Campbell on the Righteous Brothers' 'You've Lost That Lovin' Feeling' and other greats from the 1960s.[14] (In a strange-but-true moment of mutual admiration, Campbell invited Urban to play at the 2006 Midlands Music Festival, held in Ireland. He regarded Urban as a 'delightful friend' who was also currently the 'best thing in Nashville, Tennessee'.)[15]

Urban noticed one constant among his father's record collection: this mysterious word 'Nashville' appeared amid the liner notes of virtually each and every one. He did a little research and learned that it was country music's spiritual and creative heartland, located in some place called Tennessee. But this twangy nirvana still seemed a million miles from East Brisbane, figuratively and literally. In fact, it hardly seemed real at all. But Urban was a determined kid, and he soon made a pact with himself. One day, he said, he'd find his way to this place and get a taste of the city where all his favourite music was created. 'When I saw Nashville, Tennessee on the back of [Dad's] records it seemed like the natural progression to move there when I got serious about my music,' Urban said in 2004.[16] 'Call it fate,' he said in another conversation about his eventual relocation to Nashville, 'or just call it wanting to please Dad.'[17] This may have been a throwaway comment, but if Urban's relationship with his father was as troubled as at least one person close to the scene suggests, then much of Urban's career was built upon the notion of 'wanting to please Dad'.

Still, in the mid 1970s, Nashville seemed more a far-fetched dream than even a remote possibility.

Nashville did have a mythic quality, as Mark O'Shea, another country music expat who left Australia a few years after Urban, explained to me.

> It truly is a Mecca for songwriters, artists and musicians from the world over. The cool thing about this place is that you can be having a beer in a divey local bar and strike up a conversation with someone and it'll turn out they wrote 'Wind Beneath My Wings', or you'll waltz into a bar and see some old scruffy guy with a beard singing 'The Gambler' and it turns out to be Don Schlitz — who wrote it! Both true stories.

Not long after her younger son had outgrown his first guitar teacher, Urban's mother spotted a newspaper ad seeking hopefuls for the Westfield Super Juniors, a showcase of local Brisbane talent sponsored by the shopping centre giant. (Westfield Shopping Town Toombul had opened in 1967.) Urban, who was seven, auditioned reluctantly but was accepted. 'It was a little like the Mouseketeers,' he said on a segment for CMT's *Greatest Stories* series. 'Sort of an amateur theatre group, with singing and dancing, putting on kind of musical plays.' The troupe would perform on weekends and during school holidays at such glamorous spots as Indooroopilly shopping centre; their family-friendly repertoire included a take on the then perfectly acceptable *Black and White Minstrels Show*. Urban, like the rest of the team, was decked out in pinstriped shirt, vest and over-sized bowtie, although he was one of the few boys to wear his hair shoulder length. According to one shopping centre employee, he was the first performer picked for the Super Juniors, and was 'a natural entertainer', even though 'the guitar was taller than he was'.[18] Urban spent a few years with the Super Juniors and has admitted that the experience made it a little easier for him to morph into a live performer. 'It just helped being on-stage,' he said. His minstrel days, however, were soon a thing of the past.

At around the same time, along with his parents, Urban joined the Northern Suburbs Country Music Club, a congregation of amateur music lovers and the oldest country music club in Queensland. They'd gather once a month to pick and play. The club had a house band and anyone who was willing would be allowed to get up with the group and sing. 'It was just a bunch of people that loved country music, getting together,' Urban recalled. At various times throughout the more rural areas of Australia, many of these clubs would converge and 'compete' for prizes, playing in front of handmade banners on pokey town hall and community centre stages. The facilities were spartan, no doubt about it, but to the club's true believers these humble get-togethers may as well have been happening on the stage of Nashville's legendary Grand Ole Opry.

'There was a real down-home, friendly, small-town kind of vibe,' said Jewel Coburn (nee Blanch) who, along with her father, renowned country singer Arthur Blanch, would sometimes be called upon to judge music club events. 'There were a lot of these clubs around Australia,' said Urban. 'I spent my whole youth immersed in that kind of culture.'[19]

It was at the Northern Suburbs club that Urban met Angie Marquis, a curly-haired, rough-as-guts Queenslander. It was also where he befriended some likely Redcliffe locals with whom he'd briefly play in a metal band named Fractured Mirror, covering Whitesnake, Judas Priest and the Scorpions. That liaison was considerably more short-lived than his time with Marquis; they would play together as part of a duo called California Suite and remained an on- and off-stage couple for several years.

Not surprisingly, the club continues to talk up Urban's youthful membership with due prejudice. 'Many club members can still remember a very young Keith performing at our club and on the country music festival scene around Brisbane,' it is noted on the club's website. 'He was an exceptional talent then.' And then, in a neat piece of understatement: 'Keith Urban is now undoubtedly the Northern Suburbs CMC's most famous member and an industry legend.' 'Yes, we do often talk about Keith as being our most successful member, as it does help when spruiking the club,' admitted Leisa Bye, a current member.

> And most of us are huge Keith fans and love what he does. We are one of the more advanced clubs in Brisbane – a lot of the clubs up here tend to play a lot of the older style country, whereas we don't mind what is played.

'They're salt-of-the-earth people [in the club],' explained Tamworth broadcaster Nick Erby. 'It's unbelievable what they do for the kids, those people.' Urban wouldn't forget them, either, duly thanking the club in the liner notes of his debut album in 1991.

Keith Urban has often admitted to having a 'gypsy soul' and there's no doubt that his peripatetic upbringing contributed to his own restlessness as an adult. In 1977, after several years in Brisbane, the family moved yet again, this time settling in Caboolture, located about 50 kilometres north of Brisbane. It was an attempt on the part of Keith's father, Bob, to regain some of the rural spirit he'd felt when growing up in New Zealand. His younger son's first and strongest memory of life in Caboolture was the complete absence of traffic lights. 'No traffic lights anywhere,' he laughed, when asked about his life there. When the first set was installed, at the intersection of the

Caboolture Hotel and the local post office and newsagency, it made the front page of the local newspaper. These days, Caboolture is essentially an outlying suburb of Brisbane, with an always-expanding population (currently nearing 20,000), a place known to some for its role in the local bikie-controlled drug trade. But in 1977 it was a smallish dairy town, as humble and down-home as anywhere in the American South. Urban would drift down to the local dog track and collect discarded betting tickets, which he'd then bring home and distribute among his family as concert tickets. Only when they returned the tickets to him would he agree to sing and play at the 'concerts' he staged in their lounge room.

Caboolture was a locale with an interesting back-story: the traditional home of the Kabi Aboriginals – the name Caboolture is derived from Kabi words meaning 'place of the carpet snake' – it was first settled by Europeans in 1842, when land around the Moreton Bay penal colony was opened up for 'free settlers'. The Archer brothers were the area's first white residents; they established Durundur Station, comprising the entire Woodford district, on the banks of the Stanley River. This was the northernmost settlement in what was then the Colony of New South Wales. Twenty-five years on, a small settlement was established in Caboolture as a trading and supply centre for local settlers; the railway line from Brisbane was opened in 1888 (before then it had been a stop on the Cobb & Co route). Timber, which was rafted down the Caboolture River to Deception Bay, was the area's first key industry, but locals soon diversified into sugar cane, wheat and Indian corn, which was grown along the river flats. The discovery of gold at nearby Gympie also speeded up growth in the area.

By the time the Urbans put down roots in Caboolture, it had experienced another growth spurt even though its population wasn't more than a few thousand. This was due to the electrification of the train line to Brisbane, the development of the Bruce Highway and the availability of low-cost housing and cheap land. The Caboolture Shire Council permitted the subdivision of rural land into what was known as 'acreage housing estates', which consisted of blocks in three-quarter, two and five acre allotments (roughly one-third, three-quarter and two hectare lots). But the Urbans chose to live in a well-established farmhouse-cum-cottage, some 70-odd years old. It sat on two hectares, a few kilometres outside the township, just off Toorbul Road (now known as Pumicestone Road). Cows, chickens and pigs ran wild in the yard. They couldn't get more country if they changed their name to Judd.

'We were relatively self-sufficient,' said Urban's older brother Shane, when asked about life on the farm.[20] He and Keith rode horses on the property, and also hooned around the neighbourhood on BMX bikes and motorcycles. (Keith would graduate to choppers much later, when the money started rolling in.) Marienne opened a takeaway shop in Caboolture's main street, while Bob found work at the local tip. He quickly developed a reputation as something of an eccentric, cruising around town in a black 1959 Pontiac, a cowboy hat atop his head, his handlebar moustache growing wild, country music blaring. Bob also owned, and restored, a 1960 Chevy Bel Air, a massive tank of a car with huge rear fins and a hefty V8 under the hood. This was one badass, gas-guzzling ride, and must have stopped traffic in Caboolture. (Years later, when he moved to Nashville, Keith would motor around town in a hefty white Chevy and sport a licence plate that read: 'NO SHOW' in tribute to country giant, George Jones.)

'[Bob] was right into country music, like everyone then,' said Keith Chisholm, who ran the local music store. He once sold Bob a drum kit and also kept him supplied with country albums and cassettes. 'You'd have people playing Slim Dusty and coming into the shop with pig shit on their boots,' Chisholm recalled.[21] Bob was also known as something of a 'loose cannon'. It was suggested to me that he and Keith had a turbulent relationship, something that would manifest itself a few years after the family shifted to Caboolture. As one Urban friend told me, 'Keith could do no wrong in his mother's eyes, but couldn't do anything right according to his dad.'

Urban's brother, Shane, had just enrolled at Caboolture State High, and would wait for the school bus with Keith. One day, as they sat at the bus stop just outside their house, Keith asked his brother what he hoped to do with his life. Shane, who was already a competitive tennis player, swimmer and foot-baller, was a little taken aback by such a serious question, especially from a kid who hadn't yet started high school or sprouted his first wild hair. 'I want to get married, have children, own my house, get a good job,' Shane replied after a moment's consideration. 'You know, the normal things.' Keith chewed this over for a while and then tried again. 'Yeah, *but what do you want to do?*' Shane was insistent. 'No,' he said, 'that's it, that's a good life.'[22]

Keith wasn't sold on his brother's everyman response; even then he knew that he wanted something more 'substantial' from life. 'I don't want to sound cocky,' Shane said many years later, 'but I was always confident he'd make it.'[23] (To Shane's credit, he's lived out his dream; he now lives in Murwillum-bah with a wife and two children and works in the hospitality trade. Those who know him via his famous brother consider him a 'regular suburban bloke'.) Keith's dream was more ambi-tious. From those few shows he'd seen with his dad – Glen Campbell, Johnny Cash – he sensed that music truly had some magical, almost mystical power. And, frankly, he wasn't much of a student, so even then he had an inkling that music might be the only thing that he could do really well.

When the weather turned hot, which was a pretty common occurrence in this humid part of the country, Urban would skip school and head down to the local river, where he would jump off a rope swing. Other days, he'd roar around town on his BMX bike. On one particularly bold occasion, Urban emulated legendary daredevil Evel Knievel, lighting 10 apple boxes, closing his eyes and riding straight through them. At the age of 14, Urban entered a local BMX race and won, without even telling his family. He sheepishly rode into the driveway afterwards, sporting an ear-to-ear grin and carrying a trophy. When the council built a BMX track near the local velodrome, Urban spent almost as much time there as he did in the family garage, playing his guitar. Now and again he'd 'borrow' the keys to the Caboolture Civic Centre from a friend so that he could sneak in after hours and tinker away at the piano.

By his own admission, Urban was 'a quiet kid' who spent much of his time daydreaming about 'music and the life I wanted when I grew up'.[24] The usual Aussie pastime of sport didn't hold much appeal for him; music truly was his one big obsession and provided an escape from any tension that occurred at home. He might have been quiet, but just after moving to Caboolture, aged 10, he had enough self-confidence to enter his first talent quest, which he won. He pocketed the not-so-shabby amount of A$50, which he duly lost. 'That was devastating,' he admitted.[25]

Keith Chisholm, the man who sometimes found himself sweeping the chicken shit off the floor of his music store, also gave Urban his first paying gig, as an in-between act 'filler' at the local Caboolture Tropicana Festival, at the urging of Bob and Marienne. Chisholm recalled how Urban's parents said to him, 'We've got this kid, he's pretty good,' so he agreed to hire him –

MASSANUTTEN REGIONAL LIBRARY
DISCARD

after all, as Chisholm has freely admitted, he was always on the lookout for a 'cheapie' act. Once again Urban collected A$50 (a well-known local act such as Lee Conway would usually be paid around A$1000 for headlining the annual outdoor event). Music, in its own small way, was already starting to pay off for the kid. As Chisholm has since stated, it was quite a coup, even if he didn't know it at the time. 'You probably wouldn't get Keith Urban these days for $50,' he has wryly observed.[26] Chisholm, did, however, manage to book Urban one more time, the following year – for the same bargain-basement fee.

Two key events happened during the family's first year at Caboolture, both of which left their mark on the youngest member of the family. The first was the death of Elvis Presley, on 16 August 1977, at the not-so-ripe old age of 42. The Urbans sat in front of their TV watching the bleak, mournful scene that was being played out on the streets of Memphis, Tennessee. As much as Urban was touched by the loss of the rock and roll legend, whose songs his father had once faithfully covered, there was something else about the black-and-white images that grabbed his attention. 'I remember seeing all the footage of Graceland and Memphis,' he said. 'America seemed like such a big, magical place.' The King's death only served to reinforce Urban's dream to get there one day and check it out for himself.[27]

But another development much closer to home really shook up the 10-year-old Caboolture kid. One afternoon his mother collected him from school; she had an announcement to make that once again sounded as though it was lifted directly from the most clichéd country song ever written. 'Keith,' she said, speaking softly, 'the house has burned down.' The 'official' explanation was that a faulty combustion stove caught fire, although one former Urban associate said that they'd been told Bob Urban had somehow contributed to burning down the

MASSANUTTEN REGIONAL LIBRARY
Harrisonburg, VA 22801

house. There is no evidence of this, nor has Urban or his father spoken in any detail about the fire. (Unfortunately, the Urbans/ Urbahns turned down the chance to speak to me for this book, sticking to their policy of not going on the record about their son's life or career.) Whatever the cause, the entire homestead was gone. Fortunately, no one was home, but virtually all the family's possessions were now in ashes. When they got to the site of the fire, 'I remember everything being jet black and crunching beneath our feet,' recalled Urban. But his biggest fear was laid to rest when he learned that the blaze hadn't spread to the garage, which was where he kept his guitar. To Urban, that was the fire's 'only saving grace'.[28] His father's drum kit was also stored in the garage, so the two things he treasured the most had escaped the inferno. Given that on most afternoons he would return home from school and head straight to the garage, it was as though his 'sacred place' had been spared.

As his parents set about building a new family home further back on the property – only to shift to 17 Douglas Drive three years after the blaze, the last home that Keith would occupy in his 10 years in Caboolture – Urban began to spend time in town, busking at the Caboolture Park shopping centre in King Street. The response he received was somewhat short of all-out acceptance; he'd often be shooed away by shopkeepers who feared this country crooning prepubescent might scare off their customers. Regardless, his BMX bike and, especially, his guitar, became an 'extension of himself', according to family friends. The son of the slightly eccentric if taciturn Bob Urban was becoming known around town as that 'loner with a guitar'. His connection to his guitar was so strong, in fact, that whenever he transgressed the family code, his parents would lock it away as punishment.

Darryl Cavanagh was the local bus driver who collected Urban each morning and transported him to school. 'He would get on the bus and just sit down and strum his guitar and sit by himself,' Cavanagh once said. 'He was virtually a loner.'[29] The noise from the other students on the bus all but drowned out Urban's strumming, but that didn't stop him. 'He was very quiet,' Cavanagh added, 'and never played up.'[30] His more sports-obsessed classmates often laughed at his very solitary obsession, but Urban shrugged and continued picking. Even before he reached his teens, Urban was growing a thick skin, an attribute that would prove very handy in years to come.

The Urbans continued their annual pilgrimage to the Tamworth festival, packing up the family wagon each January long weekend at the tail end of the school holidays, and driving the few hours south-west to check out the buskers and catch most of the headline acts. The event was slowly increasing in size and popularity. From the mid 1970s through to the mid 1980s, BAL Marketing (a division of Radio 2TM) launched numerous initiatives to augment the Golden Guitars awards. These included the *Country Music Capital News* newspaper and *Festival Guide*, launched in 1975; the Roll of Renown, which was introduced the next year; and such things as the Hands of Fame, the Tamworth Songwriters Association, the National Bluegrass Championships (for banjo, fiddle *and* flat pick guitar, no less). Most important for the music-mad Urban, though, was the Star Maker Quest, which was launched in 1979. Though little more than *Australian Idol* with a wardrobe from R. M. Williams, Star Maker would kickstart some notable country music careers, none more so than Urban's. In 1977, Urban won a CCMA Special Encouragement Award for under-10s. Oz country music icon Smoky Dawson, Australia's answer to singing cowboy Gene Autry, handed the trophy to a starstruck Urban. (A polaroid of the moment can be found in Tamworth's Walk A Country Mile museum exhibit.)

Urban was soon making inroads at the Queensland Country

Music Awards. Aged all of 14, in 1981 he won both the Junior Male and Open Duo awards. In the latter he played as part of a combo called Silver Spirit, alongside Angie Marquis; they wore matching black-and-white outfits, Urban's outrageous flares all but covering his black dress shoes and revealing hints of a fledgling fashion victim. A photo from the ceremony shows a pint-sized kid with shiny hair and an even shinier silk shirt, beaming a smile as he accepts the award. He's all grace and good manners, but you can just detect a certain confidence beneath the perky facade. Look closer and you can spot the intense stare of an obsessive in his eyes. 'This looks good,' Urban could almost be saying. *'So what's next?'*

In the same year, during the Tamworth festival, Urban won several talent quests, and while in town he made the acquaintance of another country singer, Jewel Blanch, who was 21 at the time and had just claimed her first Golden Guitar. Blanch, who'd acted in TV series *Fantasy Island* and *Mod Squad*, had only recently returned to her native Australia after spending several years in Los Angeles. With her flowing fair hair and ethereal good looks, she could have easily passed for Stevie Nicks's kid sister. (While in Hollywood, citing 'language' and the 'vomiting' as reasons for her decision, Blanch knocked back the lead role in *The Exorcist*, which made a star of Linda Blair.)

Just like Urban, Blanch was reared on country music; her father, Arthur, had been raised on the family sheep property at Wollun, NSW, 'about 50 miles [80 kilometres] north-east of Tamworth as the crow flies', as his official biography declared. He built a crystal set so he could listen to country radio as he mustered sheep and cattle, and would make one of the first country music recordings in Australia, cutting six 'sides', as they were then known, for Rodeo Records in July 1952. Arthur was a frequent Golden Guitar winner, and during a lengthy stay in the US he recorded for Capitol Records, the future home of Urban. His daughter would become a close and important confidante of Keith's.

Jewel talked briefly with Urban after the Tamworth awards. Now the 50-year-old co-president of Ten Ten Music, a publishing and management firm located right in the heart of Music Row, Nashville, Jewel still fondly recalls that first encounter with Urban. 'I remember watching him [before meeting him],' she told me. 'He was a very talented kid. He was polite, very respectful.' This would prove to be a key bond for Urban. For one thing, the Blanches would hire Urban to play guitar. He backed them – their family act was called Lady and the Cowboy – at various shows throughout Queensland and at the Wondong Music Festival. Although barely in his teens, Urban 'was a professional already', according to Blanch. And many years later, Blanch, who founded Ten Ten with her husband, Barry Coburn, whom she met backstage at a Wondong Festival, would catch an Urban showcase and subsequently become Urban's music publisher, lifeline-giver and yet another dedicated champion of the sometimes troubled singer. (She would later hire him as a staff writer, putting him on a weekly wage, an advance against future royalties, handy dollars at a time when he couldn't get arrested in Nashville. The Coburns' support 'got him through some very lean times here,' one Ten Ten staffer told me.)

Nick Erby, the long-time host of the weekly syndicated radio program, *Country Music Jamboree*, interviewed both Urban and Blanch in 1981 as part of the local television coverage of the Tamworth festival. Erby was confronted by a smiling blond-haired kid holding a 'guitar as big as he was', but he sensed something deeper. To Erby, Urban was 'quiet yet confident and had a definite aura about him even then'.[31] 'I would grab people in twos,' Erby said, when I asked him in 2008 about the interview.

The story was that Jewel had just been through it [youthful success] and he was now going through it, which was the main reason for doing them together. He was winning all the talent quests and she had just come back [from America, returning in 1980].

Pardon the pun, but Urban legend has it that even then he had his eyes on a much larger prize than the Tamworth spoils. Erby, however, isn't so sure.

A kid of that age can tell you that he's going to do this and that — and I've seen it plenty of times before — but all he knows is that he's got heroes that he admires, and he had the opportunity to meet some of them, and he wanted to be like them. But he didn't win because he was cute; he won because he could play a guitar, he looked good and he had a stage presence. He may have said, 'I'm going to do it,' but that's a kid thing.

While Urban had been scooping the country music prize pool, he wasn't blinkered when it came to musical taste. He and his brother, Shane, bonded over mutual likes which included the overblown pop of the Electric Light Orchestra and the sweet melodies of Fleetwood Mac. 'And there was always Eagles [being played],' Shane recalled. He also fell hard for the way-over-the-top pop melodrama of Queen, and was obsessed by their mincing, prancing front man, the gay-and-proud Freddie Mercury. Years later, whenever Urban needed some 'retuning' of his live show, he'd flick on a DVD of Mercury 'conduct-ing' a full house at London's Wembley Arena, and watch and learn as a true master reminded him what performing was really all about.

A major record for Keith was Dire Straits' self-titled debut long-player, which was released in 1978 and transformed a rootsy English bar band into global stars on the strength of the memorable breakout single 'Sultans of Swing'. For a kid such as Urban, deeply in love with his guitar, the chime of Mark Knopfler's Fender and his grasp of rock, blues and pop must have sounded like a clarion call. According to Urban's mother, 'Mark Knopfler was his idol.'[32] Urban had been introduced to Dire Straits by local guitarist Reg Grant, who'd asked Urban to bring together some youthful musicians for a show called 'Kid's Country'. Grant impressed Urban – he could play Mark Knopfler's licks note for note. Urban would play the *Dire Straits* album so much, in fact, as he attempted to emulate Knopfler's distinctive finger-picking style, that he almost wore a second groove into the vinyl. He'd also recorded the album onto a reel-to-reel tape player so that he could slow it down on playback and analyse Knopfler's playing.

Another (less likely) guitar hero for Urban was AC/DC's rhythm man, Malcolm Young (the Young who didn't wear the school uniform, in case you were confused). His earnest study of Young's rock-steady rhythms, as heard in such benchmark records as *Back in Black* and *Highway to Hell*, would prove handy not far down the line when Urban, as part of a band peddling Oz-rock classics to rowdy drinkers, began plugging in and playing at a selection of Queensland beer barns. Urban even had a plan to start a band named Rock Fever, despite not having any other willing starters. All he had was the name, which he thought was brilliant. He asked his parents if he could paint the words 'Rock Fever' on the wall of their garage. They passed on the idea.

Urban's first love remained country, but he was never mad for the local variation. As much as he respected the troubadour spirit of someone like Slim Dusty who collected Golden Guitars seemingly by the handful, songs about beer-swillers named Duncan and poisonous spiders in outdoor dunnies (as immortalised by Slim Newton in his quaint 'Redback On The Toilet Seat') didn't strike a chord with Urban. He much preferred the epic sweep of such songs as the Jimmy Webb-penned, Glen Campbell-crooned 'Galveston' and 'Wichita Lineman'. Many years later, when pushed, Urban admitted that he felt disconnected from what he saw as Australia's 'out-of-date perception of country; they even refer to it as "country and western" still'.[33] Sherrie Austin, another expat Aussie country singer who shared some stages with Urban in the 1990s, was somewhat more blunt when asked about her Tamworth past. 'When I won my first country music awards,' she wrote on her website, www.sherrieaustin.com, 'we were in a tin shed. There was actually a sign that said "livestock to the left, artist entrance to the right". You can't get more country than that.'

The more Urban listened to such acts as Dusty and bush balladeers like John Williamson and Ted Egan, or tried to relate to songs about 'the Warrumbungle mare', big-hearted stockmen and the simple desire to find a 'home among the gumtrees', the more he figured that his musical future lay elsewhere.

The domestic live music scene had been undergoing its own not-so-quiet revolution as Urban retreated to the garage and worked on his Knopfler-esque licks. A thriving network of sweaty beer barns, including Sydney's Bondi Lifesaver and the Sylvania Hotel, as well as Bombay Rock in Melbourne and numerous venues dotted in and around Surfers Paradise and the Gold Coast, was providing a handy financial lifeline to such bands-on-the-rise as the Angels, Cold Chisel, Midnight Oil and Rose Tattoo. Hosted by Ian 'Molly' Meldrum, a well-connected prat in a very large hat, the cheesy but massively influential TV show *Countdown* also played a key role in spreading the word about homegrown rock and roll. And the introduction of Australian quotas on local radio guaranteed healthy airplay for such era-defining albums as Cold Chisel's

East, the Angels' *Face to Face* and Midnight Oil's *10, 9, 8, 7, 6, 5, 4, 3, 2, 1*, as well as one-hit wonders like the Choirboys and Moving Pictures. Meanwhile, Urban's own rockers of choice, AC/DC, were rising from the ashes with their epochal *Back in Black*. Oz-rock, clearly, was in its boozy, sweaty ascendancy. The sound was aggressive and masculine, powered by bass, drums, guitar, screamed vocals and window-rattling volume – Oz-rock truly was a boys' club – and beer was the drug of choice, which made publicans very happy (and wealthy, in some instances). It seemed that the louder the band played, the more punters drank. Pretty soon, a mullet-sporting axegrinder by the name of Keith Urban would be finding his own way in this world of black T-shirts and scruffy jeans, Sandman panel vans and carpark punch-ups. But first he had to finish school.

In the early 1980s, Urban joined his brother at Caboolture State High School. Sherry Rich, another Caboolture High alumni, was a friend of Urban's. She would later become a singer herself. As she remembers it:

> The school had a lot of kids from the tobacco, pineapple and avocado farms in the surrounding areas and also from Bribie Island, which is where I grew up. The town of Caboolture was fairly conservative and had a healthy dose of the rural, redneck element. There was however one good record store that would order in our hotly anticipated imports from the UK new wave scene.

While at Caboolture High, Urban accidentally discovered another useful by-product of music: girls paid way more attention to him when they realised he was a performer (of sorts). Up until then, meeting members of the opposite sex had seemed about as likely as relocating to Nashville and morphing into the next Glen Campbell. Urban auditioned for, and scored, the lead role in a high school production of *Oliver!* and then played drums in the band during a production of *Bye Bye Birdie*, and girls began to take notice of this pimply, skinny, wild-haired kid, rather than staring straight through him. As Urban said in 2001:

> All of a sudden, there were hordes of women around. [But] I learned early on that they weren't interested in me, they were interested in something else. That has helped me keep a reality check on who I am and what people want from me.[34]

This awakening, however, didn't stop Urban from continuing to get lost in music. He was also lucky as he moved into Year 8 at Caboolture High to study under a keen, green music teacher, Megan Grimmer — she was only 22 at the time — who was able to recognise his raw talent. She described Urban as a 'bit obsessive [and] never distracted from music'. She still wasn't quite sure if he was talented or just moody when, on a typically sticky Caboolture afternoon, he stepped forward and warbled Dolly Parton's 'Apple Jack'. This grabbed Grimmer's attention; it didn't really matter that his voice hadn't quite broken yet. 'I thought, "Oh, that's who you are",' Grimmer commented.[35] Not only did she encourage Urban's nascent talent, but he in turn introduced Grimmer to the more palatable aspects of country music, a form that she had been raised 'to despise'.

Said Sherry Rich:

> She was a wonderful teacher, not much older than us, and a mentor in the sense that she gave me the confidence to believe in my talent and use it. She also shaped my musical tastes by introducing us to more alternative music — new wave and post-punk pop that was coming out of England at the time. So my brother [Rusty] and I had the crazy haircuts, skinny ties and coloured shoes with our school uniforms.

Keith, on the other hand, looked pretty much the same as he does now except with a more pronounced mullet, tight jeans and a fierce love of Dire Straits and Iron Maiden. Even so, we had a lot of common ground musically. My mother was a guitar teacher/country folk performer so we grew up around that music and I remember going to see Keith play at his country music club.

Megan Grimmer wasn't a pushover, however, when it came to grades. Even though she wrote a forward-thinking musical entitled *Music Is, Music Was*, that gave her students enough freedom to demonstrate their chops, she was still forced to flunk many of her charges, Urban included, because *Music Is* fell outside of the state music curriculum. Urban bore no grudge, though, praising her in his entry in a commemorative edition of the school's yearbook – in fact, he considered Grimmer 'my favourite [Caboolture] memory of all'.

Urban wrote in the yearbook:

She knew she had a class full of gifted musicians who couldn't read music, Mrs Grimmer did her best to change the school's mind, but 'rules are rules'. It was truly radical thinking for a teacher, and despite my F in music, I have a music career that I couldn't have dreamed of, thanks in a large part to a passionate teacher who only wanted her pupils to succeed, a teacher at Caboolture High School.[36]

Caboolture High produced several famous alumni apart from Urban, including golfer Ian Baker-Finch, world champion axeman Bruce Winkel and jockey Glen Boss, but it was Sherry Rich's brother, Rusty Berther – now one of the musical-comedy combo Scared Weird Little Guys – who got relatively tight with Urban during his few years there. (Berther also failed music class, incidentally.) Even then Berther could see that

Urban was no academic. 'He didn't do a skerrick of school-work. [Instead] he used to come and stay over at our place and we used to rehearse and muck around recording.'[37] Urban formed one of his earliest and most short-lived bands with Berther and his sister. They called themselves Obscure Altern-atives, even though it's likely they were more the former than the latter. Their name was lifted from an album by slick UK electro-pop outfit Japan.

Rich recalled:

> My mum made us all matching red bomber jackets with sequined initials but we only played a few times, at the Bribie Island Festival and the Caboolture High School social, which was a huge success and gave us a taste of the performing high — as well as lifting us briefly out of nerd status.

Their setlist, like their name, was very much of the time, including their take on the Vapors' 'Turning Japanese' and Mental as Anything's 'The Nips Are Getting Bigger', as well as 'oldies' like the Monkees' 'I'm a Believer'. Rich's most vivid memory of Urban, however, is the time he arrived at school with his new guitar:

> I clearly remember the day that Keith opened a guitar case in class — and there was his beloved, brand new, red Fender Stratocaster. Even at that tender age he definitely had the skill to play impressive technically proficient guitar. It seemed to me that performing and playing guitar was his great singular passion and path in life; luckily he realised it early on.

Rusty Berther admitted that he and Urban didn't necessarily swap albums and bond over shared musical loves, despite playing together in the Alternatives. 'He had crappy taste,'

Berther said in 2006. 'He used to like the worst commercial aspect of country music.' His sister felt likewise; Rich told me how she didn't make the effort to check out Urban's post-Alternative acts because 'it wasn't my cuppa tea'. For one assignment, Urban was required to come up with something to be used in a school radio broadcast. He duly went home and taped a selection of ads directly from the TV onto a cheap cassette and handed them in. 'He loved that whole commercial aspect,' said Berther.[38] Urban would sometimes stay with the Berthers on Bribie Island. The three of them would fiddle about with a dual-speed Marantz stereo, 'recording and playing it back extra slow or fast and rolling around laughing 'til it hurt,' said Rich. 'I'd say Keith had a happy-go-lucky air about him as a teenager, with an infectious husky giggle.' The Berthers' mother was especially fond of Urban. 'Mum says he was such a well-mannered house guest,' Rich recalled.

But by the middle of Year 10, music teacher Grimmer noticed that Urban had turned inwards; school clearly held no interest for him. 'Kids like that who have those sorts of abilities are often emotionally fragile,' she said, looking back. 'I'm not a doctor, but you see it.'[39] Urban dropped out without completing his School Certificate, which was fairly common practice in Caboolture. He was 15 at the time. When asked about high school, Urban wasn't especially nostalgic. 'I would have left sooner if I could,' he admitted. 'It was a terrible inconvenience.'[40] Urban's parents, who'd been driving him to paying gigs on the weekends, knew that he wanted to get out, and they could also see that there might be some money to be made playing music, so they reluctantly accepted his decision to bail. Urban, meanwhile, was set to undergo another type of education, this time in a selection of sticky-carpeted Oz-rock dives.

Two

STICKY CARPETS

[We had] a healthy mutual regard bordering on competitiveness. I then found out that Greg [Shaw] had set sights on moving me out of the road so the path was clear for them. I was like, 'Fucking hang on, I was just being friendly.'

James Blundell

If Urban had to choose someone to steer him through the bacterial beer barns of Oz-rock, he couldn't have picked a better guide than a fellow who called himself Rusty Ayers. He became the guitarist's surrogate guardian a few years after Urban left Caboolture High. Ayers had a back-story that seemed like pure invention: he was an American, a chef by trade, whose real name was Rusty Hammerstrom. He and his partner, Lisbet, had drifted into Australia in the late 1970s, spending several months camping near the Northern Territory landmark and Aboriginal sacred site Uluru (aka Ayers Rock). The pair was staying there when Azaria Chamberlain disappeared in 1980, and even helped in the forlorn and

43

much-whispered-about search for the missing child.

Before working with Urban, Ayers had formed a group in Sydney with percussionist Dave Parle and guitarists Steve Cornwall and Rob Fisher. The latter, who more recently wrote songs for dynamic pop duo the Veronicas, remembers Hammerstrom as 'very charismatic'. Not so charismatic, however, as to be invulnerable to visa problems, because this band split after six months when their leader was asked to leave the country and return to his native USA.

Hammerstrom eventually drifted back to Brisbane with his partner and a 12-string guitar and reinvented himself as the front man of a hard-working band called Rusty and the Ayers Rockettes. They were billed as 'Australia's Best Party Band'. Clearly his experience at Uluru had left a sizeable mark on his psyche, hence the name. And in keeping with their tag and Hammerstrom's past, the Ayers Rockettes pumped out songs with such 'authentic' titles as 'Kakadu' and 'Gondwanaland', along with the usual Oz-rock covers. Their numbers at times included guitarists Brad Hooper (now part of an outfit named the Sugar Daddies), Darryl Mitchell, and Brisbane-born drummer Peter Clarke, a solidly built tub-thumper fond of wearing sleeveless singlets – aka 'wife beaters' – while playing. Clarke would eventually keep the beat for Urban, first in his Australian band and then in The Ranch. They first met on New Year's Eve 1987 and would work together for more than a decade. While on tour with the Rockettes, Clarke and Urban would share a room (while on tour with The Ranch, they'd sleep together in a converted van). They became close, on-stage and off.

In the early 1980s, band leader Hammerstrom was very much aware of Urban's growing local reputation as a guitarist, sometimes driving to a Caboolture country club to check him out. Urban was playing as part of a duo called California Suite, with romantic partner Angie Marquis. They took their name from the 1978 Hollywood flick based on the Neil Simon play about four groups of guests and their misadventures at the Beverly Hills Hotel. The permed, no-nonsense Marquis had known Urban since she was 10 years old, having met him through their country music club. (Like Hammerstrom, who now lives in Florida, Marquis remains friends with Urban.) As he did with the Berthers, Urban often stayed over at the Marquis's home and would write letters to Angie's mother, Daphne. Like most people from Urban's past, Daphne Marquis remembers Urban as both polite and ambitious. But it's unlikely he mentioned the proposal he and her daughter made to photographer John Elliott – to shoot them nude. Elliott declined.

His appearance at the time, though, was off-putting, at least at first glance: it was part suburban bogan, part country-rock stoner, with his mousy blond hair straggling past his shoulders. He was so gaunt that he seemed to have no flesh at all on his face; he was all bones (and hair). Urban's wardrobe looked to be comprised entirely of snug jeans, T-shirts and bib–and–brace overalls which he would wear, sans shirt, while playing. In 1986, he and Marquis entered the Star Maker event, finishing in the Top 10. Urban was so chuffed that he still has the certificate.

California Suite was doing OK, playing mainly local clubs and pubs. According to Urban, they would usually collect around A$250 for a night's work. 'We didn't make a lot,' he admitted, 'but enough to pay the rent.'[1] According to more than one report, Urban was 'deeply' in love with Marquis. 'He was so in love with his girlfriend, he came to Kirsty [Meares] and I one night and said that he wanted to marry her,' said Peter Blyton, a fellow Queenslander who later produced Urban's first solo album.

> We said that it was very sweet, but he was also very young. But he came from Caboolture, where there was nothing going on. He couldn't afford to buy her an engagement ring, so he gave her his Telecaster instead. It was everything he had in the world. Of course, things didn't work out.

Meares can't recall the conversation, but does remember Urban as 'lovely'.

California Suite's shows would usually run for four, sometimes four and a half hours, with the twosome doing their best to be heard above the din of drinkers. 'They were all different clubs,' Urban said. 'Rowdy pubs. A lot of people didn't want to listen. You had to *make them listen*.'[2] He and Marquis covered songs from Fleetwood Mac, Linda Ronstadt, Nicolette Larson, the Eagles – 'tons of Eagles' – as well as slipping in such country favourites as George Strait's 'You Look So Good in Love' and 'Dixieland Delight' by Alabama. Urban knew his way around everything from Jackson Browne's 'Somebody's Baby' to the Beatles' 'Ticket to Ride', Little Feat's 'Cajun Girl' to Brian Cadd's 'Angry Words'. James Taylor's 'Handyman' and John Mellencamp's 'Jack & Diane', as well as songs from UB 40 and Creedence Clearwater Revival also fleshed out their shows. Playing a set full of originals was still a long way off for Urban.

Nick Erby was one long-time Urban supporter who caught some of California Suite's gigs.

> They went out, got some work and sang some covers, because you couldn't only sing your own stuff in that sort of environment, sitting on a stool with a girl singing. That [duo] was purely money-making; that was just making a living.

As busy as Urban was, he never stopped being a music fan. He fell especially hard for the fleet-fingered string work of

guitarist (and Muswellbrook native) Tommy Emmanuel; sometimes he'd sneak into Emmanuel's dressing room and leave a
bunch of flowers for 'the maestro'. Urban was still in his teens
the first time that they met. It was straight after Emmanuel had
played a set at a Brisbane festival, and was taking the night flight
back to Sydney. He found himself seated alongside Urban and
Angie Marquis.

'He had pink hair, he looked like a little punk,' said the
doughy-faced Emmanuel, a world-class guitarist who speaks
with a respectful, sagacious tone, and is now a close friend
and Nashville neighbour of Urban's. (They've also shared what
Emmanuel refers to as 'the disease of addiction', so their relationship is based on more than music.)

> We had the conversation on that flight where he told me what
> he wanted to do and how hard it was to do that in Australia.
> I said, 'What you should do is get the hell out of here and
> do what it is that you know you want to do.' I think he felt
> that he had bigger dreams than he could dream in Australia,
> and I encouraged him in that, because I had the same dreams.

Emmanuel hadn't heard him play yet, but was drawn to the
kid's enthusiasm.

> I told him that everything he'd seen me do to that point was
> handmade; I'd gathered the right people around me. I told him
> that you needed to be surrounded by people you trust and
> you have to give it everything you have every time you go out
> to play.

Urban nodded in agreement and set about doing just that.
Roughly a month later, Emmanuel boarded the same flight and
had almost the exact same conversation with James Blundell.
Urban didn't lose his sense of wonder at Emmanuel's

playing, either. Many years after that in-flight pep talk, they were jamming at a Nashville club, trading licks on their acoustic guitars, when Emmanuel slipped into one of his trademark lightning-speed solos, tapping out percussion on his guitar in between flourishes. Urban's eyes widened and he pretty much stopped playing, opting instead to watch Emmanuel explode and the small but rowdy crowd erupt. 'He's a good player,' Emmanuel insisted, when I mentioned that show.

One night at a gig in Caboolture, Rusty Hammerstrom was among the few punters actually tuning into California Suite. He'd recently lost a guitarist and immediately recognised that Urban was the perfect replacement: he was young, which was no bad thing, and could pick and shred like a pro. 'Even back then, Keith was an awesome guitar player,' he said in 2005, 'his music was superlative. And he always had that country edge to his playing.'[3] Hammerstrom approached him after the gig, offering him the guitarist's spot with the Rockettes. Urban accepted, even though it meant he had to maintain a juggling act between Hammerstrom's band and his duo with Marquis. He would remain a Rockette for the better part of two years, playing the covers circuit which included such Queensland venues as the Salisbury pub, the long-gone Brisbane Hotel and the Orient.

Hammerstrom likened the Rockettes to a 'Vegas show act where everyone gets to show off. We brought him out of his shell, taught him it was OK to show off a bit. [But] he was pretty cool back then, a shining star.'[4] Urban, years later, continued to pay dues to his apprenticeship served under Hammerstrom, acknowledging that it was a hard, though necessary, path to pursue. 'Australian pub audiences are not a forgiving crowd,' said Urban. 'You've gotta work for it.'[5] With every gig, his skin grew just that little bit thicker. James

Blundell, a Queenslander just like Urban, caught the Ayers Rockettes' set one night at a pub in Mossman, not far from Port Douglas. 'Keith must have been 18 at that stage of the game,' said Blundell, a handsome man with a sharp mind and an ear for a melody. 'It was one of those things; I'm watching the band and thinking, "Fuck, that guy can play guitar." I've always had a high regard for his ability.'

As Urban learned to deal with rowdy drinkers and crowds more interested in the football score than his take on 'Peaceful Easy Feeling', American country music was undergoing one of its periodic upswings. Based on the Broadway musical of the same name, the breakout Hollywood hit of 1980 was *Urban Cowboy*, a film starring, in no special order, John Travolta, Debra Winger and a feisty mechanical bull. The film's tag line, 'hard hat days and honky-tonk nights', became almost as common a catchphrase as the pre-coital line uttered by Debra Winger's Sissy Davis, when she gasped: 'I got a real cowboy.' The film grossed US$54 million, a substantial sum for the time. It featured a hit country-pop soundtrack with tunes from middle-of-the-roaders Kenny Rogers and Anne Murray, as well as fiddle-driven firestorm 'The Devil Went Down to Georgia', from the Charlie Daniels Band – a barn-burner that Urban would cover live, sometimes picking it while blind-folded – and 'Stand By Me', which was sung by Mickey Gilley. Mickey also owned a bar called Gilley's, which was where much of the film's wild bucking action took place.

It was hardly a great piece of cinema – one critic wrote that 'aside from Winger, this soap opera is utterly dismal' – but this popcorn western helped to shift everything country right into the mainstream. The number of country radio stations in the US doubled between 1978 and 1982, while sales of country albums reached a new peak of US$400 million, about 20 percent of the market. Even *The New York Times* deemed it necessary to declare that the form had 'supplanted rock for the time being as the dominant commercial mode of modern music'. Country's poster boy was the ubiquitous, avuncular Kenny Rogers, who had three huge singles in 1980, while the *Urban Cowboy* soundtrack set up camp in the Billboard Album Chart, riding high in the saddle for almost six months. By the end of 1980, *Kenny Rogers' Greatest Hits* had spent three months in the upper reaches of the same chart, a stretch that continued into March 1981. The genre was red hot, even if back in Australia a cheery bar-room singalong about some bloke called Duncan was the pick of what passed for home-grown country.

Country's temperature jumped a few degrees soon after, when ageing American country singer Stan Hitchcock, along with a group of investors, bought a fledgling video production and broadcast company based just outside of Nashville, in a suburb called Henderson (nearby Madison is known to locals as the 'butthole of Nashville'). The purchase price included some two million subscribers and a selection of bargain-basement country music videos. So it was that Country Music Television – CMT to its many million devotees worldwide – was born, a cable station that introduced a fresh-faced roster of artists to a totally new country-loving audience. Suddenly the genre had a much younger demographic than ever before.

In much the same way that MTV gave a slumbering beast called rock and roll a few sharp jolts, CMT added a whole new dimension to country music: it was now necessary to look good, not just sound sincere and play with all your heart. (Heaven knows how an artist as credible as Johnny Cash would have fared if he was born 30 years later. The Man In Black had a face like a roadmap, which might have scared away poten-tial CMT subscribers.) Record labels now began to add substantial video production costs to typical production budgets. CMT's preference for acts that could fill their 501s and flash million-dollar grins would eventually prove to be a blessing for Keith Urban, as much as he preferred to downplay his sex symbol status. Billy Ray Cyrus's execrable 'Achy Breaky Heart', with its accompanying bump-and-grind dance moves, was only a few line-dancing steps away.

Urban Cowboy's success and the gradual if unstoppable rise of CMT didn't fully rub off on Queensland audiences. They were still yelling for covers of the Swingers' 'Counting the Beat' and pretty much anything from Cold Chisel or the Angels when Urban and Marquis (aka California Suite) set up to play yet another gig at a Brisbane venue. One of the few people in the small crowd looking on with any interest was Greg Shaw, a local who ran several venues, including General Jacksons which was located beneath the Crest Hotel in the city. Shaw was in dire need of a new act for Thursday nights. A cheerful character with modestly cut brown hair and sensible glasses, he had once been the star water-skier at Brisbane's Sea World resort. He'd also been the first person to show some interest in the music of James Blundell, and has recordings of the Oz star dating back to when he was 16. (The two also battled over the affections of Rebecca Williams, whose father owned Sea World. Williams would appear in the lyrics to Blundell's 'Down on the Farm'.) Shaw had pretty much the same response as Rusty Hammerstrom when he stood and watched Urban work his way up and down the fret-board: this was just the guy – the kid, actually, because Urban wasn't yet drinking age – that he needed.

Shaw recalled how, after only a few minutes, he turned to his then girlfriend (now his ex-wife) and not only said that Urban was perfect for the Thursday night gig, but declared: 'I'm going to manage that guy and take him to Number One in the US.' His partner thought he was just blowing smoke – people in

Shaw's position needed to talk up their artists, even acts they hadn't yet hired – but Shaw was genuinely sold on the Caboolture kid. 'I could just tell that Keith had that special quality, that "it" factor,' he said. 'His obvious talent just shone through.'[6] When Urban accepted Shaw's offer to manage him (and only Urban, significantly), he set in motion what was probably the most significant professional relationship of his life.

Like almost everyone else from the time, Shaw found Urban to be quiet – more a listener than a talker, the kind of person who only really shone when he plugged in and started playing. The way Shaw read the situation, all Urban needed was some experience fronting a band rather than playing sideman, and pretty much anything could happen. 'The guy's a superstar,' Shaw told those close to him, and duly set to work turning Urban into one.

It was a bustling live music scene in and around the southeastern parts of Queensland at the time even if, as one musician told me, most of the Brisbane clubs were 'run by some shady characters' who had connections with the notorious Sydney venue, Whisky a Go Go. But when a regular pay cheque was on offer, most players felt it unnecessary to ask too many questions. Glen Muirhead, a Brisbane local who was a friend of Greg Shaw's and would play keyboards on Urban's 1991 debut album, made a solid living from that scene in the late 1970s and early 1980s. 'You'd get a residency in a covers band and work six, seven nights a week, especially on the Gold Coast,' he recalled.

> We'd go down and do six weeks at the Grand Hotel in Southport, where we'd play every Sunday to 1200 people, then six weeks at clubs at Coolangatta, six weeks at the Paradise Room in Surfers Paradise. That'd be with a six-piece band, a truck, a good PA, the whole bit. It was all about big pubs and big discos, tourist dollars.

Although Muirhead hadn't yet seen Urban play, he did hear some whispers about 'this talented guitarist/singer' playing with Rusty and the Ayers Rockettes. The word had started to spread.

In 1985, Shaw managed to book Urban a tour of New Zealand, then in 1987 secured him an opening slot for hirsute Scotsman Billy Connolly. Given the diehard following the manic comic had (and still has), this would have challenged the most seasoned road warrior, let alone a green teenager. Urban played a 30-minute slot, strumming the type of covers he'd mastered over the past few years – Creedence Clearwater and the rest – and was doing reasonably enough, when he snapped a string on his guitar. Urban was working on the fly – he only owned one guitar – so rather than break for a string change and come off as amateurish and inept, he kept strumming. The guitar drifted increasingly out of tune and his set (and possibly his fledgling career) seemed headed for disaster. As a nervous Urban readied himself to play the next song, he looked into the wings and noticed Connolly's tour manager standing there, cradling an acoustic that the headliner sometimes used during his act. He raced on-stage, guitars were swapped, and the show went on. As Urban recalled, 'I played, and I came off-stage and said, "Thank you for doing that." He said, "Thank Billy. He did it. He heard that you broke a string, so he sent his guitar up and restrung yours".'[7]

Urban's trophy shelf, meanwhile, was starting to sag under the weight of awards. In 1980 he was crowned Capital Country Music Association's Best Junior Guitarist and in subsequent years he won CCMA Jamboree gongs for Junior Male Vocalist, Best Junior Guitarist (again) and Best Duet. Along with Angie Marquis he was one half of the Best Duet in 1982, while the year before he had been crowned Best Gospel singer, which wasn't a bad effort for a teen who spent most nights singing decidedly profane classic rock covers. In 1983 Urban also won the CCMA Junior Male Vocal award.

But the CCMA was hardly country music ground zero, at least to someone like Urban who was hell-bent on getting to Nashville and seeing if it really was some kind of twangy nirvana. In the 1960s, what was then known as the Modern Country Music Association held its inaugural meeting in a hayshed. This wasn't quite how Urban dreamed his career would play out.

While the rise of *Urban Cowboy* and CMT might have made some hefty inroads into mainstream American culture during the 1980s, and also put a little shimmy into the genre's conservative two-step, the same couldn't be said for Australian country music. Slim Dusty, an avuncular journeyman with a slouch hat and a sideways grin, still ruled the roost, filling venues from Bourke to Bundaberg and topping the local country charts. As much as Urban respected Dusty – he never missed the chance to speak with due reverence of the man – he couldn't imagine himself replicating his folksy, homely style of musical storytelling.

Rising country star James Blundell – more of whom later – experienced the same dilemma when asked by his father, of all people, why he chose to be a musician. *Was he planning to be the next Slim?* 'I said that I can't be a Slim clone,' Blundell replied. 'As much as I love his music, I can't do it with conviction. It's not me.'[8] Former *Perfect Match* host Cameron Daddo, another expat now living and working in the USA – Urban was guitarist-for-hire on Daddo's solo record *A Long Goodbye* – told me of a similar conversation he once had with Urban. 'We both agreed that we had more to do than was on offer in Australia,' he recalled. A very telling image from the time shows

Urban riffing on his guitar in yet another RSL club while seated amid some less-than-impressed locals. They look on, sipping beers, decked out in their uniform of checked shirts, R. M. Williams boots and Akubras. Urban's flashy showmanship was totally lost on the crowd.

Slim Dusty's championing of Urban, however, should not be underestimated. The Dusty seal of approval definitely helped his progression through the local country ranks, and eased the distress that many conservative true believers felt on first seeing Urban. As Nick Erby read it, they had more in common than a glance would suggest. 'It just so happened that Slim and Keith hit it off. Slim had immeasurable respect for the youngsters like Keith who were taking the music forward,' he said.

> [And] 30 years before, Slim had been in that position. When he started recording he was pushing and kicking to get a band on his recordings. In the mid 1950s he had a rock and roll band in there, so Slim wasn't foreign to that as a concept.
>
> Slim always had an interest in young people and he accepted his mantle as the senior citizen of country by the beginning of the 1990s. The relationship between Slim and Keith began on that premise but ended up being a personal thing between the two of them; their mutual admiration developed into friendship.

Both enjoyed a beer, too, which only helped the friendship develop.

Joy McKean, Dusty's widow and a fine songwriter herself, couldn't recall the first time that she and her husband met Urban, although Urban reminded them how, when he was 10, he approached Dusty at the 2TM Roll of Renown display in Tamworth, clutching the sheet music for 'Lights on the Hill' (which McKean wrote), requesting the great man's autograph.

He duly wrote: 'Slim Dusty, all the best. 1977.' 'I know Slim was amused at Keith's "way out" attitude and appearance,' McKean wrote in an email.

> And coupled as it was with his obvious talent and drive, it made us notice him. The whole establishment 'noticed' Keith when he made his appearance on the [Tamworth] awards one year wearing cut-off jeans as shorts during his act. We were not quite as shocked as most others, actually.

(Years later, Urban played a reworked acoustic version of true-blue trucker's anthem 'Lights on the Hill' at the Chairman's Dinner, a high-profile industry event at Tamworth, that 'just staggered' everyone there, according to one witness.)

'Slim liked to see someone "pushing the envelope" the way he sometimes liked to do himself,' McKean continued, 'though he always wanted to see enough ability and talent to justify it.'

> He also expected to see respect for and knowledge of country music's heritage and background incorporated within that pushing. Keith seemed to have all that, and therefore he interested Slim. Perhaps they did share something like a maverick streak in some ways, but with Keith I am more inclined to think that he was always looking towards the USA and modelling himself towards that style, which did make him seem at odds with the Australian style of music of the time. Whereas with Slim, the maverick streak came out in a different way, directed towards extending the scope of what he was singing and writing.

When Dusty took Urban on a lengthy tour, along with drummer Peter Clarke, Urban was apprehensive as to how Dusty's audience would accept him, a long-haired outsider. His multi-coloured leather jeans probably didn't make the assimilation any easier. Urban held himself back for the first few shows, fearful that his more rocking approach might offend Dusty's fans. At the midway point of the tour, before going on-stage, he asked for Dusty's advice (something he would do at various key stages of his career). 'Should I keep holding back?' he asked. 'Just go out there and do it your own way,' Dusty told the kid. 'Just be yourself.' According to McKean:

> Keith had not realised that in the first place, the audiences would be prepared to give him a go because Slim was backing him, and in the second place, by the time he got into his stride he would have them on his side simply by virtue of his remarkable talent and music. That was what happened, and it all worked out fine.

There's no doubt that the confidence Dusty showed in him was soon channelled into Urban's own playing. 'It was actually quite a big deal for Keith,' said one colleague of Urban's. 'Keith definitely thought it was an important moment in his career.'

'It was wonderful to be on the road with Slim,' Clarke said in an email. 'He was a mentor to us all.' To mark their time with the icon in the slouch hat, Urban and Clarke wrote a song for Dusty, entitled 'Born a Travellin' Man', which he eventually cut. It was nominated for the 'Heritage Song of the Year' Golden Guitar at Tamworth and became a hit single. (In 1998, when Dusty visited Nashville, Clarke and Urban backed him during his only appearance at the legendary Grand Ole Opry, the spiritual home of country music. Clarke still considers it a high point of his career. When Urban was asked to have his name etched into a Royal Easter Show display entitled 'The Slim Dusty Heritage Centre Project', Urban simply wrote back, in his typically rounded, flashy handwriting: 'God bless you, Slim and Joy. Your mate, Keith.')

McKean added:

> The ambition, drive and talent in Keith was obvious from the
> start, especially to Slim and to me. It could not be mistaken.
> An artist can have all the talent in the world, but without that
> burning, single channelled drive and 'stickability', that artist
> may never realise his or her full potential. Keith had all that.

'What Slim did in the 1940s and 1950s was inspiring,' Urban
once said.

> He had a lot of people who said he was doing an injustice
> to country music and he really fought a hard battle to be
> himself, but he stuck to his guns and followed his heart.

As Urban would discover, the path that Dusty had blazed both
within and outside the mainstream would become a useful
roadmap for him over the next couple of decades. They may
not have played the same music, or even covered the same
territory, but their attitude was remarkably similar.

A cursory glance at the Australian country music charts
from the 1980s, and the manner in which the form was
relegated to several notches below mainstream pop and hairy-
chested Oz-rock, proved just how little potential there really
was for someone as quietly ambitious as Urban. Bush ballads
like 'On the Road to Gundagai' and such quaint novelty ditties
as 'Who Put the Roo in the Stew?' and 'One Armed Bandit'
(seriously) were deemed worthy of Golden Guitars (the former
in 1980, the latter pair in 1981 and 1982), while such stalwarts as Dusty, TV show host Reg Lindsay and everyman
Johnny Chester still dominated the field. John Schumann's
'I Was Only 19', the spooked recollections of a battle-scarred
Vietnam vet – which collected two Golden Guitars in 1984 –

was a rare instance of a more edgy work making inroads. But in the main, Oz-country comprised songs about life on the land sung by earnest men and women of the bush. It was a parochial music made for an audience that felt isolated, both culturally and geographically, from the so-called 'big smoke'. And it was a cold fact that apart from Brisbane's 4KQ and Sydney's 2SM, which adopted a country format well past its commercial prime, most country radio stations were based outside of the capital cities and didn't even bother trying to compete with the major broadcasters.

Urban was dreaming a little larger than spending his life rubbing shoulders with the fellow who sang 'Old Man Emu'. (John Williamson, as it turned out, didn't have much time for Urban, either.) In America, as Urban well knew, there was the potential for a country singer to share chart space with such superstars as Prince, Madonna and Bruce Springsteen. In Australia that seemed about as likely as Slim Dusty covering the Sex Pistols. In fact, Dusty's cheery, beery 'Duncan' was the only Australian country song to come anywhere near the top of the Australian mainstream charts during the entire 1980s and it would be many more years before Kasey Chambers gave country some left-of-centre credibility.

Urban may have been something of a guitar-loving dreamer, innocent to the workings of the music biz, but his manager, Greg Shaw, was a pragmatist. He began to explore what was needed to get Urban to Nashville, at least for a taste of the country music capital, despite the protestations of Urban's parents who weren't convinced there was any good reason their son should leave Oz. According to Rob Potts, Urban was very keen to go, mostly to pursue what he saw as his musical 'destiny', but also because 'he was stoked to be away from the family'. When Urban did make his first trip, in 1989, visa restrictions meant that he could only stay a short while –

but it was enough to sell Urban on the idea of not just returning, but relocating. 'Oh gosh, I have to move here,' he said as
he did a whirlwind tour of the city, slowing down to check out
the Grand Ole Opry and the Exit/Inn, where crooner George
Jones, mid-bender, once drove through the front door in a
ride-on lawnmower. 'I love it here, I just want to be here,' said
Urban, wide-eyed.[9]

Back home, Shaw and Urban looked and learned as James
Blundell, the square-jawed Queenslander raised on a cattle
station, with a high-wattage smile and a solid understanding
of country music, started to build his career. Just like Urban,
Blundell was an early starter, playing guitar at four and penning
his first lyrics at the age of seven. Blundell, who was raised on
a steady diet of country and Eric Clapton, Jackson Browne and
Creedence, also did hard time early on playing covers. As he told
me in 2001, a typical setlist for him was 'the Angels, Springsteen,
James Taylor and John Denver, mixed in with a few originals'.
His first completed song was a 'what-a-bitch-she-left-me' tune
called 'Silvery Shadows'. 'It was about a chick I was fighting over
with a guy called Peter Jackson, the football player.'

Blundell won the Tamworth Star Maker Quest in 1987,
which led to a recording deal with label EMI; he also collected
a pair of Golden Guitars in 1989. And Blundell, like Urban,
was looking Stateside too, even if his initial foray there in 1989
was relatively unproductive, thanks to a corporate pogrom at
Capitol Records. Subsequent trips to the US proved equally
disastrous.

As anxious as Urban was to relocate to the States, he and
Greg Shaw – who would later manage Blundell – also knew
that some domestic success could only help their case when
it came to applying for what was known as the 'Extraordinary Alien' visa, which would allow Urban to live and work in
the USA.

His time spent with Rusty and his Ayers Rockettes may
have taught Urban the basics of bringing an audience into
his world, but he was a long way off mastering the art of songwriting. (The Rockettes did, however, gain him some studio
time, as Urban played on tracks that the band recorded and
then sold on cassette at their shows.) Shaw was savvy enough
to see this and managed, via a deal secured with Joanne
Petersen at MCA Publishing in Australia, to get Urban into a
room with some of America's most seasoned tunesmiths
during his first tentative forays into Nashville.

Petersen herself had an impressive track record: she had been
personal assistant to Brian Epstein, the manager of the Beatles,
and her first signing to MCA was no less a band than INXS.
Her husband, Colin, a drummer, was the first non-Gibb
member of the Bee Gees. She was standing alongside Don
Spencer, another MCA signing and the future father-in-law of
Russell Crowe, when she first saw Urban playing at a half-full
Tamworth Leagues Club. Petersen sensed straight away that he
was a special talent, even before he plugged in and started
playing – and she was no country music fan, either. She
couldn't take her eyes off him as he walked through the club
in the direction of the stage. Afterwards she went backstage
to meet Urban, but was prevented from doing so by Angie
Marquis. Undaunted, Petersen called Greg Shaw, who told
her that MCA was the only publisher he and Urban had ever
considered signing with, on the strength of their impressive
Nashville roster. Resistance from within MCA was almost as
strong as Marquis's backstage muscle, but Petersen eventually
cemented a five-album deal for Urban (although they'd drop
him after one record, in a chronic act of short-sightedness).
Petersen, a key player in the Urban story, still remains close to
him; as recently as 2008 he stayed at her family home in Byron
Bay while playing the East Coast Bluesfest.

Deal in place, Petersen travelled to Nashville with Urban and Shaw – using promised MCA 'seed money' that never actually materialised – and hooked Urban up with an influential trio of songwriters. While the results were mixed – only two co-writes, 'A Little Luck of Our Own' and 'What Love Is That Way', actually made it onto future albums – the experience was hugely formative. Unlike rock acts, very few country singers, with the exception of such mavericks as Steve Earle, Lucinda Williams and Lyle Lovett, wrote their own songs without the guidance of co-writers. Such songwriting legends as Harlan Howard were treated like royalty; whenever Howard walked into a bar, he was guaranteed the best seat in the house, a fawning audience of acolytes *and free beer*. It was a good life, and it was essential that Urban get tight with these tunesmiths, even if the response during this first trip to Music City was pretty frosty. Urban, along with Shaw and Petersen, was told it would take five years before he could make any kind of impression in Nashville, if it was ever going to happen – and then it would require him to relocate. This harsh prediction turned out to be slightly optimistic. Urban slowly grew to understand this, actually referring to Music City's 'five year syndrome' in a 1994 interview, where he emphasised that it didn't matter how many hit records he'd had at home, 'you still have to start from scratch in Nashville'.

Urban had plenty to learn. There were strict rules, as Jody Williams, the head of MCA Publishing with whom all Urban's co-writers were employed, told writer Dan Daley. 'It's a lyric town,' Williams said. 'You can't be too esoteric or artsy.'[10] Men were allowed to drink in country songs, but it was frowned upon in women – Gretchen Peters's 'radical' anthem 'Redneck Woman' was still way in the future – while African-Americans and most 'outsiders' were best referred to in an avuncular way. As another hit songwriter, Bob McDill, also told Daley for his book *Nashville's Unwritten Rules*, 'Breaking up's still fine [in a country song], but there shouldn't be any children mentioned.'[11] Censorship was pretty commonplace. The line 'kiss my ass' was excised from Garth Brooks's breakout 'Friends in Low Places', a good example of how conservative country radio could be. (Years later, Urban would ditch the word 'damn' from an album title, fearing the wrath of southern wowsers.) These were rules that Urban needed to memorise if he had any hope of making an impression in Music City, USA.

But he was in good hands. All three songwriters – Gary Burr, Trey Bruce and Dave Loggins – certainly had experienced some days in the sun by the time they worked with the very green Urban. Originally a New Englander, Burr relocated to Nashville in the late 1980s, primarily on the strength of the song 'Love's Been a Little Bit Hard on Me', a hit that he penned for Juice Newton. A much-sought-after writer, and hit-maker for Randy Travis, LeAnn Rimes, Patty Loveless and George Jones, Burr had been named Songwriter of the Year by three key institutions: *Billboard* magazine, Nashville Songwriters' Association International and the American Society of Composers, Authors and Publishers (ASCAP). He was a major player, and probably the most productive early collaborator for Urban.

Trey Bruce was originally from Memphis, and he'd done hard time in the club scene of that very musical city before shifting to Nashville in 1989. His subsequent track record was just as impressive as Burr's, as he pumped out tunes for Shelby Lynne, Trisha Yearwood, Faith Hill, Reba McEntire and Gary Allan (a brooding, sexy Californian who'd share a few stages, and beers, with Urban).

Dave Loggins, however, came from a slightly different background: he'd actually been a pop star himself, albeit briefly, with his Top 5 US hit from 1974, 'Please Come to Boston'. A year later the song scored him a Male Vocal Performance Grammy. He was a little older than the others – Loggins was in his forties when he met and wrote with Urban – and probably impressed Urban as much with his tales of meeting Beatle John Lennon at the 1975 Grammys and writing with Kenny Rogers at his ranch, as he did with his understanding of the basics of a great country song.

At around the same time, James Blundell was in the midst of his own Nashville co-writing experiments. He first travelled there in 1989, and would return at least once a year for the next five years. And while some great tunes came out of his co-writes, including 'Walk On', one of the best songs he has ever recorded, Blundell found the experience of writing with a complete stranger very artificial and more than a little un-settling at times.

'I was always put with interesting writers,' Blundell admitted.

> But one of the less productive songwriting sessions I had was with a guy called Skip Ewing [who later had major success with Urban, funnily enough]. He was the only guy I clashed with because he wouldn't move an inch off the stereotypical formula. We started off with something that I thought was good and he said, 'No, that won't fly, they won't play that at radio,' and I said, 'How about we just write the song and worry about that afterwards?' He kept referring to 'Way Out West' and said that was a hit, why didn't I just write another one of those? *And this was a song I didn't write in the first place.* There was a problem straightaway. I realised that there are two very different schools in Nashville: one is the artist and the other is the songwriter. That was tough.

Blundell also learned that the stereotypical view of Southern-ers as conservative rednecks, swigging moonshine and blasting shotguns while hooning around town in their pick-ups, was a long way from the truth. On one occasion, he met up with American Billy Dean in a songwriters' room at the EMI building on Music Row. They were introduced, shook hands and got to work. 'Just to show how these types of situations can sink or float very quickly,' Blundell said, with a chuckle:

> I'd picked up a newspaper that morning and read how the KKK had a meeting that day in Knoxville. I went, 'For fuck's sake, are these people still at it?' So I went to the session thinking that Billy was a covert member of the clan.

Blundell and Dean set to work on a six-pack of beer, 'to break the ice', and just as Dean reclined on a couch, beer in hand, the thing collapsed beneath him.

'Fuck me!' Dean shouted. Blundell was stunned.

> I said that I was surprised he swore, and then he looked at me as though I was from outer space. He said, 'Yeah, and I drink, too.' So I had to ask him about the Klan and he looked at me as though I was really fucking odd. He said, 'No, mate, we're all fucking normal people here.' One of the things that I think is problematic is because you're thrown together, sight unseen – you'll get some kind of resumé about the person and what they've written, little more – and you're trying to be creative and discern someone's character at the same time. I used to come away from writing sessions mentally tired.

One lesson learned by Urban – but especially by Blundell, who was a far more recalcitrant character than his Aussie peer – was that you should never laugh at a co-writer's suggestion. Said Blundell:

> They were always too polite to do that, but there would be a deafening silence at times. 'Try this,' I'd say, and then there'd be nothing. I guess not, I figured, and carried on another way.

But the key difference between Urban and Blundell, whose careers would dovetail, for a time, during the late 1980s and early 1990s, was that Urban desperately wanted to re-create the American music he had so loved as a kid, whereas Blundell thought there was something unique in his take on Oz-country music that could fly in Nashville. Urban and Blundell would share backstage downtime and talk music, and Blundell clearly recalls Urban saying to him: 'I like this kind of music; I like American country music.' Blundell was more inclined towards what he saw as the 'older brigade', singer/songwriters with a worldly bent such as Kris Kristofferson, Johnny Cash and Willie Nelson. 'There were people who Keith was hip to that I just didn't know at all,' said Blundell. '[Nashville] was a much better fit for him and it made better sense.'

'I thought that what we had here in Australia, and still have, was very strong and unique,' Blundell continued.

> The nexus for me was colliding with the American mindset where I was literally told, 'First of all, you sing lyrics that go over the head of the audience, and secondly, if you want to compete in this market, you have to play this game.' So first up you're going to be given songs from about a hundred people, and then have to work your way into a position of being able to record your own songs. I certainly didn't have the patience for that and I didn't think that being sent over as an Australian artist entailed having to change what you do in order to fit in.

Blundell was also given some advice as to how to conform in Nashville. Basically, he was told to roll his 'r's and wear a hat. Neither sat comfortably with the man, although the former was a compromise that Urban was willing to make. As Blundell explained:

I was in the studio with an engineer one day and he told me that I was getting criticism because I didn't sound like I came from there. I said, 'No, mate, I come from a completely different part of the world.'

Blundell duly agreed on an experiment and attempted to sing a verse and a chorus using an American accent.

He stopped me quickly and said, 'I take your point.' It was a big call on his part; he was a young engineer who'd been appointed by Capitol and he then had to go back and tell them that it didn't work

Even though Greg Shaw was doing his best to build a case for Urban's Extraordinary Alien visa, and MCA's Joanne Petersen was also championing Urban, it was still a frustrating time for this star-in-the-making. He and Shaw were doing the immigration two-step: every time they travelled to Nashville and made some inroads, they'd be forced to return to Oz when his existing visa expired. Urban compared the experience to being stuck in the longest checkout line at the grocery store:

You're almost at the register and someone goes, 'Oh, you have to leave.' So you go, 'But I'm just about to . . .' and they say, 'No, *you gotta go.*' And when you get back you find out that the line is twice as long and you're right at the very back again. You start to think, 'God, this is never going to get anywhere.'

Urban was shrewd, however, and would leave a few more belongings behind with friends back in Nashville each time he visited. True believer Shaw, meanwhile, continued to talk up his new charge every chance he got. Once, while speaking with the manager of another prominent Australian country act, he boldly stated: 'My guy's got what it takes to go all the way.'

Shaw's fellow manager, at least initially, thought the comment was arrogant, but soon figured that he was speaking the truth. Of all the rising stars of Oz-country, Urban seemed the most likely to adapt to the demands of Nashville – and with youth, ragged good looks and musical chops on his side, he had plenty to offer Music City.

Former Sydneysider Jeff Walker had shifted to Nashville in 1974; it was the home of his father Bill, an arranger/conductor. He'd swiftly established himself in Music City, first with indie label Con Brio Records and then, from 1980, with his own company, Aristo Music Associates, Inc, a promotions firm. He'd also had some chart success, co-writing a pair of Top 20 country tunes, 'The Feeling's So Right Tonight' and 'She's the Girl of My Dreams'. Walker would do a weekly phone hook-up with Nick Erby for his radio show, reporting on the Nashville scene. When he heard that Urban was considering a move to Tennessee, he admits to 'being excited about the prospect'. Walker could certainly help an up-and-comer like Urban.

From his own experiences, however, Walker knew that the Caboolture kid couldn't just jet into Nashville and expect a limo to collect him from the airport, with a record company exec in the back seat brandishing a chequebook. As he explained to me:

> I feel that anyone who wants to make it in this country has to roll up their sleeves, work hard and be prepared to take setbacks. In this regard Keith and I are similar. In terms of 'fuelling the dream', I think we both strive for perfection – me on the business side and Keith on the musical side.

Within a couple of years, Walker would be the go-to guy on the ground in Nashville for both Urban and Greg Shaw – he became one of the singer's earliest 'boosters' in America. His support was crucial, especially when he was able to get Urban's music into the hands of massively influential radio DJs at a flashpoint when corporate power plays at Urban's US label took precedence over the wellbeing of their acts.

Back in Oz, as a new decade began, the homefires continued to blaze just that little more brightly for Urban despite his occasional absences. He had his sights set very firmly on one of Tamworth's key events, Star Maker, which was held during the first week of the festival. No money changed hands, but the pay-off from winning the quest was twofold: you scored some recording time *and* gained an instant 'profile', at least among the country music community. As the founding fathers proudly state on their website:

> Star Maker opens doors of opportunity for the young winners, helping them move into music as a career. This is achieved by 12 months heavy promotion of the winners to both fans and industry resulting in an extremely high profile for the current Star Maker. Many winners have gone on to enjoy enormous professional success.

Since its inception in 1979, Star Maker had helped establish James Blundell and Lee Kernaghan, while Troy Cassar-Daley had been a grand finalist. (Just like Urban, Cassar-Daley sprang from humble musical beginnings, busking on the streets of Tamworth. In 2008, Urban flew him to a show in Phoenix on a private jet.) Even though Urban had once shocked the sedate regional crowd by playing in shorts – it was January, after all – and his lank hair was now an interesting shade of Billy Idol white, he was crowned Star Maker in 1990. Cassar-Daley was runner-up and Tania Kernaghan, one of the female members of that Oz-country music dynasty, also reached the finals.

Urban sang two self-penned songs in the grand final, 'Homefires' and 'I Never Work on a Sunday', a boot-stomping, hand-clapping, the-boss-sucks-and-I'm-ready-for-the-weekend singalong that was really more a showcase for his Knopfler-derived finger-picking than some wellspring of human emotion. The song had evolved from a guitar riff and pretty much stayed that way. 'Sunday' was pleasant and good-natured, but it was no 'Galveston'. Nick Erby, who'd met and interviewed Urban almost a decade earlier in Tamworth, was on the scene, and noticed how 'focused and determined' Urban was about winning the event. According to Erby:

> Of 29 Star Makers there has never been anyone else as ready as Keith was to take advantage of what it offered. The thing about Star Maker was that the prize wasn't cash or a car or a night on the town; the prize was opportunity. It was all about career building. There has never been anyone since then who has been more ready to exploit the opportunities presented by Star Maker than Keith. He had a road album out there, he was already working with Rusty and doing gigs, he already had management support, he had the American plan in place, he'd already been there. No one had ever come into the event more ready than Keith.

Erby, in fact, realised that Urban was unlikely to lose Star Maker as soon as he ran his eyes over his entry form which contained a list of his many competition victories and his lengthy live rap sheet. 'I saw what he had been doing,' Erby laughs, 'and I went, "Shit, no one else is going to win this." He had a track record, something he didn't have [when he won junior Tamworth awards] at age 11.' Urban's parents, Bob and Marienne, were standing at the back of the room when their son was declared the winner, as was Rob Potts, who ran booking agency Allied Artists. Within days he would sign

Urban and subsequently represent him for the next 18 years. Their relationship would run deeper than client and agent – they shared a fondness for life-sweeteners.

The head of the Star Maker judging panel, ABC Rural broadcaster Colin Munro, was equally impressed by Urban, even if his ball-hugging, skin-tight denims and sharp black jacket didn't necessarily match Tamworth's Akubras-and-R. M. Williams uniform. Accordingly, Munro stated that Urban was country's 'image of the nineties' and compared the 22-year-old hopeful with American star-on-the-rise Dwight Yoakam. Even mainstream dailies such as *The Sun-Herald* got on board. 'Australian country music found itself a new sex symbol this week,' the paper declared, tagging Urban 'a smouldering young singer from Brisbane'.[12] As uncomfortable as Urban would be with the 'sex symbol' tag, it stuck with him. Nick Erby admits that some of the more conservative elements of Tamworth frowned upon Urban's 'rough trade' look – they still do, in fact – but he knew that Urban was part of a new, image-savvy generation of country artists:

> This was the renaissance period, the new generation, which had started a couple of years before with James [Blundell]. The industry was waiting for it but was on the lookout to see who was driving it forward and it turned out to be Keith. And it's spurred on the others. The mid eighties period also saw that renaissance in America which gave Keith the confidence to go, 'OK, I can fit in here.'

While Urban was busy 'sexing up' staid Tamworth, another soon-to-be supporter of his, American Garth Brooks, was kick-starting his own quiet revolution. The two shared similarities, though you'd hardly sense it by looking at them – Urban was gaunt and bleached, while the paunchy, Stetson-wearing Brooks tended to wear his Wranglers three sizes too small, which made him resemble an overdone muffin. Both came from unlikely spots for country music success: Urban from semi-rural Caboolture and Brooks, who was five years older than Urban, from Yukon, Oklahoma, which he once described as 'an average city in the middle of average Oklahoma in the middle of average America'. According to country music mythology, a 'real' country act should be raised on a dirt floor in a backwoodsy tarpaper shack, or something even more hardscrabble, ideally hundreds of kilometres from the nearest phone. *And then your dog gets run over.* That wasn't Yukon. Nor was it Caboolture.

If Brooks was any type of cowboy at all, he was a suburban cowboy, which would lead to accusations of him being inauthentic, a charge also directed at Urban. And Brooks and Urban shared tastes that, although steeped in country – they were big fans of George Strait, a clean-cut figure whose surname summed up his entire persona – sometimes strayed far from the fiddles-and-mandolin formula. Both loved touchy-feely singer-strummer James Taylor and were huge Eagles fans. Brooks also had it bad for the big-haired stadium rock of Journey, Foreigner and Styx, which would become very evident in his later arena shows. Brooks, again like Urban, had his human frailties: caught cheating on his wife, he opted for 'full disclosure' on the usual round of TV chat shows to publicly patch up their marriage. It worked, or at the very least she caved and took him back.

Brooks and Urban also shared a misconception: they naively felt that acceptance by the closed-off Nashville community – and the fans themselves – was as simple as plugging in, playing and being discovered. 'I thought Nashville would be like Oz,' Brooks told Bruce Feiler for his book *Dreaming Out Loud.*

[I thought] you came here and all your prayers would be answered. You'd flip open your guitar case, play a song and someone would hand you a million bucks [and] tell you, 'Come into the studio right quick, son, we got 10 songs we want you to cut.' People would be asking for your autograph that night.

It took several 'missions' to Nashville, a stint as a bouncer, and one failed band effort before Brooks made any inroads. But after being spotted by a Capitol records exec, the late Lynn Shults, at a Bluebird Café showcase (Urban would also play there in time, and one day also sign with Capitol), then really striking paydirt with a hand-on-heart hit called 'The Dance', Brooks became the Bruce Springsteen of country. He had made it as an undeniable, multi-platinum-plated star, with ego to match, whose record and ticket sales in the early 1990s reached numbers never before witnessed outside of rock and pop.

Soon enough Brooks – who didn't so much see himself as a superstar as a superhero with a Stetson in place of a cape – would play his role in both helping and inadvertently hindering Urban's progress Stateside. As for Shults, he was one step away from granting a US release to James Blundell's second album, *Hand It Down*, when a corporate coup at the label left him without a gig, and Blundell minus a supporter.

Nick Erby was right: by the time Urban returned to Tamworth in 1991, he had taken full advantage of the spoils of his win the year before. First up, he'd cut his debut single, 'I Never Work on a Sunday', with 'Homefires' on the flipside, as part of the Star Maker prize. The song was a good-enough start for Urban, even if the cover photo was a contender for worst single art of all time. The photographer caught Urban in classic 'Thinker' pose, his mullet freshly cropped and swept back like the crest of a wave, his hand poised under his chin, some pimples scattered across his exposed cheek. If that image wasn't clichéd enough – the sensitive artiste in repose – he was shot while wearing a very conventional drawstring bowtie which was pulled tight around his neck. The look was one part rent boy, one part poor man's Rhinestone Cowboy, and did little for the guy's credibility or his rep as someone not quite fitting the twangy stereotype. Regardless, in 1991 Urban was nominated for his first Golden Guitar, as Best New Talent, on the strength of the single and the country chart momentum it had collected – it was the first of his four subsequent country number ones in Australia. (The 1991 Star Maker winner was blue-eyed songbird Gina Jeffreys, a Toowoomba hairdresser, whose toothy smile and polite tunes indicated that Urban's rougher, earthier sound and edgy look hadn't inspired a legion of soundalikes.)

Urban had taken several steps in the right direction over those past few years leading up to his Best New Talent nomination. He'd started songwriting in earnest; 'The River', one of his earliest efforts, dated back to 1986, while 'Love We Got Goin'' came together in 1988. 'Future Plans' was written a year later. Urban was not what you'd call prolific – he never would be – but he was gradually weaning himself off his dependence on classic rock standards and country staples. Urban's track 'There's a Light On' was also prominently featured on ABC's 1990 compilation, *Breaking Ground: New Directions in Australian Country Music*, along with songs from James Blundell, Anne Kirkpatrick (Slim Dusty's daughter), Mary Jo Starr (who would marry Paul Kelly) and The Happening Thang. Urban had also moved on from the Ayers Rockettes and California Suite – though he would remain tight with Angie Marquis for some time yet. Gradually, his own band, who were sometimes known as Three Magic Words, fell into place. Drummer Peter Clarke was along for the ride, as was bassist Marlon Holden, who had formerly played in the Greg Shaw-managed Oz-rock act Skintight, one-time favourites on the Brisbane circuit. 'Skintight played to large pub crowds of 1000 to 2000, even during the week,' Holden told me. 'Those were the days.' (The band played, on average, five nights a week.) Like Urban, the burly, straight-talking Queenslander Holden was an early starter, first picking up the bass way back in 1972. He was an uncomplicated character, who once listed his favourite things as 'women, Thai foods [sic], Jack Daniels and originality'. When asked about his accomplishments, he replied: 'I'm still alive. Now that's an achievement.'

Alan Cameron, Robert Stevenson, Neil Wickham and Jeff Wickenden would also, at various times, either play in Urban's own band or be part of his live crew. Steve 'Flo' Law, who knew Urban from Caboolture days, was the band's sound guy, who would work with Urban both in Australia and the US. Today he still controls the 'front-of-house' sound at Urban's shows and is one of the singer's 'inner circle'.

A promo flyer from the time summed up Urban's musical stance. 'He is a top MUSICIAN and a great ENTERTAINER' it screamed. 'Keith is an amalgam of all that is positive in music combining strong influences from the past together with playing styles that are very much part of today.'

But not only had Urban brought together a 'proper' band, he and Shaw had also stitched up a legitimate record deal with a 'real' record label. Rob Walker, the head of A&R at EMI and a strong supporter of local country music, had signed Urban to record his debut LP for the major. Walker was an interesting character, a wiry, good-natured Kiwi with a thing for the epic novels of Cormac McCarthy, gas-guzzling American cars and the good life. He'd started out with EMI in New Zealand in the 1970s and had worked his way slowly but steadily through the ranks.

Walker first saw Urban play at a club in Tamworth when he

was sharing the stage with Angie Marquis. The label guy was immediately impressed with Urban's playing and 'the timbre of his voice'. But he had one big concern. Backstage, he spoke with Urban's parents, Bob and Marienne. 'I want to sign him,' he admitted, straight up, 'but I have to ask, "What's the deal with Angie? Does she have to stay in the picture, musically speaking?"' He considered her a typical Queensland suburban girl, nice enough, but without a great deal of talent. He figured she was there purely because she was Urban's girlfriend. Urban's mother, Marienne, very much the rock of the Urban family, said no, it wasn't a package deal. When Walker asked Urban the same question he agreed, albeit with some compassion towards his girlfriend. Marquis has never spoken about her rejection, nor has Urban ever outlined how he broached the subject with his ballsy, cut-the-crap girlfriend.

EMI's local roster included world-beaters Crowded House, country king Slim Dusty and new star-on-the-rise James Blundell, another Walker signing, so Urban was keeping some good company. (When Dusty died in 2003, the label's Chris O'Hearn stated: 'We call EMI in Australia the house that Slim built.') It wasn't long after his signing that the head of EMI, Brian Harris, caught an Urban set at Tamworth. He was just as impressed as Rob Walker. The now-retired Harris told me:

> I always considered Keith more rock and roll — I felt sure that one day he'd 'cross over' into the mainstream. He was a brilliant young talent who could have gone in any direction. When I first saw him play, I knew he had a great deal of talent but was very raw and needed a lot of guidance.

Harris readily agreed to Walker's plan to sign Urban, despite being cornered by one exec who said: 'What did you sign this guy for?' He grew close with Urban who played at his wedding, even though his friends outside the music business had no idea who the Billy Idol-lookalike actually was. (In 2007, when Harris turned 60, Urban sent him a congratulatory DVD and mentioned the wedding gig. A few years earlier, during an ARIA acceptance speech, he described Harris as a 'freakin' living legend'.)

'A lot of people forget that [Keith and I] were direct commercial opponents, vying for the same space, signed to EMI by the same A&R guy, Rob Walker,' recalled James Blundell when we spoke in 2008.

> There wasn't so much antipathy between us but a healthy mutual regard bordering on competitiveness. I was dumb enough not to worry that there were other people doing the same thing and then found out that Greg [Shaw] had set sights on moving me out of the road so the path was clear for them. I was like, 'Fucking hang on, I was just being friendly.'

Neither Walker nor Harris considered it a problem to sign two rising stars of country. As far as Walker was concerned, they represented 'the new face of Australian country music. Blundell was the eloquent modern poet, Urban was the maverick guitar-slinger. Both were young, smart and good-looking.' It also helped that Slim Dusty continued to record cheaply and sell strongly; his ongoing success meant that reasonable budgets could be allocated to the albums of Urban and Blundell.

All the time, though, Urban and Shaw had never lost sight of their bigger goal: to make some real noise in Nashville. Shaw badgered label boss Brian Harris, to the point where:

> Greg used to drive me nuts about it. But he played a massive role. Keith was quiet, understated, not a good schmoozer. Greg did that hard work. He also lent Keith a lot of money, financing him all the way along.

(Harris would play his part, too, advancing Urban A$50,000 from his record deal to help him establish himself in the US in 1992. 'And we didn't get the money back for a long time,' he laughed, looking back.)

Urban also deserves due credit for his commitment to the cause. He wrote to all the major players at Nashville record labels and elsewhere, 'shopping' himself and his music. Very few replied, but one response would tell Urban that his American dream wasn't some folly. Maybe he didn't have to remain a biggish fish in a tiny pond called Australia.

The letter came from Mary Martin, a legendary talent scout, who'd championed such edgy country acts as Rodney Crowell (with whom Urban would one day work) and Emmylou Harris. Martin was also instrumental in steering Albert Grossman, the imposing, bear-like manager of Bob Dylan and Janis Joplin, in the direction of four Canucks and an Okie who called themselves The Band. Martin was a Toronto native who had moved to New York to begin her career as Grossman's receptionist in the mid 1960s and more than 20 years later was still actively involved in the 'biz'.

Her letter to Urban read: 'I listened to your music and really enjoyed it. Unfortunately, country is enjoying a traditional time at the moment' − the so-called New Traditionalists, led by stony-faced crooner Randy Travis, dominated Nashville and country radio at that time − '[and although] I feel your music doesn't fit . . . I hope you come back to Nashville and find a home here.' Urban didn't feel rejected; in fact, he felt encouraged by her comments. 'What I read from her letter was,' he said:

'Come here and when the pendulum swings you'll be in the right place.' I thought about that letter over future years. To me it meant, 'Stick to your guns and be patient.'[13]

But Urban had other things on his mind that night in Tamworth during January 1991, when the nominees' names were read out by Anne Kirkpatrick for the Best New Talent Golden Guitar. One of the things weighing most heavily on him was this: 'I wonder what they think of my jacket?' The quiet kid from rural Queensland, the bogan loner with the loose-cannon father and imposing girlfriend, was sitting there expectantly, wearing a sharply cut, candy-apple-red jacket with black brocade on front and back (and now a popular display at the Walk a Country Mile exhibit). His blue jeans stuck to him like a second skin, while his bleached mullet was topped off by a skyscraping quiff. In a room full of oilskins, denims and Akubras, he was one rare bird. Then, finally, the moment of truth, delivered with due rustling of envelope and pregnant pause: 'And the winner is . . . Keith Urban.' As the entire room turned his way, the look on Urban's face was pure joy. It was his first Golden Guitar. Now it felt as though he was really on his way.

Three

SADDLE-POP

Keith was living in a dodgy neighbourhood and having all that around, while fighting disappointment and self-esteem issues, is trouble.

Mark Moffatt

When Urban had finished re-reading Mary Martin's talismanic letter, he headed into the studio to record his debut long-player, another essential step along the path to Nashville. An impressive cast of players and pickers was assembled, and not all from within Urban's inner circle. The Urban engine room of drummer Peter Clarke and bassist Marlon Holden were the only members of his working band to play on the LP, and even then Holden only contributed to one track. '[Marlon] was a buddy of Keith's who did his best,' said someone who worked on the album, 'but he didn't have the fingers. He did do a lot of co-writes, though.'

Keyboardist Neil Wickham, who was part of Urban's touring band, was also overlooked. According to his studio replacement, Glen Muirhead, Wickham was annoyed by his exclusion. 'I got to meet him and got to know that he felt a little burned by being left behind, but musicians get used to that. People move on.' (It's possible that the scars remain. I approached Wickham, who is now the Head of Learning [Performing Arts] at Queensland's John Paul College, for an interview, to which he initially agreed. Then, after being briefed as to what I'd like to ask him, he backed out, claiming he didn't realise it was an unauthorised biography. One of my questions asked whether he'd felt dumped by Urban, both with the album and his relocation to the US.)

Urban wasn't totally dependent on a country-savvy crew, either. Pop singer/songwriter Rick Price – who would break out in 1992 with his singles 'Not a Day Goes By' and 'Heaven Knows', both Top 10 hits – put in cameos on several tracks. Price's memory of the session is fleeting, at best, as he told me:

> I'm afraid there's nothing to tell really. I sang some background vocals on a track for him and I'm not sure that he was actually there for the session. It's quite some time ago.

The album's producer, Peter 'Huggie' Blyton, also seemed an unlikely contender. His recent production credits included records from pub rockers the Radiators and the Choirboys (including their chart-topping Oz-rock anthem 'Run to Paradise'), amped-up garage punks the Lime Spiders, the psychedelically inclined Max Q (which featured a moonlighting Michael Hutchence) and synth-pop dandies the Machinations. He'd also worked with hair metal pretenders the Candy Harlots and had actually played in the Tim Gaze Rock Ensemble. Blyton's first production credit was as unlikely as anything else on his CV; he produced a record of Burt Bacharach covers by creamy-voiced Malaysian native Kamahl. (Blyton can still pull off a near-perfect impression of Australia's favourite caftan wearer.) There was nary a tear-in-beer or anything resembling a twang on Blyton's resumé, at least up until then – and it was a long way from the Candy Harlots's 'Red Hot Rocket' to pedal-and-steel Tamworth.

However, Blyton was a Brisbane native and a close friend of Greg Shaw; they'd been on opposing sports teams in high school and knew each other very well. Blyton attended Brisbane Grammar, as did pianist Muirhead, who played on much of the album. The Queensland connection was strong; Blyton had played in a band called Big Red whose numbers included Chris Lloyd, a former member of the Shaw-managed Skintight. Blyton also had a reputation for 'capturing the moment' in the studio and was known as a fast worker. And he was dead keen to work in music's A league. 'I was very young and kind of thrown into that production,' the now 50-year-old Blyton said to me over a Sydney harbourside lunch.

> But I wanted to get more work with the majors and [EMI's] Rob [Walker] was very nice and said that he wanted me to do it, even though I'd never done country before.

There was a reason for that, too. 'Australian country music makes me want to vomit,' Blyton admitted. To him, country was something best heard in the honeyed bluegrass of Alison Krauss, taken straight from the Appalachians. Tamworth was not the epicentre of what he understood country to be. Piano man Muirhead felt exactly the same:

> I was a Herbie Hancock fan, a fusion aficionado, so I'd always hated country, I didn't like it at all, but I found I had a knack for doing it. In Queensland I'd done a lot of jingles. And Queensland being what it was in the late 1970s, early 1980s, there was still quite a bit of country in the advertising.

Urban clearly liked Muirhead's work, referring to his playing as 'keys from hell!'

Before signing on, producer Blyton saw Urban play beneath Brisbane's Crest Hotel, on the urging of Greg Shaw. Blyton had no hesitation telling his old friend what he was witnessing:

> I said, 'The guy has the voice of an angel and he can play guitar like Tommy Emmanuel.' He had spiky blond hair, pimply face and was skinny as a rake. He was semi unmarketable, an unassuming dude. He was playing rock covers but he had this country yearning.

Blyton immediately agreed to produce the album.

However, Blyton and Urban were up against it from the very beginning. Rob Walker, a flamboyant character who once dated former Miss World, Belinda Green, and was Tina Turner's tour manager for five high-flying years, had just left EMI. (Sick of the music biz, Walker opened an antiques and collectibles store, only to return eventually to work for Roadshow Music, where he signed Savage Garden. He now lives in blissful isolation in the NSW Hunter Valley.) Walker was replaced by a new A&R boss, Neil Bradbury, who had little time for country music. A few years later he died, allegedly of a drug overdose.

Upon Walker's departure, Blyton's original production budget of A$64,000 was slashed by about 50 percent, which meant that he and Urban – despite the many cameos on the album – were forced to play and record much of the material by themselves. The contributions of guests like Price and guitarist Kirk Lorange came about by chance and were done very much on the fly. 'When Rob left, [Greg Shaw] was shattered,' said Blyton. 'It was now like trying to push a four-tonne truck up a hill.'

Initially, Blyton had wanted to record in Starsound Studios, which was located at Channel 9 in Brisbane. It was ideal because Urban, of course, was Brisbane-based, as was Shaw. And Starsound had all the right equipment. Blyton was initially told that they didn't take 'outside work', but he talked the studio owners around.

> I told them it was for EMI and they agreed, but they insisted there was to be no drinking, no smoking, the whole thing. I've had everyone flown up from Sydney and put them in accommodation, it's all ready to go, when I got a call from EMI – not from Rob Walker but from some pompous bitch, who said: 'Rob Walker's no longer looking after A&R, it's now Neil Bradbury. Your budget is now halved.' I was told to send everyone packing. I was just about in tears and sent half the crew home.

They were instructed to fly back to Sydney and work in EMI's 301 Studios. The demos they had recorded while in Brisbane effectively became the 'finished' backing tracks for the album. 'We were gutted,' Blyton recalled.

> The only reason I'm playing all these parts on the record is because I had to – there was no one else but Keith and I there – with the drummer and two old mongrel dogs. Everything was hurried and rushed, and we were ushered from the big studio in 301 to the little studio they used for overdubs. We had to make silk purses out of sows' ears.

It was the kind of unfortunate record company intervention that would stall Urban's progress more than once early on in his career, and give him and Shaw added motivation to leave Australia. Regardless, Blyton, some 15-plus years down the line, remains very proud of what they achieved with so little.

'I think the record still stands up,' he told me in 2008. 'To this day, I still think it sounds great.' Blyton was paid about A$2500 for four weeks of recording and another two weeks of mixing, which didn't even cover his costs.

Pianist Muirhead, who played on almost all the 15 finished tracks, was struck by Urban's intensity in the studio. He may have been young, but Urban seemed to know exactly what he wanted.

> One thing that has stuck with me was just how focused he was. And he was very quick to help in terms of guidance – and he was quite good at it, too. He pulled me back from the bluesier thing, which is what I loved playing, and got me into a really good place, actually, for doing country-rock, as that was. He was obviously hearing those tracks very clearly in his head and it's a great talent to then communicate that to the other people in the studio – and he could do that, he was great.

As the sessions continued, those close to the record came up with a tag for Urban's musical blend of twang, melody and sugar: they called it 'saddle-pop', though not within earshot of Urban.

Muirhead also noticed that Urban, unlike most studio novices, wasn't prepared to sit back and let producer Blyton do his thing – he was more a co-pilot than a trainee. 'He rode Peter pretty hard; he pushed him to get his way,' Muirhead said.

> Peter had a great talent for organising things and getting things happening quickly. One of his real skills was keeping a good vibe in the studio and getting a good result. I never saw any conflict, but Keith wasn't sitting back while Peter ran the show. He was right alongside him, pushing buttons and sending directions back into the studio, almost as much as Peter did.

If the union of producer Blyton and star-on-the-rise Urban, at least in theory, seemed unlikely, then the album's opening track, the sweetly melodic soft-pop of 'Only You', hinted that Urban was shooting directly for the heart of the mainstream. The song was a co-write between the hulking co-founder of Dragon, New Zealander Todd Hunter, and his partner Johanna Pigott (who's played in such pop-punk acts as Scribble and XL Capris). The pair – a couple away from music – were on a hot streak as songwriters, having recently written the runaway smash 'Age of Reason' for the airbrushed king of pop, John Farnham, as well as Dragon's comeback hit 'Rain'. That success, as Hunter told me, gave him and Pigott the luxury of retiring to the country for a couple of years, where they divvied up their time between music-making and baby-rearing. 'Only You' was one of the tracks to emerge from this idyllic time. 'I think it was one of the better songs,' Hunter says today, looking back. 'It worked across different genres.' Producer Blyton agreed. 'It's more of an MOR record,' he said of both the opening track and the entire album. Saddle-pop, in other words.

Todd Hunter readily admits to having no great knowledge of country music apart from the Glen Campbell songs that he and his brother Marc – Dragon's sexy yet doomed lead singer – once sang together on the way to school. He knew little of Urban when he got the call to head down to Sydney's 301 Studio and play on the track. Hunter and Pigott had actually written the song, which became the album's first single, with a female voice in mind, so he was taken aback to hear that some guy called Keith was about to cut it. His curiosity aroused, he drove down to Sydney to see what evolved.

The session was one of the easiest Hunter had ever been involved with. 'They actually used the demo's rhythm track,' he recalled, which was probably as much a result of fiscal restrictions as anything else. 'We were asked to bring our stuff into the studio — whatever primitive computer stuff we had then — and Keith just played guitar over it.' Hunter was satisfied by what he heard upon playback of the track; clearly, the song also worked with a male voice. 'He's always had this thing where he was never hardcore country; he's been able to skip across genres,' Hunter said.

Even though they'd never met before, a bond was formed between Kiwi behemoth Hunter and skinny country kid Urban. So much so, in fact, that a few years later Hunter asked Urban to help out on an album called *Incarnations*, where guest vocalists added their own twist to a swag of Dragon standards. It was recorded in Hunter and Pigott's country hideaway. As Hunter recalled, things didn't quite work out as planned for those sessions. Urban, who was on a flying visit from the States, wasn't in the best shape. 'He came down to sing on a few songs [but] he had a terrible flu and he couldn't sing.' Hunter didn't know Urban as a guitarist, but asked him to play anyway — after all, he'd travelled a long way, he might as well contribute *something*. He was startled by what he heard.

'He played guitar on a few tracks and he was incredible,' Hunter laughed, thinking back. 'He played on "Rain" and "Are You Old Enough?" and a really slow version of "Speak No Evil" that Renee Geyer sang, where he played wah–wah guitar.' Hunter had based the new arrangement on the Motown classic 'Papa Was a Rolling Stone' — and Urban nailed it first take. 'He played such impeccable stuff,' said Hunter. 'I was taken aback by how tasteful his stuff was. His influences were very wide because no matter what track you played he'd be right in the pocket. It just worked.' Urban may have only been a few years into his Nashville journey, but Hunter sensed that he was already a little damaged by the experience.

I got a feel that for him it was like *The Odyssey*; he knew it might take him 10 years to succeed but he was going to do it. And he seemed to know of the pain he would have to go through. And when he did it, I thought, 'Fuck, incredible, here's a man who lived out the whole thing.' He was wearied by it, even then, but he was determined.

Back in EMI's 301 Studios in Sydney's Castlereagh Street, a curious assortment of guests continued to make their way through the doors as Urban's album – which, in a classic act of record company confusion, was originally self-titled but then changed to *1991* on its re-release five years later – took shape. They included highly regarded banjo plucker Mark 'Bucky' Collins, fiddler Paul 'Pixie' Jenkins – who was so impressed that he said Urban was his 'hero' – and even producer Blyton's former bandleader, Tim Gaze, who'd also played in Rose Tattoo for a time. Stringman Rod McCormack, soon to establish himself as a key player in the 'country music mafia' located in and around the NSW Central Coast, added some tasty banjo to an updated 'I Never Work on a Sunday', the song that had won Urban Star Maker a few years earlier. Most of the guests worked for the minimum fee, some for even less. The track 'Got It Bad' was co-written by Heather Field, a blind songwriter who worked a lot with Rick Price (and who was, incidentally, yet another Queenslander).

Though not quite an all-star cast, it was just about the best that could be assembled at the time, especially for an unproved recording act like Urban and given the recent shake-up at EMI. And these weren't strictly country guys. As mentioned, expat Canadian slide guitarist Kirk Lorange, who'd played alongside Marc Hunter and was best known for his work on Richard Clapton's benchmark *Capricorn Dancer* and *Goodbye Tiger* albums, also contributed. Urban was a keen fan of the moustachioed Lorange's band, Chasin' the Train, an ensemble of musicians' musicians which also included future members of Tamworth favourites The Flood. Urban would sometimes turn up in the crowd at their gigs at Gladesville's Bayview Tavern, eagerly looking on, scrutinising their moves, ever the fan (although this time he wasn't clutching flowers, as he'd done at Tommy Emmanuel gigs). Interestingly, EMI boss, Brian Harris, once showed at an Urban gig at the Bayview – he admitted to being 'dragged along' – where there were more people on-stage than in the audience. 'He still played great, though,' said Harris. What's funnier still is that as recently as March 2008, when Urban was playing to a full house at Sydney's Hordern Pavilion, he recalled those Bayview shows, chuckling at how 'six people would show up and we knew five of them'. Mind you, by that stage in his career he could afford to laugh at his earlier failings.

Another unlikely onlooker at an early Urban gig was Sherbet founder and crack pop tunesmith, Clive Shakespeare, who had done some home recordings with James Blundell and was developing an interest in country music. He was invited by Rob Potts to an Urban set at the long-gone Sydney venue, the Saloon. Potts, as Urban's agent and friend, was interested in why Urban wasn't pulling more punters to his Sydney shows and thought Shakespeare might have some answers. 'We rocked in and Keith's playing,' Potts recalled.

> At the end of the gig, Clive and I went away and talked, and he said: 'He doesn't know how to put his set together. He doesn't know how to communicate with his audience. He's brilliant, but he doesn't have a clue.' I'd thought it was great, but then he told me how Keith didn't construct a set with real dynamics.

Potts raised his eyebrows and kept listening. 'I didn't have a clue myself,' he admitted. Potts tried to get Urban and Shakespeare

Keith Urban at home in the early 1970s, not long before the family home burned down. According to his schoolmate and friend, Sherry Plant, 'The town Caboolture was fairly conservative and had a healthy dose of the rural, redneck element.' *(Both photos: Newspix)*

Alongside his first music teacher, Sue McCarthy (now Crealey), whom Urban met purely by chance. After several lessons, she approached Urban's parents with a confession: 'I just can't teach him any more – I just know the basics.' *(Photo: Newspix)*

Urban *(middle row, centre)* during his last year of school at Caboolture High, 1982. When asked about high school, Urban wasn't especially nostalgic. 'I would have left sooner if I could,' he admitted. 'It was a terrible inconvenience.' *(Photo: Newspix/Annette Dew)*

Urban on stage with brother-and-sister act Rusty Berther and Sherry Plant, at the
Bribie Island Festival in the early 1980s. Their set, as Plant recalled, 'gave us a
taste of the performing high – as well as lifting us briefly out of nerd status'.
(Photo: Newspix/Brianne Makin)

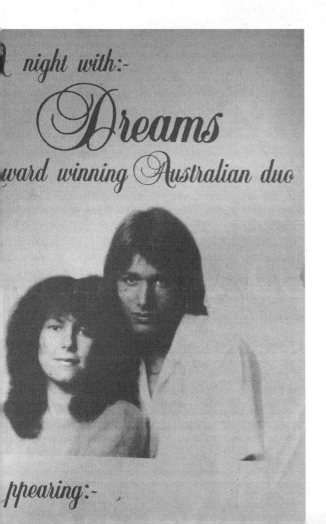

A poster for a duo comprising
Urban and his on- and off-stage
partner, Angie Marquis. 'He
couldn't afford to buy her an
engagement ring,' recalled
record producer Peter Blyton,
'so he gave her his Telecaster
instead.' *(Photo: Newspix/Brianne
Makin)*

Urban's parents, Marienne and Bob. When EMI's Rob Walker wanted to sign their son, he asked them, point-blank, 'What's the deal with Angie? Does she have to stay in the picture, musically speaking?'
(Photo: Newspix/Nathan Richter)

A star in the making, 1989. Urban already had a manager, Greg Shaw, and a booking agent, Rob Potts. The next year he won Tamworth's Star Maker comp. 'No one had ever come into the event more ready than Keith,' said broadcaster Nick Erby. *(Photo: John Elliott)*

Urban and band Three Magic Words, 1990. Drummer Peter Clarke is far right; bassist (and later groomsman) Marlon Holden is at far left. The straight-shooting Holden listed his favourite things as 'women, Thai foods [sic], Jack Daniel's and originality'.

Playing live, also during the early 1990s, at the time he was looking towards Nashville as a new base. According to Rob Potts, Urban was very keen to pursue his musical 'destiny', but was also 'stoked to be away from the family'. *(Both photos: John Elliott)*

A fashion crisis, 1991: Keith Idol – or Billy Urban? Urban was fresh from a significant in-flight conversation with Tommy Emmanuel. 'He had pink hair; he looked like a little punk,' the guitarist recalled. (Photo: John Elliott)

On the streets of Tamworth with Lee Kernaghan, 1992. When then country king James Blundell caught Urban live for the first time, he was stunned. 'Fuck, that guy can play guitar,' he said. 'I've always had a high regard for his ability.'

With his mentor and hero, Slim Dusty, in Moree, 1993. Urban admired and trusted Dusty. 'I know Slim was amused at Keith's "way out" attitude and appearance,' said his widow, Joy McKean. '[But] we were not quite as shocked as most others, actually.' *(Both photos: John Elliott)*

With manager Greg Shaw, backstage at yet another gig. Their relationship was the making of Keith Urban. Shaw, allegedly, sunk as much as two million dollars of his and his family's money into Urban's career, before being sacked. Nothing, to date, has been recouped.

On stage at Brisbane's Festival Hall, 1994. 'An artist can have all the talent in the world,' said Joy McKean, 'but without that burning drive and "stickability", that artist may never realise his or her full potential. Keith had all that.' *(Both photos: John Elliott)*

together to record, but it didn't pan out. And when he told Greg Shaw what Shakespeare had revealed, Shaw looked stunned. 'He didn't grasp it at all,' said Potts.

'We did some jamming and hanging out together in Tamworth one year around that time,' said Kirk Lorange, when I asked him about working with Urban. 'As I recall, he was in and out of Studio 301 for that album and I was always in there doing various sessions.' Lorange can't recall too much of the session, which took place in Studio D, typically used for recording jingles and overdubs, although he's pretty sure that:

> . . . various mind-altering substances were ingested first, as was always the way back then. I'm sure we just bumped into each other in the hall and he would have said something like, 'Kirk, you're the guy I need for this track I'm working on, when can you come in?'

Apart from the fact that Urban was a fan, Lorange liked the guy's drive and couldn't help but be charmed by his youthful spirit.

As Lorange explained:

> He was quite a bit younger than most of us, so he was always that super-talented kid that we knew. He was very outgoing, very charming and always smiling, full of energy, full of country music.

Lorange was nonplussed, however, not long after working with Urban, when he bumped into him blithely walking down the main street of Crows Nest, his dyed blond hair at full attention and his face smeared with pancake makeup. Did Urban have some dark secret that he'd just let out of the bag? Not quite. It turned out that he'd come straight from a recording of the

Midday Show at nearby Willoughby – where he appeared many times, as did James Blundell – and had forgotten to have his makeup removed. Not that Urban minded the attention from passers-by, Lorange admitted. 'I'm sure the people wondered,' he said, 'but I think Keith would have been OK with them staring.'

The standout track for producer Blyton was the bluegrass-flavoured, tearaway instrumental 'Clutterbilly', a track that gave Jenkins, Collins, Clarke and – especially – Urban, the chance to really cut loose. 'It's virtuoso guitar playing; he could make a Tele[caster] sound like a pedal steel,' said Blyton. 'He had this incredible bluegrass influence; it could have just been heaven sent, I don't know.' When not tapping into his heaven-sent talent, Urban spent much of his time on the phone, cooing words of love to Marquis. 'He always wanted to be married to someone,' figured Blyton, who'd already had his 'marriage' discussion with Urban by this time. 'He wanted someone to cuddle with and come home to. He's always loved the ladies.'

'Blue Stranger', a moody Paul Kelly ballad that Urban covered, was another standout for Blyton:

> As a producer, 99 percent of the time you're looking through the glass and there's a singer on the other side. You're looking at the lyrics and listening for the performance and appraising, whatever, especially back then when we didn't have digital recording. But with Keith I started to forget what I was doing; it was like being a punter in the front row, just listening. That's only happened to me a few times: with Chrissie Amphlett and Marc Hunter. Keith would be singing 'Blue Stranger' and I'd be sitting there with goosebumps – then I'd go, 'Oh, shit, that's right, we're making a record,' and get back to work. That's when you know you're onto something special.

Urban's *Midday Show* cameos and his ever-escalating public profile inevitably led to mainstream media zeroing in on country's 'newest sensation', even if EMI's support of the album was negligible apart from a few live showcases and a typically gushy press release in which Urban, somewhat disingenuously, stated:

> I see my music as contemporary country, FM country which we don't have here [in Australia]. Hopefully it's the type of country that will get commercial airplay and the type that people will think of when they think of country music.

Australian television, however, was especially generous to a guy who dwelled on the fringes of the mainstream. In 1991 alone, Urban made two appearances on Steve Vizard's *Tonight* show (playing 'Arms of Mary' and 'Only You'), performed once on *Midday*, singing 'Love We Got Goin'' and also scored a spot on the high-rating *Hey Hey It's Saturday*, cranking out 'Got It Bad' while wearing a gloriously tacky red, gold and black shirt-cum-poncho. He later returned to the Ray Martin-hosted *Midday* and tore through a smoking take on Charlie Daniels's 'The Devil Went Down to Georgia', looking every inch the rocker in his open vest (without a shirt) and shoulder-length hair, showboating madly on his Telecaster. Drummer Clarke had now grown his dark hair past his shoulders and that, teamed with *his* soul patch, gave Urban and the band a decidedly edgier, wilder look. For an audience that thought bearded, chatty bandleader Geoff Harvey was a crazy guy, the sight of Urban must have come as quite a shock.

As this proved, Urban seemed wary of being regarded as strictly country – he knew that it was a marginalised genre at best, which didn't sell in the same numbers as, say, a saccharine pop singer/songwriter like Richard Marx (another Urban collaborator further down the line). In one of his earliest interviews with a major newspaper, in January 1991, with the album still being made, Urban referred to his music as 'con-temporary' – even though you'd hardly rate *Midday Show*'s blue-rinse viewers as part of a 'contemporary' audience.

'I agree . . . that the music can appeal to anyone, not just so-called country people,' said a surprisingly forthright Urban. 'Look at the success of the *Blues Brothers* movie and music. Much of that drew on strong country roots and established a cult following. Look at me,' he added with a chuckle. 'You could hardly categorise me as a country and western plucker.' Urban added that he'd toured with comic Billy Connolly and recorded a Paul Kelly song – and he knew for a fact 'that Jimmy Barnes even has a few country records, so it's not as if I'm something odd at 24 wanting to play it.'

His tone grew increasingly defensive when the conversation drifted to the perception of Tamworth and its stars held by 'outsiders'. 'City people look at us as freaks and oddities,' he replied.

> But we represent good things and wholesome family attitudes. It's easy to knock in these cynical days but you never hear of riots and drug taking at Tamworth. [There's] no violence, no ugly threats. Maybe the world could learn from us right now.[1]

Of course, none of his Tamworth audience were privy to the various 'mind-altering substances' probably being consumed in 301 Studios while Urban's debut LP was being made, but why let that fact mess with country's apple pie public image?

Maybe Urban was making a conscious effort to distance himself from James Blundell and his songs about the simple pleasures of the 'Kimberley Moon' and 'Rain on a Tin Roof', let alone the homespun laments of Slim Dusty and Smoky Dawson – a man who in 1991 stated that 'if Saddam Hussein listened to country music there wouldn't be a Gulf War today'.

You could read Urban's solo debut as a statement of intent. Sure, there was plenty of twang, but there were also moments of pure pop, sappy middle-of-the-road ballads, some slick production and very little in the way of cattle dogs, utes and/or celebrations of honest working folk doing it tough on the land. Unless, of course, there was a subliminal message hidden away in the warp-speed 'Clutterbilly'.

The front cover image, as usual, did Urban few favours. Posing in a sawn-off 'western' shirt and snug blue jeans, a heavily accessorised Urban – a peace symbol hung from a chain around his neck, a hoop was in his ear – glared at the camera (and his female fans) like some kind of bad boy that you could still bring home to meet mother. Yet the photo, like much of the mistake-ridden album sleeve – the surname of Urban's long-time buddy Marlon Holden is misspelled as 'Holdern', while Chris Lloyd's surname picks up a superfluous 's' – only served to illustrate his record company's lack of effort. 'It seemed to us,' said Blyton, 'that EMI did everything in their power to knock this on the head. Even the fucking artwork is bad.' This also contributed to the unfavourable reputation engendered by the Australian office of EMI. To some, the label's name meant: 'Every mistake imaginable.'

Still, much of the music stood tall. 'Only You' opened with a few notes of mellow acoustic guitar – Gypsy Kings, anyone? – but then locked into the kind of smooth groove that had made Perth's the Eurogliders chart-hogs for much of the mid 1980s. Combined with the honey-sweet harmonies of co-writers Hunter and Pigott, and the occasional subtle piano fill, the song had 'tasteful' written all over it. Urban headed back to more familiar territory with 'Got It Bad' where, to the ring of a razor-sharp, bluesy guitar lick, he sang of how he 'hit the highway' and 'stopped for coffee in a nowhere town'. It was the archetypal driving song, a style way closer to what his growing fanbase – Urban preferred to call them his 'friend base' – expected to hear from their Golden Guitar-winning hero. Kirk Lorange's burst of slide guitar coloured what was effectively a few minutes of likeable, sharply produced country-rock. 'Without You' also drew from the same musical well; it was crisply played and smartly produced, but stuck pretty tightly to the twang-pop template, even if a Knopfler-like guitar solo from Urban added some heat.

Urban's cover of Paul Kelly's 'Blue Stranger' typified the record's more downbeat side; this late-night ballad was duly 'twanged-up' by Mark Collins's banjo (soon enough, Urban wouldn't need to hire banjo pickers; he mastered the instrument himself and would use it with extreme prejudice). 'Arms of Mary', one of the songs Urban would regularly croon for Ray Martin's superannuated audience, was another of the album's covers. This mid-tempo weepie had been a Top 30 hit in 1976 for English folkies the Sutherland Brothers and Quiver. The Sutherlands, brothers Ian and George, also wrote 'Sailing', an equally soppy tune that supermodel-shagger Rod Stewart navigated to the top of the charts in 1975. 'Mary' was a favourite of Blyton, who insists that he played it for Urban and encouraged him to cut it.

> We were having trouble filling up the record because Keith was still a budding songwriter. I asked him, as a favour, to record 'Arms of Mary', my favourite song in the world. That was a request from me, and I think it's one of the standout tracks.

During the recording of the album, it would also prove to be something of a marriage-saver for the producer. Urban, Blyton and Shaw had been on a boozy night out and upon returning to Blyton's Sydney home found that the producer had been barred from the marital boudoir. Clearly in a fix, he handed Urban a guitar and asked him to play the song loud enough so that his enraged partner, Kirsty (sister of Jodhi) Meares, could hear it from the other side of the door. 'Arms of Mary' was also a favourite song of hers. The move worked, Blyton was welcomed back into the bedroom and Urban and Shaw stumbled back to their hotel, laughing all the way.

When I spoke with Blyton, he knew Urban only as a drinker, fond of a 'few Bundys', although he would get a taste of the faster, druggier crowd that Urban moved with on a subsequent visit to Nashville. (Blyton himself is no wowser, it should be said. As recently as March 2008, a thoroughly trashed Blyton was escorted from an Urban gig after trying to make his way backstage.) Piano player Muirhead also spent some nights out with Urban while the album was being made; they'd often roll into notorious Kings Cross venue, the Manzil Room, a dingy nightspot that welcomed studio musicians, true creatures of the night. (Goldrush, whose numbers included guitarist and Urban hero, Tommy Emmanuel, often played there.)

'There was a distance he maintained, but maybe that was because he was in Sydney, away from home and his band,' Muirhead said. 'We went out a lot after sessions, but he always kept this distance. We had a few drinks, had some fun, but we were never matey.' More than once, Muirhead watched as Urban moved away from the group, leaned against one of the Manzil Room's pillars, which were positioned smack dab in the middle of the room, and scrutinised the band on-stage. 'And I never saw Keith with any girls,' he laughed.

Maybe Urban's mood was summed up by another of the album's ballads, 'Yesterday', a co-write between Urban and his bandmate/buddy Marlon Holden. It was a surprisingly hangdog reflection for a guy barely into his twenties. Urban might have had some premonition of what lay ahead for him in Nashville when he lamented how 'yesterday / everything was easy / now everyday memories remind me / how good things used to be yesterday'. It wasn't Wordsworth, nor was it a notch on Paul McCartney's ditty of the same name, but Urban's world-weary tone came as a surprise. Wary of overdoing the 'sad bloke at the end of the bar' persona, Urban then launched into another co-write with Holden, 'Don't Go', a song that was far more upbeat, even if it was an uncertain take on a romance that could go either way. 'Hold on to Your Dreams', however, was pure pop-rock escapism, a blue-collar anthem for working stiffs who dragged their weary asses out of bed on Monday knowing full well that 'Friday seems so far away'. Producer Blyton added some funky, chunky bass which, when combined with the Hammond organ fills of Glen Muirhead, gave a fairly pedestrian song some real juice.

From there, *Keith Urban* (aka *1991*) headed into the home straight, the best moments on its back half being the freewheeling finger-picking instrumental 'Clutterbilly', a live showstopper, and the sombre, reflective 'The River'. While it wasn't a debut to rank with Steve Earle's incendiary *Guitar Town* or even Garth Brooks's self-titled first offering, this was an album that valiantly attempted to reflect Urban's catholic tastes and cover most bases: pop, rock, twang, a little funk and some heavy-hearted balladeering, quite consciously moving him out of the shadow of Tamworth. And there wasn't a mention to be found of 'the land', flame trees, wild-eyed jillaroos with trouble in mind or venomous creepy-crawlies hiding away in outdoor dunnies: Urban's lyrics were deeply personal – he was looking inwards for inspiration, unlike most of his country peers. All up, it was a grown-up, genre-jumping collection that raised a few eyebrows among Urban true believers. In fact, newcomers like Glen Muirhead couldn't see any connection between Urban and the rest of the 'Oz-country' pack.

> He never really fell into that scene at all. I'm sure he's professed a love for Slim Dusty but I've never heard much of Slim in Keith's music. But there was a drive that he had that was really discernible while working with him in the studio. I saw a desire to succeed and an immense talent.

Yet Urban's association with all things country probably hindered the album's chart progress, while the lack of anyone singing his praises in the corridors of EMI clearly didn't help its momentum either. Released in October 1991, *Keith Urban* hung around the higher-numbered end of the local album charts for three weeks, peaking at a lowly 92, and selling just a few thousand copies. The single 'Only You', which preceded the album by three months, didn't fare much better, stalling at number 93 even though it hit the top of the local Country chart (an indication of how few records he needed to shift to burn down that particular Top 40). Urban and Shaw could only look on and shrug as such vacuous fodder as Bryan Adams's '(Everything I Do) I Do It for You' or Julian Lennon's odious 'Saltwater' dominated the charts and the airwaves, while 'Only You' was restricted to high rotation on such far-flung stations as 2TM.

If Team Urban wanted a reminder of why they should maintain their focus on getting to the USA, and quick, it was there in the tepid corporate support and commercial response to the album and its lead single. 'That's when Greg put plans into motion to get Keith out of [Australia],' said Blyton, who remains friends with Shaw. 'And that was pretty scary for Keith; he was this small-town boy. But Greg knocked down walls to get him over there.'

Nor was his label pumping hard cash into the only video made for the album, promoting the single 'Only You'. With the exception of the obligatory female model caught in various states of rapture and repose, the only extras in the clip were an eagle and an owl, both shot in a soft-focus, slow-mo style that would have made David Attenborough proud. Much of the clip was taken up by an awkward-looking Urban – in full bogan chic – and band playing 'live' on a soundstage, doing their best not to notice the ever-present camera. 'I personally don't think he would like this [video],' understated one YouTube viewer, 'because it probably brings up bad memories for him.' None of these setbacks stopped Urban marking the occasion of the album's release, and his twenty-fourth birthday, by splashing out on a tattoo of an eagle. To Urban, this inkwork symbolised two key things: freedom and America. 'My freedom at the time was America,' he explained, 'so I felt the eagle was appropriate.' He paid his dues with the album's credits, too, dedicating the album to 'Bob, Marienne, Shane, Angie and Greg' – his parents, brother, girlfriend and manager.

In spite of EMI's tight-fistedness and mainstream radio's resistance to Urban's melodic wiles, his self-titled debut did produce four local number ones: 'Only You', 'Arms of Mary', 'The River' and 'I Never Work on a Sunday', while at the 1992 Tamworth awards he picked up a pair of Golden Guitars, for Male Vocalist ('The River') and Instrumental of the Year (thanks to 'Clutterbilly'). As one newspaper reported, 'Australian country music was [now] dealing with a cross between the punk good looks of Billy Idol and the country-rock of John Mellencamp.'[2] Urban looked genuinely stunned when Gina Jeffreys called out his name as Best Male Vocalist – he'd beaten Slim Dusty, among others, for the gong – and stood on the podium for many seconds, giggling nervously, getting his shit together, before attempting his acceptance speech. 'It was pretty amazing,' he admitted the next morning, speaking on *Good Morning Australia*. 'To be nominated was great, but to win was something else.'

At the same time, Urban and Shaw had closely studied the stop–start American progress of EMI labelmate and rival James Blundell, whose second LP, *Hand It Down*, was finally granted a US release in 1991, after navigating all the political machinations of Capitol Nashville. (In an interesting parallel, Blundell, at least early on, kept a step ahead of Urban, winning Star Maker three years before Urban, and claiming two key Golden Guitars in the year Urban won Best New Talent.) It was the first time an Australian country artist had received a 'proper' US release and it must have been more than enough encouragement for Urban and his manager to pack their bags, this time for good. What's more, Urban's US visa had finally been granted, allowing him to live and work in Nashville.

Before boarding a plane, however, Urban did take time out to pay some more dues. He made a vocal cameo on the album *Out of the Blue*, the breakout recording for Slim Dusty's daughter, Anne Kirkpatrick, which won her both an ARIA and a Golden Guitar. It was during those sessions that Urban met producer Mark Moffatt, another Queenslander (he was from Bundaberg) and yet another old friend of Greg Shaw. Moffatt's track record was virtually without parallel, at least in Australia: he'd worked on hit records from Tim Finn, Mental As Anything, Mondo Rock and the Eurogliders, and was soon to begin producing Yothu Yindi's landmark *Tribal Voice* LP.

Moffatt, a studio 'gun' and the kind of guy who seemed to live in sunglasses, was, like Urban and Shaw, also looking towards the States. 'I had reached a ceiling professionally,' he told me, 'and also wanted to live in the South among the musicians who had inspired and influenced me.' Moffatt, like relocated Aussie Jeff Walker, would become an essential go-to guy for Urban (and Shaw), as he struggled to find some traction in Nashville. Finally, Urban, Peter Clarke and Marlon Holden left for the USA on 28 September 1992. Clarke paid for his ticket with cash raised when he and his wife Lauren sold their house.

Urban could have picked a far worse year than 1992 to settle in America. There were more than 2200 radio stations nation-wide playing solely country music – a record high – while the unstoppable force of nature called Garth Brooks was slugging it out in the Billboard Top 200 chart with grunge trailblazers Nirvana, a mournful Eric Clapton, breakout R&B acts such as En Vogue and TLC, and funky punks the Red Hot Chili Peppers. Country stalwarts like Alan Jackson and super-duo Brooks & Dunn were also enjoying stellar years (Urban would work with both). The domestic sales of MCA Nashville, the label of choice for A-listers Vince Gill, Trisha Yearwood and George Strait, came to a record-breaking US$120 million-plus. It was the best of times, it was the country-est of times.

Brooks's commercial impact was so substantial, in fact, that during the lengthy chart reign of his mega-selling album *No Fences*, he accounted for almost 20 percent of all country music record sales. Even the stadium-filling U2 couldn't claim those kind of stats. Just like Urban's, Brooks's album had generated four domestic number one hits – 'Friends in Low Places', 'Thunder Rolls', 'Unanswered Prayers' and 'Two of a Kind, Workin' on a Full House' – but unlike *Keith Urban*, *No Fences* sold in serious numbers (currently 16 million and counting).

Urban had far more pressing concerns to deal with on his arrival than calculating record sales by the million. He led a five-piece ensemble in Australia but, as he explained in a special episode of CMT Loaded's *Greatest Stories*, 'I couldn't afford to bring my whole band.' His rhythm guitarist and keyboardist may have been handy all-rounders – they could sing harmonies for one thing – but he opted instead to take Peter Clarke and Marlon Holden to the US because they could operate as a more traditional three-piece of guitar, bass and drums. It also helped that Holden and Clarke were tight with Urban off-stage. Holden, however, didn't last long. 'He wanted to go back, anyway,' was Urban's explanation, but one insider has suggested that Urban's decision to carry on without him reflected Holden's lack of bass-playing skills as much as his inability to adapt to life in America.

> Marlon had the same reaction as Pete [Clarke] had, but a little earlier on. 'Fuck, there's six years of hard work that went nowhere.' But there are reasons for all that, I'm sure.

Holden returned to Australia on 10 November, not even two months after arriving in the USA. He married his partner, Cheryl, another Brisbaneite, in Dubai in early 1993. The final time he played with Urban was at the Sydney Christmas party of EMI in 1992.

Shaw, despite commitments back in Oz as a husband and father – he had two young sons – spent much of his time in the USA with Urban as they tried to get some career momentum happening. According to Peter Blyton:

> Greg Shaw, bless him, had the balls to mortgage his house and give up his family and go mow lawns in Nashville for years to help Keith chase his dream. Keith had all the talent and was a star, while Greg had all the motivation. He made Keith Urban. No Greg, no Keith.

And Shaw's marriage duly fell apart; on one of his return trips to Oz, he sat his boys down and explained why he was spending so much time away from home. He believed in Urban that strongly. An American, Richie Compton, was brought in to replace Holden on bass but Compton's place would soon be taken by Jerry Flowers, a lanky, laconic West Virginian with a chunky twang to match, who would become a devoted Urban sidekick for most of the next 15 years.

These early Nashville years were incredibly tough, remarkably educational and more than a little fucked up for Urban. He'd gone from being the newest, blondest kid on the Tamworth block to just another Nashville contender, and the adjustment was tough. And while the Garth Brooks era had moved country much closer to the musical mainstream there was a downside, as producer Mark Moffatt, who'd prove to be an incredibly handy contact for Urban in Nashville, explained to me:

> The boom period really attracted a lot of dross to Nashville from all over the US, so there was a huge increase in the number of artists in the game. It also concentrated the power of the major labels here, and was really the beginning of the lockhold they held until the recent emergence of well-funded indie labels like Big Machine, Broken Bow, Montage and Equity. And there's always a tendency for people in powerful positions in the country industry to try and prevent anyone else from getting lucky. That was heightened during the boom period of the early and mid 1990s.

This only made it that little bit harder for the skinny Queenslander with a Fender to make an impression.

Jimmy Bowen, a Los Angeleno who'd recently taken over at Capitol Nashville, had a similar conversation with James Blundell about the winds of change that were currently blowing away the tumbleweeds that had gathered along Music Row.

Nashville has the opportunity to catch the world mid-yawn and we can re-create what we had on the West Coast in the 1970s, with Little Feat and CSNY and The Band. But I also have the sickening feeling they're going to go down the colour-by-numbers road.

According to Blundell:

He turned out to be exactly right; they then went through the 'Garth Brooks and clones decade'. They ended up taking the worst of pop and country and stuck it together. A real shame.

There was also another cultural shift occurring in Nashville that would have a major impact on pre-superstar Keith Urban. Recreational drugs were making inroads on a town that once relied on 'weed, wine and reds' for a good time. 'Blow [cocaine] was quite available in Nashville in the 1990s when the city's club scene, as opposed to its music scene, was nascent and growing,' said the Nashville-based author Dan Daley.

Also, there are projects – council flats to you, I'd guess – just a few blocks from Music Row. If your club or music biz connections couldn't hook you up, you could always take a chance in the 'hood.

A Narconon report confirmed that crack cocaine was 'the most popular drug of abuse among Tennessee residents'; it was no coincidence that the Mexican border, where most supplies of the drug made their way into the USA, was relatively close by.

Urban, along with another expat muso, piano player Hughie Murray, rented a place on Elliott Avenue in a funky, downbeat end of Nashville. Although it may not have been their intention, this made access to drugs that little bit easier. 'There is more sex, drugs and rock and roll in Nashville than in any other city I've been to,' added James Blundell, who lived in Music City for a year as well as being a regular visitor.

> That's what used to make me laugh. There was this tantalising condescension towards this place as the sweet country cousin of places that made real music – and it was all happening there. It was a very exciting city.

Crack cocaine, however, which became Urban's drug of choice, was not necessarily the best thing to help a budding songwriter tap into his mojo. 'I've seen the personality change brought on by crack; people literally morph,' added an Urban insider. 'You'd struggle internally to survive that bout, so creativity would be the last thing on your mind.'

When Urban arrived in 1992, James Blundell was nearing the end of his failed 'Nashville experience'. One of the last things he did was check out an Urban showcase at the venerable Exit/Inn, seated alongside Jimmy Bowen. Even though they'd reluctantly agreed that Blundell wasn't right for Nashville, they'd become good friends. 'I just liked Bowen's directness, he was great, really blunt. He actually said to me, "I'm using you as an experiment."' As the gig progressed, Bowen turned to Blundell and asked his opinion of the gangly Urban, Blundell's friendly 'rival' a few years back in Australia. 'I said that the guy was monstrously talented,' said Blundell.

> [But] I knew that the Nashvillians had trouble dealing with the square peg in the round hole. I said to Bowen, 'I don't know how he's gonna go, because he's a strong character and has a unique style of music.'

Bowen didn't sign the up-and-coming Urban, although his decision probably was based on more than just Blundell's opinion, as astute as it turned out to be, at least in 1992. 'But that's where I really clocked the fact that Keith had committed to staying in Nashville and was going to succeed come hell or high water,' Blundell added, 'and *it very near did fucking kill him.*'

Also at that Exit/Inn gig – one of countless Nashville showcases Urban would play before his star began to rise – was Jewel Coburn (the former Jewel Blanch), who'd shared a stage with Urban way back in Tamworth in 1982, when she won her first Golden Guitar and Urban was blazing a trail through the junior ranks. Now, just over a decade down the line Coburn, along with her Kiwi husband, Barry, ran Ten Ten Music, a leading Nashville-based management and publishing company that had helped kickstart the career of lanky, laconic country superstar Alan Jackson. Coburn was knocked off her bar stool by Urban's Exit/Inn gig but, just like Jimmy Bowen, sensed that he wasn't quite right for Nashville – at least not yet.

'I'd been reading and hearing about Keith but we hadn't been in touch,' she recalled, when we spoke for this book. 'We were invited to the showcase at the Exit/Inn, which was put on for Jimmy Bowen. And it *was* amazing.' But Coburn had one concern about Urban: this was the so-called New Traditionalists era when such acts as Randy Travis and George Strait (a buttoned-up kind of character who wore western shirts that somehow never lost their starchy crispness) were doing their bit to strip away some of the gloss that was threatening to overrun Nashville.

'Keith was so pop for anything that was going on in this town at that point,' added Coburn.

> Barry was going, 'Oh this guy is going to be a superstar.' I thought, 'You're probably right, but I think he's just too pop for Nashville; I don't think they'll accept him, being Australian

yet almost English in his pop sensibilities.' I thought he was incredible, but just so pop, especially with his spiky blond hair and piercings. I just couldn't see Nashville going for it. This was at a point when things here were pretty country. There was no Rascal Flatts or Shania Twain; he was ahead of his time.

Coburn also found Urban drop-dead funny, a true cut-up – she was one of many people who couldn't get through his comical phone machine messages without doubling up with laughter.

Despite Jewel's reservations, the Coburns became true believers and in 1994, two years after Urban relocated to the USA, they offered him a publishing deal at Ten Ten. It would prove to be a very essential lifeline for the struggling Queenslander, even though he would unfairly dismiss it in a *60 Minutes* interview as 'a pathetic little publishing advance'. Truth be told, it was anything but. Urban approached Ten Ten with some rough demos of songs that would end up on the 1997 album for his band The Ranch, including 'Walkin' the Country' and 'Tangled Up in Love'. Even though the Coburns sensed that Urban saw himself as a musician first, then a songwriter and vocalist – 'he didn't have much confidence with his writing and singing, but that developed over the years,' said Coburn – they didn't have any hesitation signing him up as a writer. 'We knew who he was, obviously; we knew his background,' recalled Coburn.

> When he came to us about a publishing deal we said 'yes' straight away. We totally believed in him and his ability, but we also knew it may take a while. I still had my doubts about him being too pop for Nashville. But we signed him as a writer and he developed really well.

Publishing deals in the USA are structurally and financially quite different to those signed in Australia. Essentially, Ten Ten paid Urban a weekly wage, basically enough to cover the rent on the band house in Elliott Avenue (although it was subsidised by whatever menial work that the band, and Greg Shaw, could find, which included mowing many a Nashville lawn). This wage was offset against future royalties earned when songs were either recorded by Urban or other acts – and, ideally, became hits. Urban and Ten Ten would split these earnings 50/50 (a writer gets more in Australia). As Coburn recalled, 'That allowed Keith to survive and write while he was developing.'

Although Ten Ten had been set up at a time when their possessions amounted to 'two suitcases and some cassettes', they'd become real Nashville players, the leading independent music publisher in the city. When they signed Urban they had numerous 'house' writers in their HQ on Music Row; the plan was to team Urban with as many as possible and see if sparks would fly when they convened in one of the company's 'writers rooms'. Unlike James Blundell, Urban seemed a natural fit for this very Nashville methodology.

'We had some successful writers, like Harley Allen [later heard on the *O Brother, Where Art Thou?* soundtrack], who had many Number Ones,' said Coburn, 'and Keith and Harley wrote together.'

> In fact, I think [Keith] wrote with almost all our writers at one time or another, and we had as many as 13 writers. It's a process of seeing who clicks with whom. But Keith wrote much of his best stuff by himself; he was a much better writer than he thought he was.

Barry Coburn, producer/musician Biff Watson and Urban retired to a studio and cut demo versions of many of the songs that came out of these sessions. Urban and Shaw then set about the often soul-destroying, ego-deflating process of 'shopping' these recordings from one label to another, to see if anyone would 'bite'.

The Coburns's encouragement obviously played a major role in Urban's growth as a songwriter and musician, but they also became a sort of surrogate family for him, filling the gaps between visits from his parents or his infrequent trips home. 'Ten Ten was a very relaxed and creative environment,' said expat Mark Moffatt, who was on staff there as director of A&R for several years, and worked closely with Urban. 'Everyone tended to hang out together after hours.' Barry Coburn and Moffatt 'went back a long way,' as he told me, and Moffatt could see how the Coburns's support helped Urban keep it together during his lean early years in Nashville. 'Keith was very fortunate,' said Moffatt. 'Barry and Jewel are a great support team. The best, in fact.'

Jewel Coburn compared Ten Ten to a musical Mom & Pop store, an endangered species in the increasingly corporatised climate of Nashville. Coming from small-town Brisbane, Urban connected strongly with this kind of accessibility. 'I guess because we're a husband and wife team it's always had a family vibe,' Coburn said. 'It's a little like a corner shop, I guess.' Ten Ten fast became a drop-in centre for Urban. (His professional relationship with the Coburns would stretch to 2006, when he left and established his own publishing company, an inevitability the Coburns accepted without any acrimony whatsoever. They also have something like two albums' worth of unrecorded Urban songs in the vault, so there's little chance that particular cash cow will dry up anytime soon.)

Mark Moffatt, just like the Coburns, was well aware of the difficulties Urban was dealing with, both with his seemingly stalled music career and a fast-growing fondness for the various 'life sweeteners' that were available in and around his end of town.

Keith was living in a dodgy neighbourhood and having all that around, while fighting disappointment and self-esteem issues, is trouble. If anything, while at Ten Ten I was just part of a special little family who cared very much for their own.

Jewel Coburn recalled that it didn't take Urban long to become an office regular. That then extended to chill-out time at the Coburns's Nashville home, and elsewhere. 'We've spent so much time together, with him coming to the office and writing and hanging out, coming over for dinner and spending time with my kids and all that,' she said. And the explanation for Urban's strong relationship with the Coburns and Ten Ten wasn't strictly some kind of weird Tamworth deja vu. 'I think it's because we were from Down Under and had been through a lot together and had been a source of money and support and friendship for him,' she figured.

> We love Keith; he has a great, wacky sense of humour, he's always been terrific. I felt almost as close as a sibling. I wanted it to work for him and I really wanted to do anything I could to help.

As Urban struggled to unravel the labyrinth that was Nashville, the Coburns offered him some sage advice. It was so simple, in fact, that it had the feel of a mantra. They told him to keep writing and to look at his own life and feelings for the ideal subject matter. But first he had to hang out on The Ranch for a spell.

Four

GLOBAL PEACE THROUGH COUNTRY MUSIC

The whole painting houses, mowing lawns thing, well, as
a marketing guy, you couldn't write a better script.
It was like a country song, a wonderful story.

Bob Saporiti

While Nashville may have been the spiritual home for the
music that Urban wanted to make, he and the band first
had to undertake a road trip. Not long after arriving in the USA,
the trio of Urban, Clarke and Holden scored a residency at the
most unlikely of the venues, a place named The Lucky Snapper,
located in Destin, Florida. 'I kid you not,' Urban told a reporter
from CMT's *Loaded* program, when asked about the preposter-
ous name which suggested more a hangout for desperate anglers
than country music lovers. None other than Rusty Hammerstrom, Urban's former bandleader in the Ayers Rockettes, ran
the venue. Yet another lifeline had been cast Urban's way.

Destin was a beachside locale on Florida's Emerald Coast, wedged between Fort Walton Beach to the west and the better-known Miramar Beach to the east. Locals referred to it as 'the World's Luckiest Fishing Village'. The Lucky Snapper was situated on a peninsula that separated Choctawhatchee Bay from the Gulf of Mexico. It was roughly a 650-kilometre drive from Destin to Nashville but for the trio, who were then trading simply under Urban's name, they may as well have been on a different planet. 'It was a new club, just opened,' Urban recalled in the CMT program. 'We were the house band there five nights a week.' The band played there for a month.

Whenever the trio had accumulated enough cash to cover the cost of a showcase in Nashville – such as the Exit/Inn gig, which was ostensibly a performance solely for label boss Jimmy Bowen – they'd head back to Music City on the weekends. They'd hire a fiddle player and keyboardist especially for the gigs. 'Like every band,' said Urban, 'we'd blow our money on a showcase, we wouldn't get a bite, and then we'd go back to Destin and go back to work again.'[1]

Greg Shaw, meanwhile, had organised a lucrative run of shows back in Australia, which was effectively Jerry Flowers's public debut with Urban. (The Destin/Nashville grind contributed to Holden's hasty departure.) Flowers was a man mountain from West Virginia who sported a crewcut and what seemed, at least to those who didn't know him, to be the kind of menacing stare typically found in a police line-up. 'He looks like he'd kill you in a heartbeat, but he's such a gentle soul,' said James Blundell, who got to know Flowers well. 'And he's one of the best bass players on the planet.'

That was evident to Urban and Clarke pretty well from the moment that Flowers, who'd moved to Nashville around the same time as Team Urban, plugged in and began playing at his audition. He was the first hopeful through the door, and had turned up on the tip of a mutual friend. Clarke and Urban had given him nine songs to learn and when he asked what they should play first, Urban suggested the toughest song on the list. According to Urban, 'It just clicked, it was magic,' even though Flowers, who'd been semi-pro since leaving school, had more of a rock-and-roll background. The first concert he attended had featured hard-rock heavyweights Van Halen, no less, back in 1984. Urban was about to make this very green country boy an offer he couldn't refuse. 'I said to Jerry, who was this kid from West Virginia who'd never been anywhere, or done anything: "Do you have a passport?"' Flowers was nonplussed. 'Passport? Why, where am I going?' he asked. 'Australia, next week,' said Urban. Before you could say 'Clutterbilly', they were on a plane to Oz.

That road trip was absolutely vital for the trio that would eventually become The Ranch. One month of dates stretched into four, and Urban, Clarke and Flowers began to bond musically. 'It was great,' said Urban. 'We played every night and were getting ourselves oiled as a machine. Looking back, it was so predestined, as everything is.' James Blundell caught up with the trio one night back in Oz and was among many who could see how well lubricated this country-rock machine was becoming. 'I said to Pete [Clarke] that just by living in a van and playing every night they were playing really well.'[2]

Piano man Glen Muirhead, whose playing was all over Urban's solo debut back in 1991, shared a bill with Urban and his band during that Oz tour. They played, of all places, Australia's Wonderland, an isolated few hectares of pseudo American theme park on Sydney's suburban fringe, where patrons paid more attention to the high-impact waterslide than the music. 'It was rainy, and there was bugger all people there,' Muirhead remembered, when we spoke in 2008, 'but I watched them and thought, "Why isn't this guy big?" I thought that a lot during the gig. *"Why isn't he huge?"* I was gob-smacked by them.' When pushed for a comparison, Muirhead likened Urban and the band to the Dixie Dregs, an underrated Southern rock power combo that featured a very young Steve Morse, the kind of fleet-fingered guitarist who kept fusion fans drooling all over their transcripts.

With the benefit of hindsight, Muirhead, still an active live player himself, got the sense that Urban and the band were a tad too musically adroit for their own good. Stuff this good was hard to sell.

> I do remember thinking it was maybe a little too much about the 'chops'. And I always felt that they were a bit shunned by the country music industry. All the musicians worshipped those guys, aspired to their level, but the machinations of the industry didn't seem to be doing much for Keith here.

Obviously, the fact that Urban had dared to venture overseas hadn't endeared him to Australia's insular local country music community, whom Muirhead described as 'funny', but not necessarily in a laugh-out-loud way. 'It's very tight,' he said.

> They allow a new talent in every now and then and try and distribute the not-huge slice of the market among the old and new talent. There's not a lot of room for new stars. And it's all pretty much controlled by the one guy, [booking agent] Rob Potts at Allied Artists.

What's just as interesting is that Urban, apparently, was not in good physical or mental shape at the time, due to excessive cocaine use – yet the shows were still noteworthy.

During that same tour, while in Tamworth, Greg Shaw organised for a rising homegrown singer/strummer, Mark

O'Shea, to sit in with Urban and the band for a few songs. O'Shea was all of 16 at the time. 'I was – and still am – a total fan,' O'Shea told me.

> So it was a great experience. I've since opened up for [Keith] several times and he's always been great. He's never pulled any rockstar bullshit, like making it more difficult for the support act or anything like that. He's an incredible talent and a very charming individual.

A few years later, O'Shea would follow Urban's tracks and end up basing himself in Nashville.

Despite their obvious musical synchronicity, when the trio returned to Nashville they were pretty much back where they'd been 12 months earlier: nowhere special. They were entering what was to become known as their 'lawnmowing' phase. 'It's a matter of public record that they were mowing lawns and doing any menial task to get by to make any money,' said Blundell, a frequent Nashville visitor in the early 1990s. 'Their middle period was incredibly tough, and that'll put the best of men to the test.' There was, of course, a flipside to their hardscrabble existence. 'About the whole painting houses, mowing lawns thing,' said Bob Saporiti, an exec who'd become Urban's go-to guy at Warner Brothers Records in Nashville. 'As a marketing guy, well, you couldn't write a better script. It was like a country song, a wonderful story.'

Nick Erby, the country music broadcaster who'd inter-viewed a prepubescent Urban way back in the early 1980s, was another visitor to the trio's shared house in Nashville. He arrived at a time when Urban's father, Bob, was staying with them, acting as an in-house cook and caretaker. Marienne Urban would also visit when time and money allowed. 'They were starving,' Erby said, looking back.

They were renting a rundown house in suburban Nashville and every penny they had went back into their music, particularly the huge distances they were travelling to play at clubs and bars. They all had turns at doing odd jobs to get some money together.

[But] that's not the reason I remember that visit. I remember it because of the spirit in that house. These three knew they had something. They were pleasing crowds everywhere they played. The problem was, they hadn't cracked the very tight, very political shell that surrounds the opening to success in Nashville. They knew they would make it once they got inside – they just hadn't found the opening at that time.[3]

Urban later admitted that he was stunned by the endless 'thanks but no thanks' he and Shaw would receive from the labels to whom they shopped their demo. 'The constant rejection thing – I wasn't expecting that,' he told Peter Cooper of *The Tennessean* newspaper in 2005. 'They were like, "What are you doing here?"' Urban was confused; as far as he was concerned, his Nashville odyssey had been set in stone ever since the night he stood a few feet from The Man In Black at Brisbane's Festival Hall – *how could these bozos not see that?* 'What do you mean?' Urban would ask. 'This was meant to be. It was so obvious to me, and so not obvious to every other person I met.'[4]

The constant rejection also opened up a few potholes in Urban's psyche. He'd defined himself by his success; first with Star Maker, then with his swag of Golden Guitars and his deal with EMI – and now he couldn't get arrested. He'd been on-stage for almost 20 years of his life and was accustomed to applause and recognition; to now not have that on tap was a hefty slap to his ego. 'When I got to Nashville I realised that I didn't know who I was off-stage,' he said. 'I hadn't spent a lot of time with that guy, and I didn't like him very much.' By contrast with the on-stage Urban, who he knew was 'focused and centred', this new guy, who spent more time watching lawns being mowed than peeling off licks, was 'geeky . . . schizo and unorganised'.[5]

The various 'suggestions' that he and Shaw were given by Music City's tastemakers didn't help much, either. Some said Urban needed a haircut; others said he was too pop, too rock, or that his voice didn't cut it. Maybe he could lose the earrings, too. He was told that maybe he was better suited to the music scene in New York, or possibly Los Angeles. One fool even suggested that in order to 'fit in', maybe he could lose the guitar. To Urban, that was heresy. Of course, just as Blundell had experienced a few years before, if Urban really wanted to adapt, he had to take two large steps: he needed to roll his r's and wear the freakin' hat. The former was a given, but the latter was just too big a cop-out. Why have great hair when it's covered by an ugly Stetson?

Cameron Daddo was best known as host of Australian TV show *Perfect Match*, but he was also an aspiring country-rock musician. Daddo hooked up with Urban around this time when he was hired to play guitar on Daddo's album *A Long Goodbye*, which was mostly recorded in LA. Urban played on all bar two of the album's 15 tracks, adding some blazing guitar licks and backup vocals. He spent a solid week with Daddo in rehearsals and preproduction. The professional connection came via Daddo's manager, Gay Willis, but he'd become a fan when a stuntman buddy of his, Danny Baldwin (aka 'DB'), played him Urban's debut LP. In a nifty piece of payback, Daddo introduced Baldwin to Urban in his Sydney home. 'The usually outgoing DB was gobsmacked,' chuckled Daddo, who now lives in LA. 'He sat back stealing glances. He must've known the future Mr Urban.' Just like Urban, Daddo was a major John Mellencamp fan, although he preferred *Scarecrow* to Urban's touchstone LP, *Lonesome Jubilee*.

Urban may still have been at a relatively early stage in his own recording career, but Daddo insists that he acted as a sort of cheerleader during the album sessions, encouraging Daddo to write, sing and play on all the tracks. Even though Urban was a hired hand, Daddo never got the feeling that he was slumming as a session muso. 'We did get along really well, and one of my fondest memories was the music experimentation, the laughing and the support he gave me.' Daddo owned a fancy 1962 Gretsch Clipper guitar, which he brought into the studio and suggested Urban try it out. The trouble, however, was that it was a left-handed axe – and Urban was no 'leftie'. 'No problem,' said Daddo, 'just play it upside down', a la Jimi Hendrix, but in reverse. 'And he gave it a mighty shot, although in the end we abandoned that idea,' said Daddo. 'It was a bloody mess, but at 3am it was worth a shot and I don't remember laughing more than during that time.'

Daddo recalled the track 'Ain't the First Time' as a standout, especially during the track's 'play-off', where Urban 'was just ripping' on his guitar. And on the title track, a love song for Daddo's wife, Urban played her gut–string guitar, again on Daddo's suggestion. 'We felt it was a good idea,' he said. 'The challenge was to keep it in tune.'

Like many people whose paths have intersected with Urban's, either in the studio or on the road, he and Daddo have maintained a strong connection. (Daddo was in attendance at the G'Day LA gathering in 2005, when Urban met Nicole Kidman.) According to Daddo:

KU is generous, gifted and kind. He's got a wicked sense of humour and a curiosity for history. And he is the real deal as a musician/singer. I never felt judged by him, only encouraged. To me he was a simple guy, doing the thing he loved most, making music any way he could.

Despite some upbeat press – hard-to-please Sydney critic Bruce Elder tagged it 'some of the best country-rock ever recorded by an Australian musician . . . the kind of album the Dingoes used to dream of making and James Blundell dreams about still'[6] – *A Long Goodbye* was hardly a runaway success. But it did give Urban some respite from his Nashville doldrums.

While Urban's musical career seemed in a permanent holding pattern, his love life was on the improve. Although he and Angie Marquis remained close, the physical distance between them, among other issues, ended their romance. Urban was the kind of guy that women wanted to hug, shag or both, and it wasn't long before he was in love all over again. As a muso friend of Urban's told the *Daily Mail* newspaper, 'Keith is always falling in love with some girl or other. And women adore him. Even when he was broke they used to throw themselves at him – and he's never been one to turn down a polite offer.'[7] Music publisher Max Hutchinson, a one-time Nashville neighbour of Urban's who would eventually connect The Ranch with the song 'Just Some Love', backed this up, calling Urban a 'woman magnet. He charms every-one he meets.'[8] Urban himself would admit to confusing 'love and lust every day'.[9] (US country superstar, touring partner and party buddy Kenny Chesney dubbed Urban 'the Australian stud'.)

Born in 1970, brunette Laura Sigler was a Nashvillian who worked for a local vet. She was smart and savvy and, as one Urban insider told me, 'She was beautiful. She was a very cool chick.' But pretty much from the outset, apparently, Sigler sensed that their romance wasn't built to last, even though they dated for something like eight years. James Blundell – himself the type of red-blooded guy who had trouble resisting the lure of a sexy, intelligent woman – spoke with her at a Nashville party after she and Urban had split. According to Blundell, Sigler admitted that:

> . . . she adored him, but they'd broken up a couple of times [and that was enough]. She was very upset. She was a very smart woman and knew that it was an inevitable outcome. But he's an adorable guy, a very charismatic human. I felt sorry for her, but that's life, you know.

Nonetheless, there were some highs during the Urban/Sigler romance, quite literally on at least one occasion. They got it on in an aeroplane bathroom, thereby joining the Mile High Club. 'We wanted to see if it could be done,' Urban admitted, 'and it can. But you need to be very supple.'[10] Sigler would also act as Urban's muse; at least one song, 'I Thought You Knew', was about their topsy-turvy relationship. The song was written because Sigler, in an attempt to escape what was described as a 'toxic' relationship, fled with a friend to Canada. Urban worked the phones, tracked her down and pleaded with her to return. Reluctantly, she did, which pretty much summed up their desire for each other. Urban had a thing for buying cards for Sigler and other women, preferring 'the ones that don't say anything on the inside; there's a picture on the front that says everything'.[11]

When not grappling with Sigler in aeroplane bathrooms, Urban, along with Clarke and Flowers, was slowly starting to get some attention from Nashville players and tastemakers. They were establishing themselves with standout shows at such downtown dives as 12th & Porter, songwriter hangout Douglas Corner, and Jack's Guitar Bar. Australian guitar wizard Tommy Emmanuel, a close friend of Urban's and a regular Nashville visitor since 1980, saw Urban and band play several shows around this time. Emmanuel had a couple of indelible memories from these gigs, and they weren't strictly about the idiosyncratic country-rock that the trio was beginning to develop.

'There was a lot of interest from young girls,' he laughed.

> I didn't notice anyone sitting around talking about The Ranch as the great new musicians' band in town; all it was when they were playing – the place was full of young girls. But everyone knew of Keith's ability and talent, there's no question of it.

Warner Bros' Bob Saporiti, a player himself, also noticed this. 'The band was made up of young, good-looking guys,' he told me, 'so you had a great contingent of babes and musicians.' (To Saporiti, Urban's guitar style was 'a cross between Albert Lee and Alvin Lee, with a bit of Mark Knopfler thrown in. Maybe even some Jimi Hendrix.')

This female following would become something of an 'Urban curse' as his career slowly grew. While he preferred to be known as a 'player's player', Urban would often look into the crowd and see nothing but rows and rows of nubile, seemingly available women, screaming his lyrics back at him and sizing him up like he was a tasty slab of beef. It was flattering, sure, and provided some off-stage comfort, but it was hardly validation of Urban's musical skills: any halfway good-looking dude with a fringe, a Fender and a strong whiff of sex appeal could pull chicks. *He wanted some respect.*

When not distracted by The Ranch's oestrogen-charged following, Emmanuel – who, like Urban, would develop his own addiction problems, something they often discussed – could sense that this was a group with a fully functional mojo. 'God, they were a good band,' he said.

> He was really doing something different there; they were like this power trio. Most people [in power trios] only played blues

or heavy rock, but he was playing country with clean and dirty guitar, good harmonies and solid rock grooves. He was fusing rock, blues and country when nobody else was in that genre.

Acclaimed singer/songwriter Rodney Crowell was sometimes spotted in the crowd at Urban's gigs, nodding in appreciation, as was the equally revered tunesmith Kim Richey. She'd hold up the bar with Radney Foster, a Texan native who'd scored credibility and chart action as part of the duo Foster & Lloyd. He was now making his mark as both a solo act and a songwriter-for-hire, and recognised something familiar in The Ranch. 'Foster & Lloyd were sort of a cowpunk band and those guys were cut from the same cloth,' the bespectacled Foster told me. 'Keith was a great singer and guitar player and the band was raw and full of energy; they were a really cool thing.'

Jewel Coburn, another Urban 'booster' – she'd actually tipped off Foster, among others, about the band – acknowledges that there was no shortage of women in the pit at these shows but had an inkling that they also brought along their boyfriends. 'There were a lot of girls, sure, but also a lot of guys,' she recalled, 'mainly all the musicians in town and producers.'

> [Keith] was this guitar god; they wanted to go and see what he did and check out his magic. He's always appealed to a lot of people. He appeals to everyone from little kids to grandmothers – he has that Elvis thing about him.

He'd need all the charisma of Elvis, too, because this was a band whose members would live in each other's pockets: during one stretch from April to June 1997 the trio, plus their sound guy/road manager, Lee Baird, covered 24,000 kilometres all over the States, playing virtually every night. There were also several 'homecomings'; footage from a 1995 cameo on *Hey Hey It's Saturday* reveals the band at its tightest, tearing a hole in 'Walkin' the Country'. The super-sized Flowers, who was dressed like some kind of country-rock lumberjack, thumped his bass as Urban cut loose with some tasty 'chicken-scratch' guitar. Then they'd head back to the States, to their converted 15-seater van, and hit the road all over again.

It was hard going for Urban, especially considering that the country charts were clogged with fluff from pony-tailed line-dancer Billy Ray Cyrus and such bloodless crossover acts as Reba McEntire and Alabama. The Ranch was pulling small yet devoted followings, even if they were burdened with the stigma of being a 'muso's band', just like the acts that Urban stalked as a teenager in Australia. (While the recognition of your peers is a wonderful thing, it doesn't necessarily shift units or draw in record company execs waving chequebooks.) Musicians such as James Blundell were blown away by the band's sheer physical oomph. 'The power of that three-piece was fantastic,' he said. There was nothing polite or touchy-feely about them; they simply plugged in and let rip. Sometimes they let rip too much – at one show in Tamworth in the mid 1990s, Urban and Flowers 'did a Garth' – a nod to Brooks's thing for smashing guitars on stage – and when Flowers disentangled himself from the mess of wood and strings, he stumbled off-stage clutching a badly injured arm. During another rapid-fire trip back to Oz, they beefed up the soulful ballad 'Desiree' during a spot on *Midday with Kerri-Anne*, of all places; the band's raw power and musical synchronicity were obvious, even in such a civilised setting. Many still believe that Urban was at his creative peak during this commercially barren stretch of his career.

Jeff Walker, a very influential man in Music City, was

another who saw the band play repeatedly. He wrote in an email:

> I went to many of Keith's early Nashville showcases and American audiences loved him from the start. It did not take long to build a buzz and an excited group of supporters. People in Nashville realised and appreciated his talent.

Bob Saporiti compared the trio to:

> . . . a country Jimi Hendrix kind of thing. Peter Clarke, he was a real banger, man, a real animal drummer. And Flowers was really a great bassist. They really rocked; I loved it. Word got out and respected musicians would show up. It was a real insider's thing – and this is a guitar town, so I'd find myself sitting among all these great pickers.

But one hugely influential Urban convert, Kix Brooks, was drawn in purely by accident. Brooks was the darker-haired, hat-wearing half of good ol' boys Brooks & Dunn, a massively successful duo whose mere existence typified how Music City had adapted to the modern era. Nashville writer Dan Daley summed it up neatly when he wrote that they 'came together in what could be described as a marketing accident'. In 1989, Ronnie Dunn, then still a struggling solo act, won some studio time in a country music battle of the bands (the engineer on the sessions was Scott Hendricks, soon to be Urban's label head and vocal supporter). Among the tracks Dunn cut was a novelty piece entitled 'Boot Scootin' Boogie'. Hendricks had a cassette of the demo in his pocket when he was in the crowd at a football game, talking with Tim DuBois, his friend and Nashville kingmaker. When DuBois mentioned that he was on the lookout for a partner for a singer named Kix Brooks, the pieces began to fall into place. The dance remix of 'Boot

Scootin' Boogie' – just the idea of a dance floor makeover was seen as heresy by some country reactionaries – became the 1992 Academy of Country Music's Single of the Year, and one of country's biggest-selling duos was now united.

Brooks, however, was flying solo the night he drifted late into Jack's Guitar Bar, pretty much unaware of who was playing. Mid-song, Urban cast a glance over to the venue's entry – the place was tiny, and more than a little soiled around the edges – and saw Brooks standing at the cash register. 'He didn't know what the cover charge was,' Urban recalled. 'He pulled out this big wad of cash and stuck it in the guy's hand and walked in the door.' (Brooks left $75 for the startled doorman.) There were no empty seats so Brooks ambled over to the front of the stage and simply sat there, watching the threesome work their way through yet another set.

'That grubby old floor,' Urban chuckled, when he was asked about the gig.

> I just thought, 'Holy hell! Kix is sitting right there on the floor.' And he stayed there for the whole show. At the end of it, he came up and said, 'We want to take you boys out with us for some shows.' And I'm like, 'Yeah, great. Sure, sure. Yeah, I'm sure you'll be calling us.'[12]

It would take some time, but Brooks would eventually turn out to be a man of his word, hiring The Ranch for a handful of arena dates and then taking on a solo Urban as opener.

Also at the same gig were Jewel and Barry Coburn, Urban's music publishers. Even though, in Barry's words, Urban and the band were 'amazing, yet again', they were seriously considering cutting him loose from his publishing deal. Urban was now more than a whopping US$200,000 in the red; he'd barely recouped a cent of his songwriting advance and the

Coburns were unsure about renewing his option with them. He was costing them shitloads of money; while talent was a great thing, Urban needed to start writing some hits. It was an incredibly tough call; they loved both the man and his music, but so far he'd been a very ordinary investment.

'Should we keep going with him?' an uncertain Barry Coburn asked his wife, as they headed to their car after the gig. (The call was totally theirs, too: the deal was so watertight that Urban couldn't have extracted himself from it, even if he'd wanted to.) It was then that they bumped into Kix Brooks, who Jewel knew from some co-songwriting sessions in the early 1980s, when her own performing career was in the ascendancy. Brooks stopped them and said: 'You've been so supportive of Keith for so long. I'm going to talk with Ronnie about taking him on the road with us.' 'Then we knew we couldn't give up on him,' Coburn told me. 'We just had to make people aware of how wonderful he was.' (In an interesting footnote, when Brooks & Dunn toured Australia for the first time in 2008, many punters observed how *their* high-voltage show reminded them of Urban's live gigs. The apprentice had now become the master.) Urban still had some troubled financial times ahead, once declaring bankruptcy and going for many years without even filing a tax return, but the Coburns's investment was eventually returned, and then some.

'The band provided the perfect base for him,' said Urban's friend, record producer Mark Moffatt. 'Throwing it down on-stage here counts more than any office meeting, and those Jack's Guitar Bar days really built his reputation around town.' One night, at a venue called The Sutler, Urban's former Caboolture High schoolfriend Sherry Rich – who'd just moved to Nashville – came to check him out. She bumped into Moffatt, who told her how he and the Ten Ten team 'were worried about Keith and his habits. But you know, it's

Nashville and the music biz is full of those stories so I never paid it much mind.'

At the same time as he led The Ranch, Urban still thought of himself as a solo act – there was still a part of him that yearned for all of the spotlight. Even as the band's reputation built, he was returning home after shows and tinkering with his own demos, songs that, as he later admitted, were:

> . . . more palatable for radio. It's just what I did, the way I was. But when it got into the hands of the band it became something else, it became The Ranch. When we [eventually] recorded our album it didn't sound like the demos that I'd done, it sounded like the band. And I think the demos would have suited radio a lot better. They're both good, but different. One was very much me, the other was the band.[12a]

Yet at the same time, the very conflicted Urban admitted that he 'loved being in a band'. At this stage, he just didn't have it in him to go it alone.

Jewel Coburn, however, was never quite convinced that The Ranch and Urban were a natural fit. To her, he seemed like a reluctant solo act. 'He always had the qualities that a solo star needed,' she told me.

> Even though the band was great, I sometimes wondered why he decided to be with them rather than be a solo act. Obviously he was very loyal to those guys. I think in a way he felt more comfortable in the band because he didn't have to be out front as much; he was part of a band.

'I think the main focus was always Keith,' Urban's friend Tommy Emmanuel said. 'I never thought it was anything but a solo career for Keith.' Ged Malone, an Englishman based in LA, who would soon play his part in Urban's slow rise, also agreed. 'There was no question that Keith was the talent,' he said. 'Keith wrote the songs with outside writers; he needed the band to get to the next stage.'

Of course, the band's popularity didn't necessarily stretch far beyond the Mason–Dixon Line. When he was successful enough to be able to laugh at the band's mixed fortunes – and only then – Urban would recall an out-of-town show at a Boston venue called Mama Kin. He, Clarke and Flowers felt a little uneasy when they set up to play, and then realised what the problem was: there were possibly more people on-stage than in the crowd. 'It was one of those 10-people-showing-up type gigs,' Urban said. '[But] it was a rowdy crowd,' he insisted.[13] The same thing happened at the Dingo Bar in Albuquerque, where they found themselves playing to an empty room while the barman and venue owner shot pool in the corner. (At this gig, The Ranch gave up, unplugged and got drunk instead, something they did on a fairly regular basis – drink, that is.)

Another show at a long-gone Cleveland venue called Wilbert's, where only a handful of punters turned out, was a set that would stick in Urban's memory for years afterwards, mostly for all the wrong reasons. It's hard to forget an empty venue. They did have a better experience in New York, where they played the Mercury Lounge. After the show, Urban was cornered by a chatty member of the opening act. As Urban recalled, 'We talked for ages; he just loved the band.' When the name Glen Campbell came up, Urban's new admirer replied: 'That's funny; he's my godfather.' Urban had been amiably chatting with Christian Webb whose father was Jimmy Webb, the composer of such twang-pop immortals as 'Galveston', songs that Urban loved beyond words. Urban didn't know what to say.

This typified the stop–start progress of Urban and the band;

they couldn't play only at Jack's Guitar Bar for the rest of their careers, but every time they got in the van and hit the road they were met with a collective yawn from the public. It was a tough time. Urban, to his credit, stuck it out, whereas many in a similar situation might have shrugged, hocked their gear and bought a one-way ticket back to Oz. 'I was just full of that blind faith,' he said of the time. 'I was just absolutely committed; I had no intentions of failing. [But] I didn't realise it would take so long, and I'm glad that I didn't.'[14] Or, as James Blundell told me:

> I think Keith had the ability to see it as a business; he really got embedded [in the USA] and he had the wit to see that it would change. First you just had to get through the shit.

As Ged Malone put it:

> Can you imagine being told by just about everyone that went to see him live that he was amazing – and yet still be struggling? I think he was looking for the magic that would make him a star. He was trying everything.

Meanwhile, back in Nashville, there was another problem Urban had to overcome: his 'Australian-ness'. It was a tough sell in a city that frowned on anyone who didn't look and speak as though they'd just fallen straight from the pages of a Larry McMurtry novel, or were apishly copying the latest country music trend. (In the words of producer Mark Moffatt, 'Nashville is very good at taking trends and turning them into ruts.') As one retired Nashville executive told me, Urban's 'outsiderness' was a 'dual-edged thing'.

> Being Australian was neat, but you have to remember that Nashville is a pretty provincial town. Aside from Charley

Pride, name me five black guys who've made it here? Or an Asian? Sherrie Austin and James Blundell had that problem here. Olivia Newton-John succeeded here, but they kind of made her into a country person. In my opinion she never really was a country person.

'Musicians used to come out and see us,' Urban recalled, 'and everyone seemed to like what we were doing. But when they heard me talk, it just raised eyebrows. They thought I was a novelty.'[15] The band seemed condemned to remain the chosen ones for fellow players and for critics, but a much harder fit when it came to finding their place within the Nashville machine. Another Australian singer/strummer, Mark O'Shea, thought of Urban as 'the pioneer for a lot of expat Australians'.

I can only imagine how difficult it was for him continually having to convince people that someone from Australia – where is that again? – could be an American country music superstar. There's no in-built welcoming committee for Australians in Nashville. You really have to find your own way.

Ged Malone also told me that Urban's background probably worked against him. 'As you know, Nashville is a very small music community. I don't think it would have helped.'

Although he was, admittedly, a far less commercial com-modity than Urban, Tommy Emmanuel actually saw his Australian-ness as a bonus. 'I found it to be a great advantage,' he told me. 'I play Australian instruments, I wear Blundstone shoes and jeans on stage, I don't dress like an American, I don't affect an accent. It's like a secret weapon.' It was difficult, however, for Emmanuel to get this point across to his many American fans. He was once even abused by a true believer in Kentucky. 'He was almost angry that I wasn't big and famous,' Emmanuel laughed. 'But I could care less about fame, really.'

Urban and the band did have their outlets – and not necessarily the toxic substances that their leader would turn to when the wheels really started to fall off The Ranch. Every Sunday afternoon the trio flung open the doors of their band house, which sat directly beneath an overpass, and hosted marathon jam sessions as the traffic roared past. As one fellow picker recalled, 'The locals would rock up in their pick-ups and Keith and the band would set up on the porch and play for hours.' They'd try out new songs, flail away at raggedy-assed covers of their favourite tunes, whatever they felt was right. 'It was pretty special,' said one band buddy, 'but they were just doing what they did every Sunday afternoon.'[16] Urban, Flowers and Clarke were gradually developing a sound and style that Urban would call 'funktry': hard-rocking country with an R&B backbeat. 'We use a lot of different brushes on a country canvas,' Urban said with a flourish when asked to describe it. '[But] with all of it I try to maintain simplicity and musicianship.'[17]

Greg Shaw, meanwhile, had scored a coaching job with the rugby union team at Nashville's Vanderbilt University, and it was there that he met a professional landscaper. While Urban continued to hook up with Nashville's many writers-for-hire, trying to put the funk into country, Peter Clarke and Shaw (who both now also had US working visas) expanded their lawnmowing business to cover Nashville and neighbouring Franklin, doing their bit to keep the band in food money. Shaw also painted houses for cash.

Urban, as it turned out, wasn't the only act currently trying to cross the great divide that separated Nashville from the Australian country scene. Dark-haired, elfin-like singer Sherrie Austin, who was born in Sydney, had shifted in 1988 to Los Angeles where she stitched up a publishing deal with Warner/Chappell and spent several years fine-tuning her songwriting skills. She shifted to Nashville in 1994 and was signed by Arista Records. She shared more with Urban than an accent; her catholic tastes encompassed everyone from the more traditional (Johnny Cash, George Jones) to such song-birds as Linda Ronstadt and Emmylou Harris, and singer/songwriters like Cat Stevens and Anne Murray. 'I'm a bit of a sponge,' Austin said when asked about her mixed musical tastes. 'I just soaked up everything.'[18]

Things certainly seemed to be moving faster for Austin than for Urban as he and the band continued to plug in at their various favourite Nashville venues and jam on Sundays like there was no tomorrow. But their fortunes were about to take an upturn, and they'd be helped – or hindered, depending on who you ask – by Miles Copeland, a man who seemed least likely to help sell an act like Urban and co.

Urban finally signed with Warner/Reprise Nashville in 1995. This came about with more than a little help from Brian Harris, the former head of EMI Australia, who'd first signed Urban. He now had a top-level exec position with the Australian branch of Warners and loved Urban and the band. 'They played together so well,' Harris said. Harris also knew that Urban was often terribly homesick, and arranged on at least two occasions to bring him back to Australia – once for a Warners conference, and then for Harris's wedding – because Urban couldn't afford the airfare. Harris, like Shaw, the Coburns and MCA's Joanne Petersen, was going above and beyond for Urban.

Another key player in this chapter of the Urban story was Bob Saporiti, who was then the Senior Vice President of International Marketing at the label's Nashville office. He'd been with Warners since 1984. Saporiti's position was unique in Nashville: he ran the only International division based outside of LA and New York. It was his job to spread the word globally about such acts as Faith Hill, Dwight Yoakam and Emmylou Harris and he'd achieved some success, especially in Australia. His motto was: 'Global Peace through Country Music', a logo that appeared on T-shirts worn by him and his staff. He soon learned how Urban could play a role in this unique peace movement.

Saporiti was invited to Australia by Brian Harris to see Urban play during one of his homecomings, and immediately recognised his 'raw talent, although he was very green, just like a kid'. Saporiti, a musician himself, spent a lot of time simply hanging out with Urban, Flowers and Clarke, jamming in hotel rooms and drinking. His favourite memory from the several years he worked closely with Urban came from this tour.

> We were in a hotel room, I think it was in Sydney. I was playing harmonica and Keith was playing guitar, we got into such a jam, shifting keys and stuff like that, it must have gone on for half an hour. That was great.

While in Brisbane getting to know Urban's parents, Saporiti was introduced to Greg Shaw who had swung by the Urban hacienda to do his laundry, a sign of exactly how hand-to-mouth things were for Urban's manager. 'Greg was such a trip, too,' said Saporiti. 'Like Keith, he could not be stopped.'

Saporiti developed a protectiveness towards Urban, and while in Tamworth he got into what he described as a 'knock-down, drag-out' shouting match with Nick Erby on a rainy night at the broadcaster's house, over a BBQ and some beers. Erby told Saporiti that if Urban signed with an American label, he would be rendered ineligible for Golden Guitar nominations. Saporiti considered Erby's attitude frustratingly parochial and eventually talked – or yelled – the bearded broadcaster around.

> I told him that it was so provincial – an American can come down here and do well, but an Australian can't go to Nashville? I told him that he had to keep rooting for this guy. I said, 'You should stop this; you push these guys to get on the world stage and then you penalise them?' To his credit, that never happened, he backed down. It was a good meeting.

But Urban's relationship with the inwards-looking tastemakers at Australia's answer to Music City would continue to be shaky; his subsequent Golden Guitar wins were only in the relatively minor category of Best Instrumentalist. And such Tamworth stalwarts as John 'True Blue' Williamson maintained a strong anti-Urban line, sometimes speaking out publicly about Urban's 'defection' to America, much to the chagrin of Urban's family and others. (Many years later, Urban was prevented from winning a likely Single of the Year Golden Guitar because he'd co-written with an American.) The prevailing Tamworth mindset seemed to be this: if you live over there, you obviously don't need us. That couldn't be further from the truth. Of course, this didn't stop many in Tamworth from talking up their role in Urban's eventual success.

By the time they returned to Nashville, a friendship was formed between Urban and Saporiti over music, loyalty and brews. Saporiti then set about convincing his Warners boss, Eddie Reeves, to sign Urban, but as a solo act. There was some reciprocal back-scratching required, of course – there was *always* payback in the tight-knit world of country music. In exchange for his help with Urban, Saporiti was guaranteed extra support for his American acts in Australia. To ensure this happened, Greg Shaw was made his 'point man' with Warners

Australia, putting together marketing plans for various American acts, while co-managing Urban.

Even though the Urban deal was done, there was a problem from the get-go: Reeves and Saporiti had totally opposed views on what path Warners' new signing should pursue. 'I loved The Ranch, I loved the whole thing,' said Saporiti.

> My whole plan was to let it develop, just let it happen and let Keith find his own way, do his thing. Eddie Reeves, the General Manager at the time, had what turned out to be the correct vision, I have to admit. He wanted to take him more pop and was seeking outside material. It was frustrating Keith, because he wanted to rock out more.

Urban was now spending a good chunk of his downtime hanging out with Saporiti and his family, talking and playing music and picking apart his career, chewing over what path he should pursue: should Urban continue the Fender-bending that gave The Ranch such a rep as a live act, or should he soften his stance and shoot for the mainstream?

> Keith would come over and we'd have these conversations about what the heck was going on. He'd ask me, 'What am I doing here? What's my direction?' all that kind of stuff. But he was going to make it, one way or the other.

Saporiti had no real answer because, as he told me, 'Eddie [Reeves] and I were at such philosophical loggerheads about which way to go with Keith.'

Saporiti had been around for long enough to see that for all of Greg Shaw's Herculean efforts, he was way out of his depth in America. 'He was scrambling,' Saporiti told me, 'but he really put in. I used to call him "the World's Strongest Man".'

It wasn't long before Miles Copeland would play his cameo

in the melodrama that was Urban's career. Shaw grudgingly began to accept two key things: he needed to spend some time in Australia with his family, and he could use some outside help to further the career of his number one star. The original plan was to hire Barry Coburn of Ten Ten to represent Urban Stateside. It made perfect sense – he was an experienced manager (Coburn had looked after Split Enz way back when, and had helped launch the career of country king Alan Jackson). Ten Ten was becoming a well-established Nashville independent, and the family feel of the business would help Urban feel at ease. The Coburns had the connections to hook Urban up with some serious hit-makers, but they clearly cared for more than the guy's songs.

Urban actually approached Coburn and the deal was as good as done, when he suddenly changed his mind and said that he was signing with Miles Copeland's Firstars Management company. Jewel Coburn, for one, has never quite figured out the motivation for Urban's switch although it may have been related to her husband's decision to accept the role of president at Atlantic Records Nashville. 'It got right down to the point of doing it when he met Miles and decided to go with him,' she told me. Barry Coburn very clearly recalled the discussion with Urban. 'He walked into Ten Ten one night,' he said, 'and told me, "I've signed a management deal".' Coburn was a little shocked, given their recent conversation. 'With who?' the genial New Zealander asked. When Urban told him that he'd decided to go with Copeland, Coburn had one key question: 'Does he know anything about the town?' Clearly, the unspoken answer was 'not much'.

It was an unusual tactical move on Urban's part, for many reasons. For one thing, Copeland was based in LA, not Nashville, and as Coburn insinuated, he didn't understand the insular, esoteric nature of Music City. As well as that, his background was in rock, not country, so he was almost as much of an alien as his new client. But, as one reliable source informed me, 'Why wouldn't you go with the guy who managed The Police?' Fair point. The same person suggested to me that going with Barry Coburn may have led to the band being asked to conform to a more traditional Nashville approach – and The Ranch was anything but a 'typical' Nashville band. Whatever the motivation, Urban knew that he needed US-based management who, unlike Shaw, had a handle on the complex American music industry with its myriad formats, charts and go-to people. Urban had actually discussed this in the mid 1990s with Rob Walker, who'd signed him to EMI a few years back. Walker agreed; he could see that Shaw simply wasn't equipped to move Urban forward overseas. Copeland also had an existing relationship with Jim Ed Norman, who was then CEO of Warners Nashville, and this helped grease the tracks a little more.

Barry Coburn doesn't bear any grudge against Urban. His only uneasiness is with Copeland's claim that he 'discovered' Urban, because it was Greg Shaw who had plucked him from obscurity and Ten Ten who had kept him afloat – and paid for his first Nashville demos. Coburn, to his eternal credit and increasing frustration, had, in his words, 'actively encouraged' Shaw to set up a co-management deal in the USA, because the Queenslander simply didn't understand the workings of the American music industry.

'Greg was due some kind of payback, certainly, for his efforts,' Coburn admitted, 'but he didn't have the knowledge to succeed in the US. It's such a complicated network.' He pulled Shaw aside and advised him that he should put in place a deal whereby he would be guaranteed, say, 5 percent of the typical 15 percent management cut in the USA, while at the same time retaining the larger (10 percent) share for deals made back in Australia. It would be a fair and very pragmatic compromise – and ultimately, would have been hugely profitable for Shaw, no matter who he joined forces with. Coburn suggested that Shaw approach a large, reputable management firm such as Fitzgerald/Hartley, who represented golden girl Olivia Newton-John. 'He needed to have this worked out sooner than later,' Coburn added.

> But he just didn't do that. And by the time he did, Keith was beginning to happen and a lot of people from the record company and elsewhere would have been asking him [Keith], '*Who is this guy?* He doesn't know what he's doing.'

Tragically, Shaw left his decision far too late and the consequences, as we have seen, were brutal. Coburn, however, was one of many who saw the Herculean efforts Shaw made for his star. 'Greg would have walked through fire for Keith. His dedication and desire were incredible.'

Despite Urban's decision, Coburn was still actively involved in his career, and he strongly suggested to Miles Copeland that Urban and the band could go over big in the UK – why not try another music-friendly market, especially when Nashville wasn't exactly welcoming Urban like some long-lost stepchild? The Byrds had found a loyal audience there, while the late country-rock maverick Gram Parsons was revered in the UK. Coburn even offered to cover airfares for the band and a crew member but Copeland shut the idea down, much to Coburn's annoyance. 'Copeland was a big talker,' Coburn said, 'but didn't achieve much. We were the ones with money invested in Keith, in his publishing deal and those demos.'

In a frustrating yet satisfying footnote, Coburn was in the crowd on the opening night of Urban's 2006 UK tour, when he opened for Canuck pop-rocker Bryan Adams – whose manager, Bruce Allen, had also expressed interest in managing Urban. 'It was an amazing show; the house was full halfway through his set,' Coburn recalled, which was no small achievement for someone supporting an act with a diehard following like Bryan 'Summer of 69' Adams. Next week, when Urban played his own show in London, the VIP area was jam-packed with EMI 'suits', madly enthusiastic about their latest superstar. Coburn shook his head and wondered what might have happened if Copeland had listened up some 10 years earlier. Coburn also subsequently set up a songwriting session for Urban with Jimmy Webb, his all-time favourite songwriter, and helped re-introduce Urban to Glen Campbell, prior to a show at Nashville's Opryland Hotel. Unlike the cocky kid who once strutted up to the Rhinestone Cowboy and announced that he, too, could play the guitar, Urban was starstruck. 'I can't do it,' he told Coburn. 'What do I say to Glen Campbell?' But they did meet and they've also recorded together, all on the instigation of Coburn.

Miles Axe Copeland III's background made for interesting reading. He was born in London in 1944, and both his parents were intelligence officers – his American-born father was with the CIA and his mother worked for British intelligence. Much of Copeland's youth was spent on the move, as his parents' work led them to Syria, Egypt, Lebanon and other Middle Eastern hotspots. Not surprisingly, Copeland was fluent in Arabic. By the time he earned an MA in economics from the American University of Beirut, he'd already promoted his first rock concert. And rock and roll flowed through the veins of the three Copeland sons – Stewart Copeland was the fluent, inventive timekeeper for the Police, while Ian was a successful booking agent, especially in the New Wave era.

Having graduated, Copeland returned to the UK and set up music festivals and managed such name acts as Wishbone Ash, the Police and Squeeze. He later cared for the solo career of Sting (and the Bangles). But possibly his biggest success was establishing IRS Records (aka International Record Syndicate) in 1979. It became one of music's most successful independent labels. IRS was the early home of REM, and the label of choice for Concrete Blonde, Gary Numan, Stan Ridgeway and the Alarm. She-rockers the Go-Gos were also signed to IRS. (Copeland's deputy, the aforementioned Ged Malone, was married to Go-Go Jane Wiedlin and helped set up a songwriting session for Urban and Wiedlin that would generate Urban's first legitimate hit record in the USA.) Along the way, in 1989, Copeland married Adriana Corajoria, an artist and model from Argentina, and fathered three sons, Miles Axe IV, Aeson and Axton.

From the get-go he had a master plan for Urban, Flowers and Clarke: he was going to promote them as Nashville's answer to the Police. 'I think it was easy for Miles to make the comparison,' Malone told me. 'After all, they were a power trio, just like the Police.' Urban and the band would joke about it, calling themselves 'the *Pole*–eece'; Urban was duly christened 'Staaang'. The management arrangement was set up thus: Malone and Copeland were based in LA, while Anastasia Pruitt (now Brown) – who, allegedly, came from European royalty, and who would later marry A-list Nashville producer and label boss, Tony Brown – was Urban's go-to person on the ground in Nashville. It should be said that the glamorous Pruitt/Brown, who is now a judge on the *Nashville Star* TV show, was a true believer. But according to at least one insider, she faced the same difficulties that were hurting the band: critics and players loved them, but no one at radio was paying any attention. Country radio was too busy spinning the treacly ballad 'It's Your Love', from Nashville's golden couple Tim McGraw and Faith Hill (who wed in 1996), and equally straight-laced fodder from such country hit machines as George Strait, Diamond Rio and Collin Raye. And it should also be said that Urban wasn't Copeland's only business concern; he was thinly stretched.

Jewel Coburn may have been a mild-mannered, polite-natured woman but she wasn't enamoured of Copeland, just like many people in Nashville. 'I can never remember him doing anything [with the band],' she told me.

> He did have Anastasia here as his rep, and she did everything she could. She was a big believer, but it was tough to break through at that stage, for various reasons.

Mark Moffatt, Coburn's former colleague at Ten Ten, was less guarded when I asked him about Copeland. 'I don't know a lot about what Miles tried to do,' he admitted.

> [But] he was certainly dismissive of Greg [Shaw], and there seemed to be a lot of wheel spinning. Miles was kind of frowned upon as a carpetbagger by the Music Row executive crowd.

Others I spoke with for this book agreed that Copeland appeared to have little time, or interest, in Shaw's opinion, even though they were jointly responsible for Urban's career. Yet some, like Bob Saporiti, acknowledged that Copeland's 'international savvy' and connections could help to propel Urban's career to heights Greg Shaw could only imagine.

Copeland's involvement with Urban was definitely hit-and-miss: for one thing, his idea for giving the trio a 'proper name' didn't initially fly. The clumsy tag 'Keith Urban's Four Wheel Drive' was short-lived – thank God – and as we know, it soon disappeared in favour of The Ranch, a far more appropriate name for a fired-up trio of twangy rockers. But even then Urban met some resistance. 'We got pushed and pulled around so much during that time,' he recalled.

> Everyone advised me against it: don't drop my name in favour of the band. Call it Keith Urban and The Ranch. Even the band wanted to just call it that; they didn't seem overly concerned. It caused me so much grief. People didn't understand that I needed my own band, and I retaliated by calling it The Ranch and removing my name altogether.[19]

(A plan to call themselves The Farm was nixed when they learned an English band had the same name.)

By the time of the Warners deal, as Urban admitted, he was pretty close to the edge. 'It started to feel like it was wearing me down . . . when we *[he, actually]* got a record deal,' said Urban. '[But] it was like, "Cool, we did it."'[20] But what Urban didn't know was that the album they were about to begin recording would be the heaviest drama of his soap opera-ish career.

'Walkin' the Country' was the one song on *The Ranch* album that typified the seemingly never-ending saga that was its recording. As Urban revealed, Warner Bros were particularly hard taskmasters; this one track, to his memory, was cut 'in five different studios with three different producers'. The album was a work-in-progress for the best part of 18 months and when asked about the cost, Urban simply shook his head and replied: 'Way, way too much.'[20a] Every time the band emerged with a track that they thought truly captured their hard-driving sound, Warner execs would listen, shake their heads and then tell them to return to the studio. 'It was wearing us out,' Urban neatly understated.

It was a nightmare. They rejected everything we did. How [the album] has any continuity is beyond me, but it has and that's a testimony to how strong the band's signature sound was.[21]

One musician who worked on the album cut through the crap when he admitted to me that their new label 'didn't have a clue'. When Warners told Urban that the tracks didn't sound like anything currently on country radio, he blew a fuse. 'Why?' he snapped. *'Is that a problem?'* Urban explained how execs from the label then told him that:

. . . the more they can make the listener feel as though the radio isn't really on, the less likelihood there is of the listener changing the station. The idea is to keep the person on the station at all times. They are trying to make the music totally linear.[21a]

This, as a concept, was not something Urban felt comfortable with, at least not yet.

There was a further complication to this musical drama. The benchmark that Warners were using was the demos that Urban had recorded with Ten Ten's 'seed money', which were cut at the Nashville home-cum-studio of fiddle player Biff Watson, with a team that included bassist Flowers, drummer Steve Brewster and engineer Mike Pool. (Peter Clarke didn't play on these sessions.) Watson produced the four songs, which included The Ranch standards 'Walkin' the Country' and 'Tangled Up in Love'. 'I remember thinking at the time,' Watson told me, 'that Keith was the direction country music should go. He's a very talented man.' (In a noble act of payback, Watson was hired to strum an acoustic guitar all over Urban's solo debut LP, even though a guitarist of Urban's ability hardly needed any backup in the studio.)

Urban had been signed to Warners – as a solo act, significantly – on the strength of these demos (the masters of which
are still owned and closely guarded by the Coburns). Barry
Coburn even offered to sell the demos to Warners, but Urban's
co-manager Miles Copeland insisted that the band keep trying
to better them, even as the bills started to mount. Not coincid-
entally, Copeland scored co-producer credits on several of the
album's finished tracks. It came as no shock that Ged Malone,
Copeland's partner, told me how Urban would eventually
become 'fed up with Miles'.

While the many studios that were used by Urban, Clarke,
Flowers and the assorted players and pickers who helped them
out seemed impressive on paper – they worked in some A-list
joints – the sheer number of facilities visited was like the
punchline to some bad music industry joke. In Nashville, the
band recorded in Gambit Studios, Island Sound, Javelina,
Masterlinks, MCA Studios, Mid Town, Scruggs Studio, 16th
Avenue Sound, Sound Emporium, Soundstage and Woodland
Digital. In nearby Franklin, they bunkered down in Secret
Sound and The Castle Recording Studio. They even spent
time on the west coast, in LA, where they recorded at Brooklyn
Studios. The production crew details read like the credits of
Gone with the Wind: there were no less than six recording engi-
neers and 11 assistant engineers. The band, Urban and manager
Copeland, as well as Monty Powell (an Urban songwriting
partner), all shared production or co-production credits.

Urban also co-produced and wrote with Vernon Rust, who
had a deal with Copeland's publishing company, IRS Songs,
hence the connection. The Coburns, like many in Nashville,
knew Rust very well. Barry described him as:

> . . . a wild character, almost impossible to find for long periods
> of time. He could be living on a farm or in a car. He was a great,
> unique lyricist, though. Just listen to 'Ghost in This Guitar'.

Rust was roughly the same age as Urban and had a couple of kids; the two men clearly made a strong connection because Rust scored nine writing credits on the finished album. Warners' Bob Saporiti spotted both Rust's songwriting talent and his wildness.

> He was a pretty wacky guy, very right-brained, not a lot of commonsense. Definitely smoked the old 'herbage' too much, and that wasn't necessarily a good thing, but he was a pretty damned good writer.

Rob Potts also met Rust. 'He was a wild, wild boy,' he told me. During an Australian visit, Rust spent some time in detox, on Greg Shaw's dollar. He fled with a nurse a few days after checking in, self-medicating with industrial-strength Valium.

Speaking on an interview disc recorded at the time of the album, Urban talked up Rust's lyrics and their 'great visual sense. His lyrics are very graphic and you can put a picture to them immediately.' For a time, Rust was living in the attic of the band's shared house. He'd often come racing down the stairs, dressed in nothing but socks and jocks, waving lyrics and excitedly talking about a new song. 'Ghost in This Guitar', however, was different. Rust faxed through those lyrics to Urban, who curled up in a chair and announced that they 'read like a little novel'. Interestingly, Rust appears to have dropped off the edge of the musical world since the time he wrote with Urban. 'I'm not sure if he was his own worst enemy or not,' Saporiti figured. (Rust's last contact with Urban was several years after *The Ranch* record, when he dropped by Urban's house. Urban wasn't home, but Rust convinced Urban's girl-friend that Keith had asked him to collect one of his amps, which he duly sold. They haven't spoken since.)

Many of the people whose paths intersected with Urban and the band had an opinion as to why *The Ranch* didn't fly. According to Ten Ten's Mark Moffatt:

> Nashville musicians on all levels were very impressed [by the album], but the industry, as usual, rolled out all the excuses about it being too different, etc. I could see the lack of progress wearing on everyone.

Back in Tamworth, broadcaster Nick Erby had a slightly different take on *The Ranch*. 'The problem was that it wasn't Nashville enough in sound,' he told me. 'It wasn't full of all the stuff that you'll hear on a Nashville record. It also wasn't poppy enough.' Erby had hit on a valid point; in the mid 1990s, with Nashville going through another of its cyclical growth spurts thanks to the platinum-plated success of Garth Brooks, Alan Jackson and others, 'outside' producers, players and engineers descended on Music City, in the process 'thickening' the sound that was typically heard on country records, introducing rock and R&B feels and flavours. 'The music now had a lot of bottom end that you still hear,' Erby added.

> Listen to The Ranch stuff; it's just them, beating out what they were doing. I think if he wasn't selling a million records, he'd still be doing it. The Ranch went in there thinking they could do it their own way and Nashville more than anything else said, no, you have to fit into the box. That was the problem.

Others, including James Blundell, who had a reasonable grasp on the machinations of Nashville, felt that the album was too laboured (hardly the band's fault, it must be said). 'It had some real roots, that record, it was very earthy. But I just remember them wanting to finish it,' he continued.

History points out that spending two years on a record is not a good idea. The only stiff that U2 had was the one they re-recorded four times. I'm a great believer that you should just go in there and do it; the studio isn't a rehearsal room. Especially if you're a band, when they hit that red button you should have your shit figured out.

There are others who believe that *The Ranch* record is Urban's finest hour. 'Keith absolutely believes that his truest form as an artist is *The Ranch* record,' said Rob Potts.

He mightn't state it, but he believes it. To this day it stacks up. Any musician who's into Keith Urban loves that record. It's the one album that he made with all of his passion and all of his naiveté as an artist. What that record expressed was Keith's complete commitment to his own creativity, not tempered by anything.

He was at a stage in his career where he thought that his original talent was all that anyone was interested in, or would be interested in. The unfortunate thing in America is that if it doesn't get played on radio, no one is going to hear it. He had two Top 40 videos but couldn't get it away at radio and it disappeared without a trace. But it got him amazing critical acclaim and set up the belief that Capitol had in taking him away from Warners.

Jewel Coburn offered a few different reasons, although she admitted that she still doesn't really understand why *The Ranch* stiffed. 'I'm not sure that the label knew what to do,' she figured, 'and Keith was having some personal stuff that everybody knows about, and that was slowing down the process.' More on *that* shortly.

Urban was dead right – as an album, *The Ranch* did hang together well, a startling achievement considering its psyche-sapping creation. 'Walkin' the Country', the track that to Urban typified everything that was wrong with the experience, opened the album. Yet this freewheeling country-rocker, driven by Urban's slick finger-picking and its theme of escapism, packed a kick like a mule and became yet another number one for him on the Oz country chart. (A few years later, Urban rocked 'Country' with CCR legend John Fogerty, for an episode of *CMT Crossroads*, and the track held its own against the more formidable Creedence greats they jammed.) It also provided Urban with the chance to cut loose on the 'ganjo', basically an electrified banjo. It was his new weapon of choice, and he'd use it to increasingly good melodic effect as his recording career progressed. As writer Dan Daley, himself a successful songwriter, told me, Urban had tapped into a fresh, if not especially new, twist on country-pop.

> By making the banjo a percussion instrument, the country element is persistent rather than insistent, thus working well for both pop and country markets, where it acts as comfort food for the southern limbic system.

From there, the 'country Police' slipped into 'Homespun Love', a rootsy few minutes of upbeat back porch acoustica, inspired rhythmically by a chance on-the-road encounter with cowpunk outfit the Subdudes. When their drummer walked on-stage tapping away with what Urban called a 'handbourine', Clarke started to pay close attention. (You can hear the results on the track.) During 'Homespun' Urban was in especially fine voice, as he locked into a melody that wouldn't have been lost on Buddy Holly. Oddly, 'Homespun', a song that would remain in Urban's set way beyond the days of The Ranch, actually echoed David Dundas's too-cute 'Jeans On', a mid 1970s hit that Urban would rework on a future solo album. But *it was actually* a knock-off of Lieber and Stoller's 'Little Egypt', a Ranch live staple and 1964 Elvis Presley hit. Urban described 'Homespun' variously as 'a trailer park love song' and 'an ode to trailer park romance, fried chicken and flamingo yard ornaments' – in short, it was not a song to be taken too seriously. It also dealt with good old-fashioned shagging, but Urban has always been too polite to say that out loud. And although the words weren't his, the unmistakable Americana of 'Just Some Love' – 'if the Grand Canyon is just some ditch / Babe Ruth is just some guy with a glove' – proved that Urban had found his lyrical home.

The album's relentlessly uptempo vibe seemed at odds with its creation: 'Some Days You Gotta Dance', another cover and later a hit for the Dixie Chicks, was the kind of juicy, kick-out-the-jams rocker that Urban, Clarke and Flowers would attack during those Sunday afternoon marathons at their shared house. Like much of the album, 'Some Days' sounds as though it was caught on first take, it's so loose and funky ('funktry' at its best, clearly). Yet again, this wasn't quite the truth; its creation was as laboured as any other of the album's dozen tracks. When asked, Urban admitted that the lyrics weren't quite poetry, but he dug them nonetheless. 'It's just fun,' he figured. Fair enough. 'Freedom's Finally Mine' emerged from a band idea to write a jingle that a car company might embrace, which in turn could result in an upgrade of the band's beat-up vehicles. 'If you saw our cars, you'd understand,' Flowers said at the time.[22] The sponsorship didn't happen, sadly, but the song holds up just fine.

Not all of *The Ranch* is so energetic. There were weepies such as 'My Last Name', which Urban and Vernon Rust wrote while sitting around the kitchen table at Urban's house, with the rain tumbling down outside. And 'Man of the House' – inspired by Steely Dan's 'Dirty Work' – and 'Desiree' (which Urban would sing at Brian Harris's wedding, by request) were middling attempts at nailing the kind of blue-collar ballads that

Nashville and country radio had been mad for ever since the days of Patsy Cline's 'Crazy'. Urban didn't quite have enough faith in his voice to deliver the emotional money shot, but the playing was nothing less than solid and the feelings seemed real enough.

'Desiree', Urban's nod to Jimmy 'Wichita Lineman' Webb, became a centrepiece of The Ranch's live set – 'an epic song', in the words of Peter Clarke. Rust admitted that the heartache depicted in the lyric was drawn totally from his own life – only his 'object of desire's' name had been changed. This was one problem with much of *The Ranch* album – while Urban showed that he could completely connect with a lyric and sing it like he meant it, the experiences and emotions were all Rust's. Urban was just the voice. It would be some time yet before he was bold enough to write about what was going on in his heart and head. As Urban said in the album's interview disc, 'Vern lives these songs. I think he's the character in each of them.'

The Ranch truly excelled at amped-up stompers and the album was top-loaded with them: 'Hank Don't Fail Me Now' rocked like a beast while also paying dues to another country legend, Hank Williams, a neat act of rebellion *and* respect. (The opening lick was a nod to Williams's 'Lovesick Blues'.) And the 'borrowing' of the Flying Burrito Brothers' trucker's anthem, 'Six Days on the Road', both in groove and its busting-loose mood, was almost shameless. 'Freedom's Finally Mine' was essentially an opportunity for Urban to fuse Oz-rock muscle with cowpunk twang – it wasn't much of a song but the playing, especially his blistering mid-song guitar solo, was explosive. And as for the reworked instrumental 'Clutterbilly' – this time with added horns – it was even more furiously paced than the original that graced the *Keith Urban* album in 1991. The Ranch was a trio in a hurry, at least during the LP's best moments.

The Ranch emerged to very little in the way of fanfare in late April 1997 in the USA, and a few weeks later in Australia. The most telling blow of all was that Warner Bros didn't even release the record in the USA, when it was finally completed. By this time they had dropped Urban (in 1996) and sold the record to the more Ranch-friendly Capitol Records, whose label head, Scott Hendricks, quickly became another Urban champion. Urban's transition from one label to another was helped by the fact that Copeland was a member of the EMI board and was actively involved in getting Urban moved between labels. (Capitol was part of the EMI empire.)

This shift was the endplay in the ongoing tussle between Warners' Bob Saporiti and Eddie Reeves, who couldn't agree whether Urban should 'stay hard' or soften up and embrace the 'Nashville sound'. The way Saporiti saw it:

> [Label head] Jim Ed [Norman] took on the role of Solomon and said, 'Look, we're going to ruin this kid's career, let's call Capitol and see if we can get some money back and let him go.' He figured this would give Keith more of a chance and give him some direction. It turned out that the direction he ended up taking was the pop, Nashville sound, so I was wrong, but you never know what might have happened if he'd gone in the other, rockier direction. I thought it was so intelligent and gracious of Jim Ed to let him go. He really thought that we were going to hurt this kid's career if we kept him here, because we couldn't agree. It was truly 'what's best for the artist' and Warners in those days was a really artist-friendly type of label.

Sadly, Saporiti could only look on from the sidelines when Urban started doing big business some years down the line, peddling a much more sugary take on country than the music he was pounding out with The Ranch. But they remained tight; Urban even once got up and jammed with Reckless Johnny Wales, Saporiti's rockin', rootsy alter ego.

Interestingly, Warners did release *The Ranch* Down Under, thanks to the influence of Brian Harris. He was nobody's fool: when he first signed Urban to EMI back in 1991, Harris was getting ready to shift over to Warners, so he only signed Urban to an Australian deal, leaving him open to sign with any other label for the rest of the world. When Harris took the post at Warners, he put in the call to Saporiti and got the whole US deal in motion, even if, of course, it didn't quite play out as he would have hoped.

Reviews for the album were more rare than Ranch spins on country radio, and their flip-flopping between labels clearly didn't help the band gain any forward motion. *The Ranch* was destined to become the kind of album that's only fully acknowledged years after the event, long after the power trio had fallen apart. And even then it was shamelessly repackaged in 2003 as *Keith Urban in the Ranch*, an unreasonable slap in the face to his bandmates. (When *The Ranch* was released in Australia, a sticker on the cover announced: 'Featuring Keith Urban'.) One player on the record told me that he believed Urban's current manager, Gary Borman, has flexed his considerable muscle to distance his client from an album that was perceived by Nashville kingmakers as a flop – even if those same executives probably played the record repeatedly in their offices and cars. It was months after the album dropped that Capitol bothered to issue a single.

As clichéd as it seems, the cover shot of *The Ranch* neatly sums up the band's failure – and it was a failure, registering not a blip on any of Billboard's myriad album and single charts. Highly regarded lensman James B. Minchin III caught Urban, trusty Fender in hand, seated on some rustic (or just plain rusty) shopfront, glaring warily at the camera, while Clarke and

Flowers looked away, somewhere far off in the distance, as if to say: 'Where did our careers go?'

The trio stuck it out for a little longer as Capitol struggled, just like Warners, to find a place for Urban amid the sea of so-called 'hat acts' that had set upon Nashville like some success-hungry monster. In late September The Ranch played Nashville's Country Music Week, an orgy of new talent and major label shopping, where they shared bills with such up-and-comers as Gary Allan, expat Aussie Sherrie Austin and Matraca Berg, whose pithy, hooky songs Urban would one day cover. In the advance blurb for the event, Miles Copeland was in full promotional cry:

> When I first saw The Ranch play, I actually thought to myself, 'This band could do for country what the Police did for rock – world-class musicianship, quality songs stripped to the essence in a three-piece, and a positive attitude.'

Their agent, CAA's Jeff Pringle, talked them up as 'the best live show on the road'. Urban, meanwhile, quietly stuck with his 'funktry' schtick.[23]

It all failed to gel, of course, and Urban seriously started to consider dismantling The Ranch and doing what he should have done all along – become a solo act. He even despatched a letter to his slouch-hatted mentor, Slim Dusty, asking for his advice. Dusty's widow, Joy McKean, remembers this. 'Keith wrote to Slim during the time he was making the painful decision to go solo,' she told me.

> He was on tour, and we didn't know where to write back. It was a terribly difficult decision for him to make but in the end, it has turned out to be the correct one. In his usual way, Slim approved of Keith's doing what he had his heart set on, no matter whether it was something Slim would do himself.

When Urban decided to split the band in June 1998, he wasn't just ending a musical partnership, he was terminating an almost decade-long relationship with drummer Peter Clarke, who'd backed Urban since the days of the Ayers Rockettes. According to one source:

> It's tough when you do so much work with some people and then crank it up to the next level and say, 'So long and thanks for the fish.' It took Peter a long time to get over that. He went to ground for a few years, took a labouring job and said, 'Fuck it, it's all too hard.'

Urban has never commented on the personal side of the breakup, sticking with the usual homilies about 'changing musical direction' and his desire to go solo. Clarke did, however, play with Urban again, on a very informal level, as well as spending time drumming for Lee Kernaghan and the US band Big House. He appears to harbour no strong ill feeling towards Urban, even if he thinks the star's current carers might have downplayed his role in the 'Urban Legend'. Jerry Flowers, meanwhile, despite a spot of moonlighting for such acts as the Dixie Chicks, still plays alongside Urban today. You can't miss him: he's the one that could pass for a security guard.

It also didn't help The Ranch's cause when there was movement in the boardroom at their new label, Capitol Records. Their 'booster', Scott Hendricks, was replaced at the top by Pat Quigley at the instigation of Garth Brooks and his runaway ego. Quigley was a smarmy character whose music business experience was best summed up by the word 'zilch'. During a marketing meeting, Quigley once suggested that a new Garth Brooks record should be launched from outer space. 'God damn it, Garth, we need to launch this record from the space shuttle. That's what we need to do,' he stated, to

which Brooks replied: 'I love that idea – let's make it happen!'
In another legendary incident, which has also seeped into
Nashville folklore, Quigley bizarrely suggested that one of
Capitol's artists should duet with the long-dead Patsy Cline.
When a stunned staffer replied that this could present a
problem, Cline being deceased and all, Quigley allegedly
snapped back: 'Well, get me her management on the phone. I'll
make it happen!' But even Quigley's powers over reincarna-
tion couldn't help The Ranch.

Of course it wasn't just The Ranch that was falling apart:
their lead singer, shit-hot guitarist and main man, who had now
resorted to lingering at the gates of the Dollywood theme park
offering to sing for newlyweds, was coming apart at the seams.

Five

FRIENDS IN LOW PLACES

The assumption is that if you're managing an artist you
shouldn't roll down into the crack cocaine hole with
them, but you have to look at it from Greg's perspective:
he'd given Keith 10 years of his life and wanted
[success] as much as Keith.

Rob Potts

It was five o'clock one Nashville morning, not long after The
Ranch's less-than-dazzling recording debut, that Urban's
world truly began to fall to pieces. Racked with self-doubt
and completely over being told that he didn't fit in, Urban
had descended into a drug hell. In an interview with *USAweek-
end.com* in 2001 he talked about what happened next:

I [was] crawling around on my hands and knees, looking for
these little rocks [of cocaine], and I was drenched in sweat. It
was the worst. [There was] major chaos in my life. I pushed
everybody away.

As he explained in an interview with Channel 9's human haircut Richard Wilkins, 'Nashville has a tendency to grind you into the ground and destroy your soul.' That was especially the case when nothing was happening for you, career-wise. The kid from Caboolture, a 'fucking funny drunk' according to those who shared his company, a man who formerly enjoyed a few Bundys after sessions and gigs, as well as the occasional joint, had become a full-blown crackhead, a potential 'high-risk statistic', in the words of one friend. Even Urban considered himself an addict. As far as he was concerned, his life, not just his career, was as good as over.

It wasn't as though drug use and abuse were unheard of in the world of country music. Johnny Cash had done hard time on Dexedrine, Benzedrine and Dexamyl, which kept him on fast-forward for way too many years, almost to the point of death. And much of Willie Nelson's legend was built around his fondness for ganja – he was Music City's very own Bob Marley. There are also legendary stories of a fucked-up Waylon Jennings directing the traffic at a recording session with his pistol on display for all the players to see. As Jennings admitted in his autobiography:

> I prided myself on the fact that I could take more pills, stay up longer, sing more songs and screw more women than most anybody you ever met in your life.[1]

In the late 1960s, psychedelic cowboy Gram Parsons, of Byrds and Flying Burrito Brothers renown, bonded over toxins and twang with Rolling Stones guitarist and legendary junkie, Keith Richards; he eventually OD'd and died in September 1973 while on a bender in Joshua Tree, California. (Parsons's corpse was commandeered at LA Airport and taken back to Joshua Tree for an aborted cremation, but that's another story altogether.) And more recently, man mountain Steve 'Copper-head Road' Earle developed a fondness for smack, guns and wives (although he's since given up on at least the first two), which led to the occasional spell in prison. His son, Justin Townes Earle, also a musician, has spent some time chasing the dragon himself.

So getting seriously wasted seemed to be almost a rite of passage in roots music circles. But unlike this hard-living bunch, Urban was no outlaw; he was trying his best to fit within Nashville's narrow confines. And there can be serious retribution at the cash register if a country act on the rise screws up, as Bob Saporiti, Urban's one-time go-to guy at Warners, explained to me: 'That's the kind of thing that can wreck a career in such a white, Southern, Pentecostal, born-again place like Nashville.' (Saporiti and Urban shared many pints of Guinness, but nothing stronger, during their few years working together.)

Those close to Urban, especially his surrogate family at Ten Ten, knew that Urban was doing more than just dabbling with coke. Jewel Coburn told me, euphemistically, how she knew of the 'personal problems' Urban was experiencing, while Mark Moffatt admitted to being 'aware of what was happening' with Urban and drugs. 'Anyone fighting disappointment and self-esteem issues [could get] in trouble,' he added. Moffatt also noted that Ten Ten was 'a special little family that cared very much for their own', but there may have been times when even they felt that they'd lost Urban to the pipe. And though Greg Shaw has never spoken of Urban's addiction issues – he's said very little about his most famous client, come to think of it – there is obviously no way that he couldn't have been aware of Urban's gradual disintegration. In fact, according to Rob Potts, who knew them both as well as anyone else, Shaw was knee-deep in crack himself.

'It was a really out-of-it time,' said Potts, who would travel to Nashville occasionally and freely admits to sharing 'some pretty fucked-up nights' with Urban.

> But they were both getting fucked up all the time. The assumption is that if you're managing an artist you shouldn't roll down into the crack cocaine hole with them, but you have to look at it from Greg's perspective: he'd given Keith 10 years of his life and wanted [success] as much as Keith.

('Greg was known as a top tooter,' said Rob Walker, who knew Shaw well. I was related another story of how, during one of the notorious ARIAs 'after parties' at Sydney's Sebel Town House, Shaw quite brazenly 'shouted' Urban and another country star a line of coke in a limo parked in the street.)

Urban's record label certainly knew what was going down; they delivered a press release reporting how Urban's vocal cords 'haemorrhaged' and he'd be out of action for an unspecified period. Dated 8 May 1998, under the heading: 'Urban Under Doctor's Orders', the statement read that he was suffering 'a severe throat problem' and had been advised by his doctor to 'take an immediate break from singing'. It went on to report how Urban was on a strict diet, with 'instructions to speak as infrequently as possible to assist the healing process'. There was also speculation that if his vocal cords didn't respond to treatment, 'laser surgery will be required'. The Ranch was officially on a four- to six-month 'enforced break', which meant that an upcoming Australian tour was canned. Speaking – whispering, more likely – from Nashville, Urban expressed the usual disappointment about letting down the rest of the band and his fans. 'What I have to focus on now,' he stated, 'is the discipline required for me to get well as quickly as possible. My determination to continue my career is as strong as ever.'[2] It was mainly spin, of course, because Urban was coming undone and was on a fast-track to rehab. But it gave him the breathing space to deal with the heavy shit going down in his life.

Admittedly, his voice *was* shot. When 'Clutterbilly' won Urban his next Golden Guitar, for Best Instrumental, he croaked his way through one of the most heartfelt speeches he ever delivered, sounding like the skinny blond son of Tom Waits. With girlfriend Laura Sigler looking on — heaven knows what this classy Nashville lady made of Tamworth — Urban did his best to give 'shout-outs' to fiddler Pixie Jenkins, friend Tommy Emmanuel ('a man with the hands of God'), 'Shawree', Brian Harris and Jerry Flowers, while describing his recent experiences as 'hellacious'. He also took the time to talk about his decision to head to Nashville; Urban wasn't deserting anyone, he was just running down a dream. Clearly, the perception that he'd ditched Tamworth for Nashville — as small-minded and parochial as that attitude was from the Oz country patriarchs — must have been eating at him. 'It's a bloody hard slog in the States,' he said, 'and we're not abandoning anybody. We want to go there when we choose to, not when we have to.' Considering that the man could hardly speak, his address was passionate and surprisingly assertive.

Three weeks after the 'Under Doctor's Orders' press release, his label went into print again, announcing the end of The Ranch. 'It was a particularly tough blow,' the statement read, 'as the band were making strong inroads in the US with their debut album *The Ranch*, both in media, on CMT and on the live scene.' (They'd filmed videos for 'Walkin' the Country' and 'Clutterbilly' in the same small Nashville suburb on the same day, *on opposite sides of the street*, with one change of clothes between shoots.) 'After careful consideration,' it continued, the band had opted 'to part ways in what is a completely amicable decision.' As for Urban, the press release revealed that he was already moving forward, 'using the time to write new material for a solo album for Capitol Records'. He had a few hurdles to jump before he got back into the studio, though.

Max Hutchinson, Urban's one-time Nashville neighbour, admitted that Urban had begun to move in some dodgy circles as The Ranch fell apart. 'It was a low time for him,' he said in 2005. 'I saw him in some pretty bad states. He started hanging with the wrong crowd. Keith liked to smoke a bit of pot, but they got him into crack.'[3] (Crack is so named because of the popping sound it makes when smoked in a pipe.) A friend and peer of Urban's described his addiction as 'a roaring habit'. Mixing with some bad seeds, living in a dodgy neighbourhood in a city that wasn't short of supply, plus his ongoing problems with a stalled career and uncertainty about life after The Ranch, only exacerbated Urban's fondness for 'life-sweeteners'. It got to the point, in Urban's own words, where he was 'completely prepared to die – and I had no problem with that. I was heading straight down that road without a care in the world.'[4]

Urban, to his credit, has never tried to hush up these particularly dark days, and has very publicly picked apart what might have led to his downward spiral. He has said that he binged on coke to deal with career rejection. In one particularly candid confession, he stated: 'I realised that I could kill myself, [after] recognising that I'll never reach the icon status of a Willie Nelson.'[5] Urban also said he became a crackhead due to plain old loneliness. After all, it is true that Brian Harris, Urban's former Australian label head, did manage to bring him back to Australia twice in the mid 1990s, ostensibly for engagements, but in part because he knew that Urban was homesick. 'It was just a pathetic escape mechanism,' Urban admitted, several years down the sober road. 'It wasn't the greatest career move [either].'[6]

But even those who only dealt with Urban on a mainly business level, such as Ged Malone, Copeland's Firstars' partner, gained firsthand exposure to Urban's meltdown. Malone was flying from LA to attend a Ranch showcase that had been arranged in New York, where they were supporting, of all people, blues legend Bo Diddley. While in transit, Malone and Urban spoke on the phone, basically getting to know each other. It was the first time they had actually talked, and pretty much straight off the bat Urban requested that Malone score for him.

'He asked me to get him some coke,' Malone told me in an email, 'but he used a slang term I can't remember. I don't think Miles knew Keith had a problem.' Malone decided that this request went way beyond the typical artist–manager agreement and decided not to deliver. At the after-show party, Urban became aggressive and started to shove Malone, pushing him around the backstage area, clearly agitated by something – possibly his reluctance to score. The very proactive Malone did what he felt was right, given the circumstances. 'I grabbed him around the neck and told him that if he didn't stop I'd punch his face in. After that,' Malone added, 'he was fine and we got on great.' (So great, in fact, that Malone would play a key role in helping Urban co-write his first 'real' Nashville hit song.)

Finally, Urban took the advice of those around him and checked into a rehab facility, Cumberland Heights, a place that left a deep enough impression for him to give it a 'shout-out' in the acknowledgements of his solo US debut. (It has been whispered that he relapsed a few months after his first stint at rehab, but it is clear that he finally 'got sober', for the first time, by April 1999.) His friend Tommy Emmanuel, who also spent some dark days chasing the dragon, now found that he and Urban bonded over more than Chet Atkins licks. 'Yeah, we shared a common situation where we were both into alcohol and drugs and we've both been through the same kind of thing,' Emmanuel admitted to me.

> I went through treatment and have been sober for a while now. We both have that in common; our disease slowly became bigger than us. We had to go and find our sobriety and our wellness to get on with the things that were impor- tant to our life, our gift.
>
> I just liked alcohol and drugs too much and I had the disease of addiction and so does Keith and millions of others in the world. We're two of the lucky ones; we didn't kill ourselves and we didn't kill anybody else. We hurt some people along the way and let some people down, but we turned our lives around by getting the right treatment and living the right way. I admire his courage. You have to reach a point where you are ready to admit: 'I'm powerless over this; my life is out of my control.' You have to give up and let someone else take control and that someone else is God. That's the only way we can survive.

A non-profit operation, Cumberland Heights was set on 70 isolated, woody hectares on the banks of the Cumberland River, just to the west of Nashville. Opened in the 1960s, the facility spelled out their intentions clearly in their mission state- ment. Their treatment encompassed 'the physical, mental, emotional and spiritual dimensions of recovery through profes- sional excellence, the principles of the 12 Steps, and a safe, loving environment'. Unlike his guitar buddy Emmanuel, Urban wouldn't embrace God, but the New Agey 12 Steps concept – the guiding principles of the Alcoholics Anonymous organisation, with which Urban was later involved – would form a sort of user's manual for his life from here on in, despite the odd relapse (he returned to rehab in 2006). The core beliefs of 12 Steps are an admission that you are powerless over your addiction; that a 'greater power' can guide you through; that you need to adopt a new code of behaviour and, with the help of a sponsor, that you can try to make amends for your previous fuck-ups.

Although he denies being Urban's official sponsor, Rob Potts, who had been booking Urban's Australian shows since 1989, was someone that Urban confided in a lot. His Australian-based agent and friend had also lived through some dark times of his own. He and Urban had shared a lot of wasted nights – he readily admitted to me that they'd gotten 'fucked up' on numerous occasions, often with Greg Shaw as well – but now Potts was doing his bit to keep Urban off anything harder than a well-chosen glass of plonk. The connection between Urban and Potts was strong and some-times comical: way back in January 1992, Potts had covered a A$110 fine imposed on Urban by Woollahra Council, for the crime of 'the illegal exhibition of advertising displayed on power poles in New South Head Road, Rushcutters Bay'. In other words, Potts's agency had put up some flyers promoting an Urban gig at Double Bay's Royal Sheaf, and the council duly tore them down and sent them the bill for their removal.

While in rehab, Urban would sometimes make late-night phone calls to his friends. Ten Ten's Jewel Coburn received her share. It seemed that Urban just wanted to hear a friendly voice on the other end of the line. 'We used to have long discussions,' she recalled.

> He used to call me from rehab at three in the morning and we'd talk about whatever he wanted to talk about. He'd ask my opinion a lot about what he should do, but I never had the answers, so I'd just listen and try to be supportive and make suggestions if I had one. Even though he wanted help,

he sort of knew inside what he wanted to do. I tried to be a good listener.

As far as his musical future was concerned, Coburn's advice cut through a lot of crap. While it was great to sing Vernon Rust's lyrics, Urban now had to find his own voice.

> He needed to write more and think about what he wanted to say as a solo artist. He had to develop that confidence. I think he also went through some spiritual stuff, searching, and relationships, all sorts of things that helped him get to a point where he knew what he wanted to write about. My main encouragement was to keep on writing; *just keep writing*.

If there was one thing that Urban gained from this dark time in his life, it was subject matter for songs.

Urban emerged from his first stint in rehab clearly a better man – he'd detoxed both physically and creatively and was pretty much ready to assume the mantle of a solo artist. Crack not only clogs one's bowels – I once interviewed a former Red Hot Chili Pepper, who told me how his 'shit turned white' after some time on the pipe – but it can seriously jam up your creativity, too. While Urban may have finally put his cocaine blues behind him, he was now forced to deal with the damage that crack had inflicted on his vocal cords. There were numerous times in the ensuing years when he would be forced to cancel shows because of throat problems. The connection between crack cocaine and throat troubles is relatively well documented, although the link hasn't been explored with quite the same fervour as, say, the relationship between coke and collapsed septums, which tend to leave hideous, tell-tale holes in a user's nose. But there's no doubt that a connection exists.

An on-line medical forum revealed this:

One of the effects of cocaine is to cause small blood vessels to clamp down and cut off circulation. When snorted, this means the blood supply can be cut off to the mucous membranes, which causes irritation and, frequently, sores from tissue that has died from insufficient blood supply. Not unusually, this can result in actual holes in the nasal septum and voicebox as the tissue dies away.

Acetone and acetic anhydride, ammonium hydroxide and numerous other shitty chemicals and toxins that are used to turn coca leaves into cocaine are also known to damage the user's throat, as well as their eyes, nose, skin – sometimes even the wildlife around them, if they opt to hit the pipe outdoors. It's one mad, bad drug.

As if things weren't complicated enough – he'd owned up to life as an addict while his band and, seemingly, his Nashville dream, had collapsed like a house of cards – Urban's love life was also on a particularly slippery slope. He and Laura Sigler had managed to maintain a relatively workable relationship, but its demise dovetailed all too neatly with the darkest days of his life. According to James Blundell, who knew Sigler, she seemed resigned to their romance flat-lining. 'He and Laura, well, I thought that was going to be the thing and stabilise him, but look what happened.' Looking back, Urban admitted that their bust-up was a result of his 'troubles'. 'It was hell,' he said. 'If you have a partner on your side, you need to acknowledge them and bring them closer, but I was focusing too much on my career and my problems.'[7] He also had the odd affair, such as his dalliance with Dixie Chick Martie Maguire, although the closest he ever came to any kind of admission was when he told a Sydney journalist that he and the Dixies 'had all become friends over the past couple of years, out on the road'.[8] They'd first met during his days with The Ranch, when the trio's path intersected with the not-yet-huge Dixies. A future photo of Urban and Maguire, snapped in a friendly clinch at the 2000 Country Music Association Awards, hinted at more than a shared love of twang.

Urban, as he'd done in the past with Angie Marquis, had adopted an unusual method of expressing how much he was in love with Sigler (at least for a time). With Marquis he'd sacrificed his white Fender guitar as a token of his affection, but he tried something a little different with Sigler. He invited her to lunch and, without her knowledge, had arranged for a friend to stand outside the restaurant. On a cue from Urban, he would hold up a handwritten sign. So the couple took their table, his friend moved into place and Urban soon gave him a nod. Sigler looked out the window, directly at a sign that read: 'Laura, will you marry me?' There's no doubt that she was hugely flattered – and did, briefly, accept his offer – but by the time he had morphed into keith urban, lower case solo act, Sigler was pretty much out of his life.

She even retreated to Canada in an effort to keep her distance from Urban, where she roomed with a platonic male friend. But Keith phoned her constantly and eventually coaxed her into returning, even though they would break up. Sigler only spoke about her relationship with Urban long after they'd finally, irrevocably split and had long ceased speaking with each other. 'There were lots of lows with the drugs,' she said. 'I don't have any dark past – he was probably the darkest part.'[9]

What Urban needed to do was now re-assemble his life, piece by piece. There was some speculation that he might return to Australia for good, but Urban shut that down. As his mother, Marienne, said in a rare interview, 'I'm sure people thought, "Well, he'll go back home," but Keith was determined to prove them wrong.'[10]

As far as his career was concerned, Urban needed to make a major compromise. While out in front of The Ranch he'd taken a maverick stance in the hope that Nashville would recognise their worth and gravitate towards them, but now he needed to head directly to the heart of the country mainstream (although a hat was still out of the question). Broadcaster Nick Erby summed up Urban's dilemma neatly:

> When he came back as a solo artist they said, '*You get it together and do it our way.*' I'm not saying he's totally opposed to [nonconformity], but he tried one way, it didn't work and then he came back and tried it differently.

One thing that Urban did have working for him was an existing record deal with Capitol, to whom he was now signed as a solo act. But his musical rebirth – or re-configuration, if you prefer – didn't happen overnight. First up he had to make some cameos; and it's unlikely that he and Greg Shaw, who'd stuck with him throughout the whole messy rehab drama, could have selected three better acts to work with. Each of them – Garth Brooks, Alan Jackson and the Dixie Chicks – were either riding the wave of the so-called 'Gone Country' generation or, in the latter's case, were messing with the accepted notion of a woman's role in country.

If conspiracy theorists were looking for some connection between Urban's recent dark past and his future, his role in the video for Alan Jackson's 'Mercury Blues' was loaded with unintended symbolism. About a minute into the clip, a 'shadowy' figure, cloaked in darkness, appears behind the lanky Jackson's right shoulder, pulling off some slick licks and appropriately suggestive wiggles of his hips. But with his stonewashed denims and lank blond hair, Urban looked a tad out of place; it was as if he'd taken a wrong turn at a Poison video clip and somehow ended up on director Piers Plowden's set. (Keep in mind that Jackson had been 'discovered' by the Coburns at Ten Ten, so there was only one degree of separation between him and Urban.)

But if Urban's cameo with Jackson was a little odd, his contribution to Garth Brooks's chest-thumping *Double Live* LP was positively surreal. In what could easily be read as the final chapter in Brooks's quest for crossover superstar status – if Kiss can cut a double live album, Brooks figured, he sure as hell could, too – the 26-track album (well, 25 tracks plus one interlude called 'Crowd' that comprised six seconds of cheering) was culled from numerous US and international tour dates from 1998. But Urban wasn't on the road with Brooks or part of his live band – he was actually brought in to overdub guitar, *on a live album*. The gig might have considerably upped Urban's status as a guitar player but the concept, frankly, was ridiculous.

Nonetheless, Urban knew that his career was on the mend when he bumped into Brooks in a Nashville parking lot. Not only did the country star recognise Urban, but he helped him with his gear – and when they said their goodbyes, Brooks called him 'mate'. Urban couldn't get over to the Coburns's office quickly enough to share the news. 'It was a good sign,' said Ten Ten's Mark Moffatt. When asked about the Brooks cameo, Urban chose his words wisely. 'It was a trip, man,' he chuckled. 'I was thrilled to bits.'[11] Their paths would soon intersect again, but in a far more controversial fashion.

There's no doubt that the Jackson and Brooks bit parts were useful to Urban, as were subsequent studio gigs with the Charlie Daniels Band, John Mohead, Capitol labelmate Tim Wilson and the Sons of the Desert. Urban also found the time to fly back to Oz to record 'Walk a Country Mile' for the Slim Dusty tribute, *Not So Dusty*, working alongside Midnight Oil, Ed Kuepper and his former EMI partner in country, James

Blundell. (As well, Urban snagged Best Instrumentalist Golden Guitars in 1997 and 1998.) But his solo career was truly set in motion when he got a call from the Dixie Chicks to add a guitar part to their album *Fly* which, like Brooks's *Double Live*, would eventually shift 10 million copies, making it a 'diamond' record, the rarest of musical beasts.

The Dixies' bloodline was as rich with country DNA as any of their peers. Multi-instrumentalists Martie Maguire and Emily Robison started playing together in their teens, when the former was studying at Southern Methodist University and the latter was halfway through an uncompleted application to the Air Force Academy. They were originally a four-piece, playing with bassist Laura Lynch and guitarist Robin Lynn Macy, who were in their thirties and, allegedly, were forced out in favour of a more youthful image for the band. Five-foot-nothing powerhouse Natalie Maines, the daughter of pedal steel great Lloyd Maines, joined Robison and Maguire in 1995. The big-voiced Maines was a Berklee College of Music dropout who was then attending her third college in three years. These Dixie Chicks – named after the Little Feat classic 'Dixie Chicken', incidentally – clearly weren't cut out for academia.

The first long-player they released was called *Wide Open Spaces*, and even the most optimistic of Nashville's crystal ball gazers couldn't have predicted how massive a hit it would become on the strength of the yearning title track, the chart-topping 'There's Your Trouble', and the trio's smart, sexy image. When Urban received his call to work on its follow-up, *Fly* – specifically on the track 'Some Days You Gotta Dance', which he had cut with The Ranch – *Wide Open Spaces'* sales were four million and counting. And it also snagged a Best Country Album Grammy. At first, Urban was disappointed; he'd been told that the Dixies wanted to cut a Ranch song, ideally one of his own compositions, which might have helped him out of his current financial hole, but 'Some Days' wasn't an Urban original. Still, he agreed to the cameo. And it wasn't as though the Dixies were blind to the appeal of the guy who ambled in to add a few guitar parts to their record, as Martie Maguire admitted. 'There's always something sexy about a man who plays the crap out of the guitar – and a great Australian accent can never hurt.'[12] It was probably the first time that Urban had been praised by a Nashville 'player' for his 'Australian-ness'.

Urban made another important connection while hanging out with the Dixies; through them he got to know keyboardist and budding producer Matt Rollings, who was also playing on *Fly*. (The now LA-based piano player denied a claim on Urban's 'official' record company bio that he had hired him for the *Fly* session. 'We met elsewhere,' Rollings said cryptically, via email, but refused to elaborate.) Rollings was in his mid thirties and had been Nashville-based since the mid 1980s and, just like Dixie Chick Maines, had studied at the Berklee College of Music. The doughy-faced Rollings had a CV that read like some classic country mix tape: he'd recorded with Lyle Lovett, Johnny Cash, Kenny Rogers, Glen Campbell, Vince Gill, Trisha Yearwood and the late, great bluegrass master, Keith Whitley.

As soon as they started talking favourite records, Rollings and Urban bonded faster than Superglue. 'Matt and I talked about the fact that we are fans of albums, not just singles,' said Urban.[13] The two picked apart the early LPs of Elton John like a couple of true music geeks and another key relationship was set in stone. Even though his only studio credit, to date, was as producer on his own album, 1990's jazzy *Balconies*, Rollings was making a move to graduate from music-maker to record-maker, and Urban needed someone to work with in the studio.

Urban, with the help of Mark Moffatt who was now the

A&R director at Ten Ten, was gradually starting to come up with some new musical ideas. And a few were fairly radical, especially for a guy who desperately needed a record in the charts. Post-rehab and stuck on the couch – ongoing troubles with his throat meant that he couldn't sing – Urban resorted to channel surfing, flicking between CMT and other more cutting-edge music networks. What he learned was that hip-hop was on the rise; and not just the standard gangsta boasting, but slick, well-crafted grooves with some revolutionary production touches. *The Miseducation of Lauryn Hill* was every-where, as was Jay-Z's 'Hard Knock Life' and such breakout acts as Destiny's Child and Usher. Urban started to piece together a crossover song that 'sounded like a back porch stomp but with a drum machine'.[14]

Producer/songwriter Steven Jordan (aka Stevie J.) had worked with Jay-Z on his 1997 hit 'Lucky Me', but was probably best known for his slick, seamless commingling of the Police's 'Every Breath You Take' and a heavy-hearted rap from Puff Daddy. This became the Grammy-winning monster, 'I'll Be Missing You', allegedly Puff Daddy's farewell to his peer and rival the Notorious BIG, who was murdered in 1997. Stevie J. was part of the Bad Boy Entertainment Hitmen, a crew of producers and writers working for Puff Daddy's label. He was hardly the kind of character you'd expect to 'hook up' with a guy from Caboolture.

Surprisingly, the idea of bringing Urban and Stevie J. together came from Capitol boss, Pat Quigley, when he wasn't busy trying to resurrect Patsy Cline. Possibly the most unpop-ular label head in Nashville – and in that highly competitive end of the music business, that's really saying something – New Yorker Quigley had been tagged 'Garth's robot' by much of the Music City community. The strong-willed Quigley, who formerly sold skis, watches and beer rather than music, didn't make many friends when he told *The New York Times* that 'country for me in Manhattan was the Hamptons'. But because he wasn't so bound to the conventions of country music, Quigley saw no reason why he shouldn't connect Stevie J. and Urban – after all, he'd used the producer before on Garth Brooks's very odd side project, *The Secret Life of Chris Gaines* (more of which soon). He and Urban discussed the idea, Urban telling him that he wanted 'to infuse more rhythmic stuff into country. Why *don't* we try a hardcore hip-hop producer?' Urban figured. 'I don't know – what the hell?'[15]

It was quite a sight at Ocean Way studio in Nashville on the day that Stevie J. arrived for work. Ocean Way's carpark was typically a sea of pick-up trucks, yet Stevie J. and his 'people' arrived in a flotilla of limos. Urban raised his eyebrows in surprise at a sight more commonly seen in New York or LA, but soon got to work, recording some ideas while Stevie J. busied himself with programming. When I spoke with Urban around this time, he described Stevie J. as 'this well-mannered, really charming guy'. When Urban pressed him for any 'dirt' from working with Mariah Carey, Stevie J. stayed loyal. 'He just didn't tell any gritty stuff,' Urban laughed. 'He had nothing but praise for her.'[16]

Mark Moffatt, whom Urban would credit for 'A&R ideas and help with loops' on the finished album, was also in the studio with Urban. As the session progressed, Moffatt recalled, 'it came time to add the "local" component, but no one seemed to know who to use'. Moffatt, on Urban's request, brought in pedal steel player Bruce Bouton and fiddler Aubrey Haney. A short while later, Stevie J. pulled Moffatt aside. 'Can you stick around?' he asked the producer. 'My engineer has no idea how to work with instruments like those,' Stevie J. said, pointing in the direction of Haney and Bouton. The song they attempted didn't make the finished record – ironically, Urban felt it was too 'beat driven and not enough country'[17] – but Moffatt told me 'it was a fun couple of days'. Nonetheless, the album's lead single, 'It's a Love Thing', was definitely flavoured by Urban's, erm, urban experiments.

Quigley had one other sound piece of advice for Urban as his solo debut for Capitol slowly started to come together. As he related to *The New York Times*, he told Urban to 'get the female agenda and apply it to a sensitive new man'. In short, write touchy-feely songs that chicks will dig. In particular, one Urban co-write, entitled 'You're the Only One', caught the ear of the New York-born marketing man. 'Listen to that lyric,' he told the *Times'* Neil Strauss, '"You're the Only One". Doesn't everyone want to hear that?' When the album was being promoted, Capitol produced a slick press kit, featuring several soft-focus, beefcake shots of Urban – whose look could now best be described as 'Jon Bon Jovi goes to Nashville' – above the tag: 'Keith Urban, Music For All Audiences – What Every Woman Wants To Hear And Every Man Wants To Say.' Quigley clearly wasn't kidding. 'Keith has all the elements of a superstar,' Quigley said on an episode of Music Country's *True Stories*, 'but he doesn't know it.'

What Urban truly required was a ballad that barely stayed on the right side of 'icky'. And it just so happened that Ged Malone, Miles Copeland's LA-based partner, was married to Jane Wiedlin, a songwriter and former member of seminal all-girl rock act the Go-Gos. Malone and Wiedlin split in August 1999, but fortunately not before Urban had been enticed to the west coast at Malone's behest to see if he and Wiedlin, along with her songwriting partner and fellow Go-Go, Charlotte Caffey, could collaborate and come up with some musical magic. While the contrast wasn't quite as stark as that between Urban and Stevie J., there was still something of a cultural divide separating country guy Urban and Wiedlin, a dark-haired 40-year-old with an eye for retro chic and an ear for smart, sassy pop songs. Wiedlin had the street cool of a former regular on the LA punk circuit, which is where she co-founded the Go-Gos with ex cheerleader Belinda Carlisle. In true punk fashion, the band's debut set at a Hollywood club in the late 1970s lasted for all of a song and a half. But within a few years they had their first US Top 20, the timeless 'Our Lips Are Sealed'. Since the band split Wiedlin had divvied up her time between songwriting, voiceovers and cameos in such films as *Star Trek IV* and *Bill & Ted's Excellent Adventure*.

The trio wrote a few songs at the house Wiedlin shared with Malone, but the one that made it to Urban's solo debut for Capitol was 'But for the Grace of God' (the others currently languish in the Ten Ten vault). 'Grace of God' would become a key song for numerous reasons: it showcased the softer, more touchy-feely side of Urban that didn't get much of a look in on *The Ranch* album, and it also became his first legitimate US hit. And not only did it validate the Coburns's faith in his nascent songwriting ability, it also showed that he'd taken Jewel Coburn's advice to 'think about what he wanted to say as a solo artist'. It wouldn't require a degree in Lyrics 101 to pick apart the message behind 'Grace of God', as Urban sang how 'but for the grace of God go I / I must've been born a lucky guy'. In short, he knew he'd fucked up bigtime and was lucky to still be alive, let alone be working on his solo debut for a major Nashville label. Thanks to rehab and a second chance, Urban was no longer a 'high-risk statistic', but he hadn't lost sight of how close he'd come to crashing and burning.

Having said all that, the song very nearly didn't happen. Urban found that Wiedlin and Caffey, who'd already had a few cracks at co-songwriting in Nashville, held a narrow-minded view of Music City. 'They came to Nashville thinking of country a certain way – it was stereotypical clichéd stuff like rhinestones and cowboy hats,' he said.[18] Urban did his best to explain that it wasn't that way anymore, especially with the influx of 'out of town' players, producers and writers – Caffey and Wiedlin included – but still just wasn't 'feeling it' as the day progressed. He was about to shut down the session when Caffey threw out an idea: 'Does anyone like the name, "But for the Grace of God"?' she asked. Urban stopped at the door, took his guitar out of its case and began playing, humming a melody, as Wiedlin locked in and started writing the lyric. Possibly the most personal song Urban has ever recorded slowly emerged, written by a committee, ironically enough – though this was hardly the first time that's happened in Nashville.

When they'd finished the sketch of the track, Wiedlin's husband Malone came home from the Firstars office. 'How did it go?' he asked Urban, who replied that the session went, 'OK, we wrote a song, but it's not for me,' and started making his excuses to leave. Malone insisted that Urban play the song to him anyway. Malone was more impressed than Urban, at least initially. 'I think it's a hit,' he told him, a prediction that proved to be right on the money. Malone still speaks of that moment as the highlight of his time working with Urban – it had to be better than being asked to score coke or wrestling with the guy backstage.

This was the beginning of what Jewel Coburn described as Urban's 'writing spurt. He was writing a lot, songs were flowing out of him. And once that happened that helped to define who he was more as an artist.' Another song from this creative outpouring was 'I Thought You Knew', which also made his solo debut. Just like 'Grace of God', this was a song with a back-story. For one thing, Urban was collaborating with Skip Ewing, the country hit-maker who a few years earlier had pissed off James Blundell by suggesting that they should write another 'Way Out West', without realising it wasn't a Blundell song in the first place. Urban's Oz-country peer had found Ewing's style completely inflexible, but it suited Urban, which served to outline the differences between Blundell and Urban: only one of them craved US success so badly that he was willing to compromise and conform.

Ewing wasn't strictly a songwriter; he'd made some inroads as a solo act in the late 1980s, recording a handful of albums, scoring some hits on the country singles chart and touring with George Jones, Waylon Jennings and Merle Haggard. But like so many Music City contenders, he changed course and concentrated on tunesmithery. It was a smart move, too; at time of writing his songs have shown up on almost 300 albums, with combined sales of more than 80 million. Three years older than Urban, the bearded, scruffily handsome man of twang came from rural Redlands in California; his grandfather had been a thoroughbred rancher in nearby Murrieta. It wasn't quite Nashville, but his roots were pretty damned country, nonetheless. Urban was a fan, rating Ewing 'a great writer and storyteller'.

When Ewing and Urban began writing together, Urban had a sketch of a song he was currently calling 'The Man Who Assumed', which, frankly, sounded more like the title of a lost Hitchcock film than a heartfelt country confessional. The song was about Urban's on-again, off-again relationship with Sigler, which had, as he explained to Ewing, 'fallen apart for many, many reasons'.[19] (That said, it wasn't until a couple of years later that he and the beautiful Nashville vet finally and irreversibly split.) He wrote the outline of the song around the time that Sigler, weary of their torrid relationship, split briefly to Canada, only for Urban to entice her back to Nashville. Urban thought, at the very least, that it was a great song title, but Ewing wasn't convinced. During one songwriting session, Ewing asked Urban to explain the lyric.

'It's about a guy who assumes that his girl knows how he feels about her,' Urban replied, 'although he's not very good at telling her.' Ewing chewed this over for a few minutes. No fool, he could tell that the 'guy' in the song was clearly Urban. 'In what context did you not tell her?' he asked his co-writer, point blank. 'Well,' admitted Urban, 'I always thought she knew.' To which he added, 'Unfortunately, my girl and I had already gone through some rocky patches and this was not a good time to assume anything.' Ewing replied, in a very matter-of-fact style: 'Why don't we just call it, "I Thought You Knew"?'

It was, after all, a country song – so why fuck around with clever titles? It just reinforced exactly what Urban admired about Ewing; he may not have been too familiar with the Dingoes' back catalogue and wasn't one to stray from Nashville's established style of 'three chords and the truth', but he had a knack of 'getting to the simplicity of the song – the real heart of the matter'.[20]

With that, producer Matt Rollings, who was working on his first major label record, sat down at a nearby piano – he was a piano player more than a producer, truth be told – and started tinkering with a melody. Ewing, meanwhile, assumed the role of therapist: he got comfortable and asked Urban to recount everything he could that he thought was relevant to the song. 'So I told Skip my story and cried like a baby,' said Urban. 'Skip was like the psychologist, jotting down all my thoughts. It was like a therapy session.'

Maybe this outpouring was a little too close, a little too personal for Urban, who'd just endured all the therapy he needed for one lifetime while in rehab. He admitted that he found the experience with 'Dr Ewing' 'strange, something I wouldn't want to do again'. When they'd completed writing the song, Urban couldn't bring himself to sing it, at least not for the demo recording, and asked Ewing to do the honours.

Even though Urban's 'creative spurt' mean that in 1999 an album's worth of songs was rapidly coming together, neither Urban nor Ten Ten's Mark Moffatt, who was 'A&R-ing' Urban's new material, was especially satisfied with the early sketches of the songs that would eventually make the *keith urban* album. 'I was a little frustrated by the sessions I produced with Keith during that transition period,' Moffatt told me. Urban was working with bassist Jerry Flowers, various drummers and what Moffatt referred to as 'A-team of fiddle and steel guys', but the producer felt that a 'full session band' would have given the songs more colour and energy. 'But it wasn't my call,' he added. 'Nonetheless, many of the arrangements we came up with finished up on that first album.' In downtime, Moffatt hung out with Urban and his housemate Hughie Murray at their rented house on Elliott Avenue, and kicked back. 'We all shared some great times together.'

To Urban's ears, these demos and sketches 'sounded like karaoke'. He didn't feel that they captured the sound he was hearing in his head – essentially a more pop-orientated take on what he was doing with The Ranch. 'The last record,' he said of his album made with Flowers and Clarke, 'was a band record and there was a little bit of tension.'

> I love doing ballads, but I love doing the uptempo songs, too. The band represented the rocky side. I found that really restrictive and it was time to move on.[21]

But he still wasn't quite nailing his solo record, not yet, anyway. 'I didn't sound like me,' Urban said. 'It was a lot of trial and error.'[22] He'd later call these sessions 'scary and daunting'.

Bob Saporiti, who'd become tight with Urban during his Ranch days at Warner Bros, believes that Urban was uncomfortable at first about the musical shift he was making, morphing from rocker into crooner.

> I think he saw it as a compromise at first, but I think he had some good advice from Miles [Copeland] and Barry [Coburn] and some of the people at Capitol, and they settled him down and told him: 'You can be yourself later, but it's a lot easier to be yourself in comfort if you get some hits under your belt.' The early [Ranch] stuff was very soulful, but it probably wasn't as commercial as it needed to be for him to end up doing what he's doing. He's not a stupid guy. That's part of his desire to make it, the willingness to compromise the edge for the success. I think he did realise that there's no success in failure.

Then, finally, Urban had a major breakthrough. Producer Rollings introduced him to a high-energy number called 'Where the Blacktop Ends', a co-write between Nashville journeyman Steve Wariner and Allen Shamblin. Just like Skip Ewing, Indiana native Wariner was quite literally both a singer and songwriter, who started out with RCA Records way back in 1978, first as a solo act and then as a tunesmith-for-hire. (Wariner had a face that was just a little too fleshy to be handsome in the classic Nashville sense, which might explain his dual careers.) In some respects, 'Blacktop' was payback, as Urban had contributed to Wariner's most recent LP, 1991's *I Am Ready*. Urban had first met Wariner in less-than-perfect circumstances. He was due to play a set at the River Stage in Nashville, but all his gear had been lost in transit. Urban was frantically trying to tune a borrowed guitar when the well-connected Wariner walked past and made a cheeky remark. Deep in concentration, Urban snapped back:

'Fuck off.' Only then did he think about looking up, by which time Wariner had backed off. Wariner first saw Urban play in the company of WKDF DJ Carl Mayfield, who famously stated:

> The first time I saw Keith Urban play, I said to the guy next to me, 'He's not from this planet.' That guy was Steve Wariner. Two teardrops were rolling down his cheek.[23]

Although this statement appears in an official record company press release — and it does make great copy — Wariner denies it is true.

Ironically, 'Blacktop' was the type of hard, driving, country-rock song with a nagging guitar riff and swinging fiddle and banjo, that wouldn't have been wasted on The Ranch. Almost immediately, Urban locked into the song, admitting soon after that 'it was the first time in my life in the studio when I thought, "I think this is really good."' He was nothing short of jubilant; it was as if the past few years of serious dues-paying and hard times had finally led him to something truly mean-ingful and satisfying. He called Sigler once the track was done — they were still on speaking terms — and she asked how the sessions were progressing. Urban paused for effect and announced: 'I'm gonna be a fucking star.'[24] And 'Blacktop', unlike 'I Thought You Knew', was a stayer, because Urban was still playing it live a decade later.

At the same time that he was making numerous musical connections and in-studio breakthroughs, Urban was also securing some strong industry ties. Among them was silver-haired lawyer Ansel Davis, Capitol's Vice President of Business Affairs, who soon agreed to represent Urban (and would many years later attend the Urban/Kidman nuptials). Davis had kept close to Urban leading up to and during his stint at Cumberland

Heights, acknowledging that Urban 'concluded that he needed professional help'. He was also, in the words of Rob Potts:

> . . . able to keep him on Capitol during the Garth domination of that label. He kept Keith below the radar and away from Garth's 'get rid of that guy off my label and focus on me'.

Capitol's Bill Kennedy, who was the label's Vice President of Sales, was another true believer. Both Davis and Kennedy were extremely influential men to have on your side. Urban was wising up to the fact that a career can't move forward on songs and good looks alone – he needed to be 'connected'. 'I was concerned that he'd be swallowed by the machinery,' said James Blundell.

> But he just persevered and persevered and persevered. And he aligned with some really good people, like Ansel Davis. That's when it started to make sense for him. He had the good sense to keep his mouth shut and work out who was who, while I'd alienated all of them.

In July 1999, Urban slipped back into Australia for a handful of shows and the chance to talk up his almost-completed album. Using a 'pick-up band', including former Angel Graham 'Buzz' Bidstrup on drums and Mondo Rock's Paul Christie on bass, Urban was putting a massive spell on a full house at smart Sydney venue The Basement when he invited a guest on stage. It was none other than pint-sized belter Angry Anderson, the heavily illustrated front man of Rose Tattoo. Together, they furiously jammed Rose Tattoo's 'Bad Boy for Love' and as the song reached a smouldering conclusion, Urban was clearly experiencing a flashback to his Rockettes/Oz-rock past. 'Angry Fuckin' Anderson,' Urban laughed as the chrome-domed screamer disappeared stage right. 'How do you top that?' He couldn't, and his dazzling homecoming was complete.

But not long before Urban's Nashville solo debut was ready to drop, he found himself inadvertently entangled in a bizarre controversy with country superhero Garth Brooks, the same man who had recently begun calling Urban 'mate'. To that point in his as-yet-unfulfilled career, any connection with Brooks could only help Urban but in this instance it was all a little too weird, a little too uncomfortable to be milked in any reasonable way.

By the fag end of the 1990s, Garth Brooks wasn't just the highest selling country artist of all time, with sales fast approaching 100 million albums – he was also in the lofty company of the Beatles and Elvis Presley, a cash cow for his label and seemingly an unstoppable commercial force. When he decided to give a free show in New York's Central Park – hardly the epicentre of twang – on 7 August 1997, at least 250,000 urban cowboys turned up (although Brooks insisted that the crowd was closer to 900,000). Urban played his own small role on that night of nights. As part of a massive live 'simulcast' on US cable network HBO, The Ranch had played a set at Birmingham, Alabama, prior to Brooks's set. After The Ranch played, a big screen lit up and Brooks's show was aired. This happened at several cities outside the tri-state area. But even with such a freakish track record, *Garth Brooks in . . . The Life of Chris Gaines*, which emerged in September 1999, just a few weeks before the solo debut of the lower case *keith urban*, was a pretty outrageous and bizarre move. In what was best described as *Eddie and the Cruisers* meets *Spinal Tap*, Brooks 'reinvented' himself as burned-out 'star' Chris Gaines. The transformation was made complete when Brooks dropped a few pounds, lost the hat, and sported a ridiculous dark wig and soul patch (not unlike the one Urban was nurturing at the time).

Just for sheer silliness, the fictional 'Gaines story' bears repeating. 'Born' in Australia, Gaines 'appeared' in the mid 1980s as the singer/songwriter/main man of Crush, a group of Beatles' soundalikes that hit big with the 'single' 'My Love Tells Me So'. Then it all turned into a rock-and-roll soapie: Gaines's 'best friend and bandmate', one Tommy Levitz, was totalled in a plane crash, Crush fell to pieces and Gaines was left, in classic tradition, to 'pick up the pieces'. Solo albums ensued: the cock-rocking *Straight Jacket* and the Prince rip *Cornucopia*, and then somehow Gaines's path intersected with that of country king Brooks and this 1999 'greatest hits' album, produced by hit-makers Don Was and Kenneth 'Babyface' Edmonds, emerged.

Brooks, in his typically big-picture, micro-manager way, didn't scrimp when it came to the finer details of the Gaines project. The sound of the record was slick pop, very much anti-country, and he hired makeup artist Lance Anderson, best known for his work on the remake of *The Island of Dr Moreau*, to help him develop the dark, brooding Gaines look, as seen on the album's cover. Of course this wasn't some one-off: Brooks's plan was to give the Gaines concept a year to sink in and then he'd star as Gaines in a feature film entitled *The Lamb*, the next logical step for a man whose ego, if not his talent, was boundless.

Although he appeared as Gaines on *Saturday Night Live* and for a VH-1 *Behind the Music* 'mockumentary', the feature film didn't happen because, frankly, the whole Gaines idea was a stinker: he'd alienated his core audience of country fans and media and came across as simply too weird and egotistical for the pop-rock mainstream. The songs weren't that great, either, apart from 'Right Now', which neatly blended a world-gone-crazy rap from Brooks with some heavy sampling of the Youngbloods' classic 'Get Together'. The shameless Wallflowers steal, 'Unsigned Letter', was the low point of this yawn of a record. As one reviewer neatly surmised, 'As himself, Garth Brooks has sold almost 100 million albums. If he's lucky, many of those fans will forgive him for Chris Gaines.' (That was easier said than done, because Brooks's career spiralled steadily downwards from there on in, leading to his eventual 'retirement' in 2000.)

So far, so weird, which wasn't really out of character for Brooks, but then some observers started to notice the Urban similarities: the soul patch, the crossover sound, the Australian past. They even 'shared' a birth year, 1967, and both recorded for Capitol. A hefty half-page ad appeared in trade magazine *Country Airplay Monitor*, flogging Urban's upcoming single, 'It's a Love Thing', right alongside some Gaines-related editorial that included a headshot of Gaines in a very studied, Urban-like pose. It all seemed too close, too weird. And, after all, Brooks and Urban had worked together, in a manner of speaking, for the *Double Live* album. Maybe he'd said something to Brooks, who'd kicked it around and – *who knows, right?* Brooks denied any connection, of course, simply telling CNN, 'I'm hoping that Chris gets a chance, like all new artists . . . and starts to actually live and breathe like artists do.'

Urban, who was at this point no more than a major label hopeful, and in no position to make any kind of waves, was suddenly being asked whether he was the inspiration for Brooks's new project. A tad foolishly, Urban told Roger Hitts, a reporter from Florida's *The Star* newspaper, that when he first saw the CD, his immediate reaction was that it was 'a very strange and weird thing'. 'I mean, what are the chances of Garth coming up with this character, who was born in 1967, raised in Brisbane, Australia and is doing music similar to mine?' Under the headline: 'Angry rocker: I'm the real Chris Gaines', the tabloid suggested a 'major rift' had developed between the King of Nashville and this up-and-comer in the aftermath of Chris Gaines, and that somehow Brooks had 'stolen' Urban's identity for a record that *Entertainment Weekly* called 'a loopy ego massage'.

'Urban is claiming that Brooks lifted much of Gaines's story from his press kit after he played on the superstar's live album last year,' wrote Hitts.[25] Urban denied making the comment, claiming any observation he made 'was so taken out of context'. He did add, in a separate interview, that he thought Gaines/Brooks had opted to be Australian because:

> . . . the woman who has been chosen to play Chris's mother in the film is Australian. It's an unfortunate irony for Garth. I am certainly not angry or annoyed at Garth, as some media are suggesting.[26]

Brooks backed this up in a press conference, and the actress can be seen in the VH-1 'mockumentary', *Behind the Life of Chris Gaines*. Nancy Henderson, a Capitol Records spokesperson, also played down the parallels. 'Any similarities are purely coincidental,' she insisted. 'Other journalists have stated they feel Gaines resembles [Soundgarden singer] Chris Cornell.'[26a] Brooks said that he based the Gaines character on Tommy Sims, one of the key songwriters on the wacky, career-wrecking project. Sims was best known as Bruce Springsteen's bass player in the early 1990s, who had built a rep in the Nashville Christian music community as part of rockers-for-God Whiteheart. He also co-wrote Eric Clapton's Grammy-winning 'Change the World'. Given that Sims was black, it just made Brooks's admission less believable.

Eventually, Urban thought it prudent to call Brooks at home and deny the story – which Brooks hadn't read, incidentally – telling him it was 'complete crap', and dismissing the story as 'a complete fabrication by some bored journalist'.[27] 'Talk about career suicide,' Urban told an Australian newspaper soon after. 'He's one of the most powerful guys in America and here I am claiming he's a thief.' He hadn't actually said that Brooks didn't rip him off, but the ever-savvy Urban had turned a suggestion of plagiarism on Brooks's part into a personal apology – and it also generated some very timely copy on this up-and-comer. Urban told another local reporter:

> My main concern was making sure Garth knew it wasn't some sort of pathetic publicity ploy on my behalf. If that was the case, then it would have backfired drastically on me. I could be without a label deal if I got on the wrong side of Garth.[28]

When Urban phoned Brooks to explain, the Okie in the hat had a simple reply: 'Welcome to tabloid sensationalism.'[29] I spoke to Urban around this time, and he had nothing but respect for the man sometimes known simply as 'G', referring to him as 'one clever motherfucker'. Urban, and the Australian branch of Warners had the final word soon after when a press release announced: *'Keith Urban – Solo Album Released, and No, He's Not Chris Gaines . . .'*

While Urban downplayed any angst he may have felt towards Brooks's alleged 'identity theft', there's no doubt that Brooks's next move caused Urban some genuine aggravation. At the time of the release of the *keith urban* album, on 19 October 1999, the upper level of Capitol Records was in total disarray, largely due to Brooks's desire to turn the revered label into the 'Home of Garth'. Brooks's massive power play meant that virtually all the label's corporate energy and attention were directed elsewhere while Urban and many others were left to flounder.

Again, just like the Chris Gaines project, the details of Brooks's machinations bear repeating, simply to show how powerful *and* power hungry Urban's 'mate' truly was at the time. It also serves to illustrate how Nashville had morphed from a homely music town into a serious player in the music biz.

Scott Hendricks, the tall, quietly spoken Oklahoman who'd helped ease Urban's transition from Warners to Capitol, had never been Brooks's first choice as label head, despite an impressive track record. (Hendricks joined Capitol in May 1995 when Jimmy Bowen, James Blundell's confidant, retired and moved to Hawaii.) Hendricks had produced hit records for Alan Jackson, Brooks & Dunn and his former fiancée, Faith Hill. He was a 'music guy' who, as Brooks once admitted, wasn't so comfortable with the 'business side of music' – and this didn't necessarily suit a guy who was keen on selling records by the warehouse-load. Apparently, during Brooks's first meeting with Team Hendricks, he said, point blank: 'I don't believe in you guys.' Over time, Brooks slowly warmed to the then new label head, while still enforcing his rules: he demanded a US$5 million marketing budget for his album *Fresh Horses* and also insisted that the label 'ship' six million copies into stores on the week of its release. These were serious numbers for any signing, let alone a country act.

But in the week of the album's release, Brooks was up against the one act that he wanted so badly to outsell: the Beatles. And the Fab Four's *Anthology* outsold *Fresh Horses* almost two to one, shifting 900,000 copies to 480,000. Brooks immediately started manoeuvring for a change at the top of Capitol. He made the lives of the label's execs hell, putting forward extreme demands – it was even suspected that he had 'spies' embedded in the label's Nashville HQ. The wheels really fell off when Brooks went public, telling *Billboard* magazine that 'the Nashville office's handling of *Fresh Horses* pisses me off'. Even when the label dropped US$80,000 on a bash to celebrate sales of 60 million records, Brooks turned the event into a massive bummer, addressing Hendricks thus: 'Anytime something old gets new, there are going to be fights,' and then blowing the lid on the fact that the label had to order and ship substantial quantities of records earlier in the week simply to meet the 60 million mark. 'So, tomorrow morning,' Brooks said in conclusion, 'back to work.'

By Christmas 1997, not long after *The Ranch* debacle, Hendricks was out and Pat Quigley, the polo shirt–wearing transplanted New Yorker, was in the chair at Capitol. The sales-savvy Quigley signed away a whopping US$25 million to market *Sevens*, Brooks's new album, which sold more than 3 million copies in a month but then tapered off considerably. The king's crown – or more accurately, his black beaver Stetson, size seven and five-eighths – was slipping considerably.

Quigley's time at the top was short-lived, too; when *keith urban* hit the streets, he'd been replaced by Mike Dungan, a heavy-set, good-natured character. And he was yet another true believer, who once famously said: 'In my 23-year career I've never met someone with such horizontal and vertical potential as Keith Urban.' But Capitol, in the wake of Brooks's chronic interference, was still 'in disarray', according to Mark Moffatt, who'd effectively taken over as Urban's A&R guy in the absence of anyone from his record company. What this meant was that the album, and the lead single, the very upbeat, uptempo 'It's a Love Thing', had no one from the label assigned to give it the big push at radio and in the media. Most of their attention and energy was consumed trying to hang onto their jobs. Capitol, however, did come up with one not-too-shabby promotion, where two lucky winners scored a vacation in 'wine country' California and a return trip to Australia, where they'd meet, greet and be serenaded by Urban. It was a love thing, after all. Urban, however, drew the line at plugging his record in a baby shop, which is where Capitol sent him during one stage of the promo trail.

Fortunately, early in 1999, Greg Shaw had hired Jeff Walker's Nashville-based company Aristo to handle publicity for Urban. Walker echoed Moffatt when he said that at the time Capitol was going through 'a lot of instability'. Walker and Shaw met every week, devising strategies, media campaigns and items for press releases, getting the word out and building the 'vibe' on this so-called newcomer. 'It was a busy time,' Walker neatly understated.

He added:

> During that time, my relationship with Keith was more professional than personal, although we did have some great conversations. I always understood that deep inside, Keith was looking for something that he hadn't found at the time. He seemed personally restless and anxious to get to the next level. He was very driven, which is a good thing.

This burning desire was especially helpful considering the fact that Urban was getting little in the way of record company support, apart from the backing of such Capitol stalwarts as Sales VP Bill Kennedy. But this was hardly a new situation for Urban, or any other aspiring B-list artist, especially when you're on the same label as Garth Brooks.

'It's a Love Thing' wasn't a dud, by any stretch. It dropped a few weeks before its parent album, and made some inroads at various radio 'formats', America being a music industry that has taken the idea of 'formatting' songs to an obsessive level. It didn't hurt that the single was supported by a bright, shiny video, centred on Urban sitting in the back of a car, draped in a slick snakeskin jacket, smiling so much that his face must have hurt like hell by the end of the shoot. Producer Matt Rollings, meanwhile, can be spotted sitting silently at a studio control panel, 'working the desk'. The song was a smart choice on the part of label, management and 'talent', too, because, as Jeff Walker explained:

> Keith had built up a solid fanbase with his Ranch recordings and the label did not want to transition him directly into a ballad. 'It's a Love Thing' was a safe release to reintroduce him to the public as a solo artist.

'Love Thing' duly charted on the 'Country Song Recurrents' chart, the 'Country Audience' chart, the 'Bubbling under Hot 100' chart and, most significantly, the 'Country Songs' list, where it peaked at number 18 and hung about for one week shy of six months. It wasn't a smash, but it was certainly no flop, either. And Urban had some stiff competition, as he was up against new releases from such reliable hit machines as the Dixie Chicks ('Ready to Run'), Alan Jackson ('Little Man'), Kenny Chesney, George Strait and Alabama, as well as fellow newcomers SheDaisy. And beyond that, both 'Love Thing' and *keith urban* emerged in the midst of a teen-pop revolution, headed by such breakout acts as Christina Aguilera, the Backstreet Boys and Britney Spears. Yet slowly, gradually, as the new millennium loomed very large on the horizon, the name Keith Urban began to mean more to country punters than some slick Nashville-based guitar-slinger with a thing for soul patches and lower case spellings.

Urban insisted that the album was both a 'snapshot' of recent upheavals in his life and an attempt on his part, musically speaking, to keep the mood positive. The former may be true – or at least it's as revealing as an album of songs written with relative strangers can be – but it had more mood swings than a hormonal teenager. *keith urban* led with a knockout one-two punch: 'It's a Love Thing' was the perfect opener, a bright, breezy few minutes of 'funktry', a curious commingling of country sentiments and styles and some very contemporary digital-era cleverness. It wasn't George Strait, that's for sure. Then 'Where the Blacktop Ends' kicked in, a sort of updated take on Urban's single from way back when, 'I Never Work on a Sunday', a celebration of freewheeling weekends, blue skies and gnarly guitar riffs. Yet for every 'Love Thing' and 'Blacktop' there was plenty of saccharin, piled sky-high on the ballads 'You're the Only One' and a little less so on 'But for the Grace of God', the LA-born co-write that almost never was. It was pretty clear that Urban was catering for the conservative, main-stream tastes of Middle America, something The Ranch never seemed quite willing to do.

Every good album has a cornerstone track, a song that zeroes in on the key themes of the record. There was no doubt *that* song on *keith urban* was 'Out on My Own', a mid-tempo weepie co-written with Nashville wild card Vernon Rust, in which Urban spilled both his guts and his heart. At his best, Urban had a knack for coming on like a guy who's seen and felt some heavy shit – and he has, no doubt about it – so when he picked apart his life as a '30-something single / and tired of running everywhere / I haven't called no place my home / since 1994' he sang with the world-weariness of an old bluesman. Bruce Bouton's sobbing steel guitar and Urban's 'ganjo' piled on the sentiment. 'Out on My Own' remains one of the most revealing and heartfelt cuts of his career, even if it's not a song that appears on Urban's setlist today.

keith urban is still the most 'country' of the four US studio albums that he's recorded to date; there's no shortage of pedal steel, fiddle and tear-in-beer emotion. (Urban also laid it on pretty thick in the liner notes, dedicating the album to 'the four most important people in my life': Greg "Shawree" Shaw; his parents 'for taking care of me when I needed you most'; and his sometimes girlfriend Laura Sigler, 'for life, love, inspiration and faith'.) The album had its own 'Clutterbilly' in 'Roller-coaster', a furious country-rock jam that he took to introducing live with a simple: 'Say three Hail Marys and I'll see you at the other end.' He even headed south of the border during the zydeco-flavoured stomper 'I Wanna Be Your Man (Forever)', a sonic mash-up pitched somewhere between the Neville Brothers and Little Feat, featuring a cameo from Dixie Chicks, Emily Robison and Martie Maguire.

Urban's US solo debut didn't receive much media coverage outside of the country music press, a situation that would change dramatically over the course of his next few LPs. But the reviews given by the mainstream media suggested that he was more than some hatless Music City contender. Writing for the highly rated www.allmusic.com, Thom Jurek pointed out how Urban wasn't the newcomer that many country fans thought him to be, but had 'been on the radar of Nashvegas A&R men for a long time'. He heaped praise on Urban's ability to mix things up without ever neglecting a good tune. Jurek observed:

> He can marry a rock tune or a pop ballad to a country melody, and set it off with just the right amount of heartfelt emotion and masterful production touches, whether it be playing the banjo or adding strings to the mix. The album does mark the true root of his sound as a major artist wetting his feet.

Rick Mitchell, writing for www.amazon.com, drew the reasonable conclusion that it's 'unrealistic to expect down-

home country music from a guy named Urban. Sure enough,'
he continues, 'Urban's solo debut combines canned fiddle 'n'
steel licks with hip-hop-flavoured drum loops.' And then,
most tellingly, Mitchell notes that 'the rock edge that char-
acterised his previous band The Ranch has been replaced by
pretty-boy poses and puppy-love lyrics aimed straight at the
young female demographic.' It was a little harsh, although
he did add that certain songs 'hint at darker moods and adult
emotions that might be closer to the real Keith Urban'. A
review from www.cduniverse.com sat pretty safely on the
fence, stating how:

> Urban's brand of country includes soulful vocals, a nice mix
> of acoustic and steel guitars, banjos, fiddles and mandolins, and
> some fine songwriting. Overall, *keith urban* offers a taste of
> what this talented singer, songwriter and guitarist might do in
> the future.

Writing for *Rolling Stone* at the time, I praised the album,
singling out 'Rollercoaster' ('one wild motherfucker of a ride')
and 'Out on My Own' ('a gut-wrencher Jimmy Webb'd kill
for'). 'Sure, there's plenty of syrup on the ballads,' I added, 'but
they're offset by Urban's top-shelf picking, singing and a heart
so big it'd put Phar Lap to shame.' Other reviewers, such as the
West Australian's Ara Jansen, also talked up the album (which,
for about five minutes, was going to be called *3*). 'What's best,'
she wrote, 'is his confessional and very human songwriting.'

His label got on board, too, dropping a press release with a
seemingly endless supply of quotes from zealous radio DJs.
'Jeez, he can set a guitar on fire,' was the endorsement from Jim
West at WGRX. John Marks from KWNR declared that 'It's
a Love Thing' 'is a hit thing! His music is sensitive enough to
appeal to women and gutsy enough for men.' 'Keith is bright,

talented and very unique,' stated KSKS's Ken Boesen. 'He's just
what we need.' And then the clincher, from Dave Ervin at
KZLA, who predicted that Urban could be 'the Bruce Springsteen of country'.

In the wake of their positioning of 'Love Thing' as 'what
every woman wants to hear and every man wants to say',
Capitol amped up the touchy-feely, sensitive-new-age-
country-guy angle with Urban – even when he posed for
photos with a guitar, he seemed to be caressing his Fender. This
was clearly not The Ranch, a hairy-chested gang of rockers.
'At a time when so many men are confused about what
women want,' the album's press release declared, 'Keith seems
to get it. Keith has brought that knowledge to his music.'[30]

Capitol boss, Pat Quigley, drove the message home when he
spoke with *Billboard* just before the album dropped. 'We do
think Keith is clearly positioned as a young country artist much
in the same target audience as maybe the Dixie Chicks are,'
he trumpeted. Capitol's 'positioning statement' couldn't have
made Quigley's Dixie Chicks point any clearer – the marketing department even stole the title from the Chicks'
breakthrough album. It read: 'Keith Urban's music appeals to
all women looking for wide open spaces.' Not surprisingly,
there was no mention of Urban's stint in rehab or his unreli-
ability in the romance stakes. 'I realised how important it is to
have someone beside you,' Urban stated in some Capitol
propaganda, 'in your corner, no matter what may happen. A
partner. When you have that, you're free to do whatever you
need to do.' He did, however, admit to *Billboard* that he was
now on the other side of a 'black period'. 'Life just came
barrelling down on me all in one year,' Urban said. 'Everything
went wrong.'[31]

The over-riding theme in all the coverage and spin that
the album received was that while Urban could play the guitar

as though he had the devil inside – 'you can hear why acts like the Dixie Chicks and Garth Brooks tapped him to play on their CDs,' observed one critic – he was now more a sensitive singer/songwriter than an inspired Fender-bender. All he had to do was to get out there and spread the word.

Six

TOEING THE LINE

The way he handled [rehab] was brilliant. He said sorry
and people forgave him. I've seen a lot of others fall
by the wayside.

Bob Saporiti

The rise of *keith urban*, with the handy benefit of hindsight,
seems a relatively smooth and seamless affair, but in fact
it was a slow climb. Sure, it wasn't anything like the 20–odd
years it had taken for him to become a genuine country music
contender, but it still took more time for the album to really
succeed than Urban would have liked.

Greg Shaw and Jeff Walker – and Capitol, of course – knew
that they had a no–brainer second single ready to roll, but
they had to ensure that the lead–up was perfectly timed. In fact,
they had an embarrassment of riches, with no less than two
sure–fire ballads to choose from. And, as Jeff Walker recalled,
there was 'a lot of discussion' regarding which weepie would
be chosen as single number two. 'Love Thing' was easy – it was
a transitional song, nothing more, and not expected to be a

smash hit, but their next move was crucial. They also had to allow the silly season of Christmas and the New Year to pass before going hard on the song that, to the likely disdain of Urban the musician, would help define him in America. 'Your Everything' would become a monster, in more ways than just sales.

At the time of *The Ranch*, Urban very defiantly insisted that 'a good song is a good song, no matter who wrote it,' but he was now at a stage where he'd like to be known for a hit that was totally his. Not so with 'Your Everything', a treacly co-write between Chris Lindsey and Bob Regan, a one-time president of the well-connected NSAI (Nashville Songwriters Association International). Regan had written hits for one-time male stripper, Billy Ray Cyrus, plus Trisha Yearwood and Tanya Tucker, and knew his way around 'three chords and the truth' as well as any other tunesmith-for-hire.

Urban may have been able to rock like a beast when he started to shred on his Telecaster, but he still had a soft centre and a mainstream sensibility. As soon as he heard the demo of 'Your Everything', he was struck by the line: 'I want to be the wind that fills your sail.' Some might have considered it a touch too 'Wind Beneath Your Wings', but not Urban. As he admitted, 'I thought, "Yeah, *OK!*" Then it goes, "I want to be the hand that lifts your veil", and I was covered in goose-bumps.' Urban swiftly agreed to cut the track.[1] A suitably moody video accompanied the single, in which Urban crooned and looked on as a happy loving couple tied the knot (all in slow motion, naturally). And it wasn't just a wedding song in the video; on at least two occasions a proposal was made – on-stage, no less – while Urban and band played 'Your Everything'. There were times when he must have felt like the country-pop equivalent of Dr Phil, bringing couples together in a very public setting.

And it was the love song that refused to disappear, too. A couple of years after the track went supernova, Urban was setting up for a gig in Pigeon Forge, Tennessee, when he heard the syrupy strains of 'Your Everything' wafting out of a nearby church, where a wedding was in progress. Figuring 'Why the hell not?' Urban decided to drop in and sing the song himself, which would charm the almost-weds no end and maybe even win a few new converts. However, the father of the bride wasn't so sure Urban actually was who he said he was – he stopped him at the door of the church until his daughter gave the all clear. Only then did Urban get to serenade the stunned bride and groom. 'I went in and sang it, and they loved it. I charged them $2000,' he added, smirking. 'I'm just kidding. It was $1500.'[2] Getting his own love life sorted out was a lot harder – Urban was, in his own words, currently 'as single as a dollar bill'.

'Your Everything' dropped in February 2000 and began a steady rise across *Billboard*'s myriad charts. Crucially, the song's saccharine mix of hand-on-heart emotion and all-round soppiness connected powerfully at country radio. Such serious country players as Steve Wariner and Rodney Crowell – and Urban's ex-flame Martie Maguire – continued talking up Urban in a very public way but, as the man himself admitted, scoring radio backing was the clincher. It's good to be praised, *but it's great to be played*. 'Your credibility goes through the roof,' he said, as the single ascended the charts, 'when country radio stations start to support you.'[3] As so many people interviewed for this book agreed, Urban was a smart, savvy operator who grew to understand what was required to 'make it' in Nashville – personality and 'chutzpah' mattered as much as easy-on-the-ear songs. Yet again, he set about establishing himself with extreme prejudice.

The single's stats are impressive. 'Your Everything' became Urban's first song to crack US Country Top Five, and he was

the first Oz-based artist to achieve that chart high, this side of
Olivia Newton-John. (It peaked at number four.) The video
wasn't merely in high rotation on CMT; it topped their chart
for a fortnight. It also helped to kickstart the chart momentum
of the *keith urban* album, which had debuted at a modest
number 60, but began shifting some serious numbers as 'Your
Everything' became as unavoidable as sunburn and RVs in
the Nashville summer.

An in-house Capitol document from the time revealed
some interesting facts about Urban and his steadily swelling
fanbase. His biggest market, at least at the time of the first
album, was in the Mormon heartland of Salt Lake City, Utah,
of all places. Far-flung Seattle, the grunge and caffeine heartland, was his second-biggest market, followed by Nashville, and
major Texan centres Houston and Dallas. And the 'big cities' –
LA, New York and Chicago, all music centres – made appearances in the Urban Top 20, showing that his music was being
heard well beyond the Deep South. But the most telling
statistic of this intriguing fact-sheet was the demographic
breakdown of Urban's followers: a hefty 65 percent were
female and aged between 16 and 35. In short, chicks dug him.
The 'guitar god' was becoming a gold-plated Nashville hunk.

As Urban's public profile began to build, so did public
interest in his recent sordid drug-fucked past. There were any
number of ways Urban could have played this in interviews:
complete denial was one approach, obfuscation another – or
he could simply laugh it off as a momentary lapse of reason,
never to be repeated. Instead, he made another shrewd move
and opted for what Americans call 'full disclosure'. He admitted
in some detail to his crack addiction, his time in rehab and how
he nearly reached the end of the road, physically, emotionally
and every other way. It was a ballsy decision, one that could
have derailed his career just as it began to skyrocket. Bob

Saporiti, who felt 'saddened' when he heard about Urban's near-death crash, was one of many kingmakers who knew how fickle Nashville could be.

> The way he handled that was brilliant. He said sorry and people forgave him. I've seen a lot of others fall by the wayside. But times are changing and people are so used to stars going into rehab. More people seem to be in rehab than out, so it's hard not to be cynical about that. It's like if you don't do it, it's not cool.

Soon enough, it would become a standard question in every Urban heart-to-heart: 'Keith, how did it feel to be a drug addict?' He handled it brilliantly, but at times the constant reminder of his 'troubles', and the requisite pressure to give the 'right' reply, must have tempted him to get back on the pipe.

'In this country it's better if you come clean and tell the truth about stuff like that,' figured Urban's friend Jewel Coburn.

> He was tortured for a while but I believe he's through it and wants to hang onto what he's got. He doesn't want to screw up and I don't think he will.

Urban collaborator Radney Foster agreed.

> I am neither an alcoholic nor a drug addict but have lots of friends who are, and the guys I know who get through that are straight up from the word go. They have to be honest about that: 'I just got my 60-day chip' or whatever. And I think Nashville has changed an awful lot, and for the better. People applauded Keith for being straight up. We've got a long history in country music of pills and booze; there's nothing new to country music about that. But I give Keith a tremendous amount of credit; it's difficult to be that honest.

Urban barely stopped to take a breath throughout the year 2000. During March he scored a spot on the prestigious Country Radio Seminar New Faces show, held at the Nashville Convention Center, where he played a 20-minute set before an audience of 2000 radio tastemakers. This was an annual bash that had helped launch the careers of Tim McGraw, Mary Chapin-Carpenter and Urban's buddies the Dixie Chicks. (Brad Paisley, whose career trajectory would closely shadow Urban's, was also a starter in 2000, while Alan Jackson headlined the Super Faces Show, another key part of the seminar.) A few weeks later, Steve Wariner, the same Nashville player who Urban had suggested should 'fuck off' a short while back, gave Urban the pleasure of his company during a private show in Nashville. They tore through 'Where the Blacktop Ends', the cut that Wariner had 'gifted' Urban for his album, and then jammed a fast and furious 'Rollercoaster'. Urban clearly had friends in high places, a necessity in Nashville.

In June, Urban made his first on-stage appearance at the madness that is Nashville's Fan Fair, the same spot where I'd bumped into him backstage a couple of years earlier. This week-long orgy of meet-and-greet, grip-and-grin, sign, smile, sign, smooch – oh, and maybe sing a few songs, too – was another part of the rite of passage that elevated you from contender to superstar. Urban was also getting to know the same country radio DJs who had been championing him in print; he estimated that he visited 250 radio stations during 2000, relentlessly flogging the product, smiling through inane questions and cutting innumerable 'station IDs'. He established himself as a dependable opening act as he warmed up crowds for Music City's current golden couple, Faith Hill and Tim McGraw, as well as guest-starring for Martina McBride and Dwight Yoakam, mainly as an acoustic, one-man band, known to many of the huge crowds purely on the strength of one song.

There was an interesting ritual to these support slots. Urban would walk out on stage, play 'Love Thing' and the crowd would respond with a collective '*OK.*' Then he'd start strumming 'Your Everything' and they'd light up like a Christmas tree. '*Oh, he's that guy.*' 'You never stop working,' Urban figured. 'You really end up being rewarded if you work hard.'[4] Urban began to get a sense of just how much his star was rising when he stopped in several off-the-map towns for yet more shows, and was held up after each gig for two hours, sometimes longer, signing autographs and smiling for snapshots. Clearly, his decision to embrace the soft-pop sound that prevailed in Nashville had been a smart one, at least as far as the all-powerful cash register was concerned, because his album continued to sell, and 'Your Everything' clung to the charts like a limpet.

Urban did, however, find the time to revisit his past, at least for a couple of nights. Now based in Sydney, drummer Peter Clarke was one of many residents who'd already grown tired of all the talk of the Sydney Olympics, even before the torch was lit. (Clarke had relocated to Sydney at the end of his stint with Nashville band Big House.) He and his wife decided to head to the States, ostensibly for a holiday. Nashville was one of the spots they planned to visit, which also provided a chance for Clarke to revisit his recent past with The Ranch. He put in a call to Urban and suggested playing a couple of shows at one of their old haunts, 12th & Porter. Straight away, Urban was on board: if nothing else, it would provide an escape from the relentless promo and touring grind in which he was currently embedded. Country DJs could hang fire, just for a bit; The Ranch were back in town. And it took just one phone call for Jerry Flowers, who'd joined the Dixie Chicks touring band, to entice him back into the saddle.

Almost as quickly as the word leaked that The Ranch were (sort of) reforming, tickets to the two shows sold out. To add to the Australian flavour of the gigs, Tommy Emmanuel, Urban's mate and future Nashville neighbour, opened the two concerts. On the night of 20 September, as soon as the 'power trio' of Urban, Clarke and Flowers plugged in, they tucked into 'Walkin' the Country' as if they'd never stopped gigging (even though Urban made a point, early in the set, to acknowledge that it had been 'two years, three months and seven days' since the trio had shared a stage). As www.cmt.com reported, the band's raw power hadn't been diluted by Urban's recent pop makeover. 'The high-energy performance,' they declared, 'offered proof that the band hasn't lost its edge as a unit.' Freed of both commercial pressures and the heavy influence of Miles Copeland, The Ranch rocked hard and long, and those who managed to get into the shows went away wondering why no other Nashville act had jumped on the Ranch bandwagon. (The Ranch would plug in again during 2007, upon Urban's suggestion, at a remote Northern Territory soundstage during the 'wrap party' for the Baz Luhrmann film *Australia*, which starred Nicole Kidman. And given Clarke's guarded assistance with this book – he described himself to me as one of the few 'gatekeepers' to Urban's past – it's hard not to get the impression that, just like Greg Shaw, he's holding out for a golden handshake from Urban.)

The paths of Urban and Tommy Emmanuel would inter-sect again just weeks after the Ranch reunion, when the latter played at the closing of the Sydney Olympics and the former did his thing at the Paralympics. Urban's brief homecoming should have presented the opportunity for him to kick back, check in with family and friends and celebrate his recent US success, but that was hardly the case. While in Oz, Urban played 11 shows in 10 days, redefining the term 'hit and run'. Urban smoothly deflected veiled hints from journalists that he'd both sold out and 'deserted' Australia, carefully explaining that relocation, *and conforming*, were essential steps to Nashville success. When confronted with that old journalistic standby: 'Where's home – America or Australia?', he coolly replied that there was no reason he couldn't spend time in both. 'My goal,' he said, 'is to buy a house in Australia, somewhere in Queensland. [But] in an ideal world, I'd like to live in both places.'[5] That sounded great – it was the perfect response, really – but Urban was actually entering another phase of his 'gypsy life', where he'd virtually live on the road in the tour bus, with the band, a schedule – and a chilled bottle of Coopers Ale, his beer of choice, never far out of reach. (When Urban returned home to Nashville for any stretch of time, he'd ask his local liquor store to import Coopers especially for him.)

Back in America, the third single from the *keith* album was ready to roll. 'But for the Grace of God' was another heartsick ballad with enough fiddle and pedal steel – and syrup, laid on thick – to have country radio programmers smiling as they reached for the 'repeat' button. Admittedly, it was a much stronger song than 'Your Everything' and also a track that Urban helped write (even if, as documented elsewhere, it almost didn't happen), so his creative connection with 'Grace' was stronger. And, given that the straight-shooting lyric chronicled his recent past, the song obviously meant far more to Urban. Also, how could his ultra-conservative fanbase not relate to a song with the word 'God' in the title?

The video once again cast Urban as a brooding loner, walking down some lonely, dimly lit street, a soulful look permanently etched on his face. Intriguingly, the original cut of the clip ended with Urban returning home to his lady friend, but during the edit it was felt that his love interest bore too close a physical resemblance to the woman playing in his video 'band', so it was snipped from the final cut. It was just too confusing: was he getting it on with a woman in his make-believe band? Urban was destined to stay sad and single, at least as far as CMT was concerned. Clearly it worked, because as one Youtube.com viewer neatly put it, 'Who else can sing as well as being eye-candy?' 'He's so gorgeous,' declared another. 'I love his voice. His hair. *His nose*. Everything about him.' You know you've made it when fans start declaring their love for your schnoz.

As for the song, which hit US radio in the middle of October 2000, it was a bona fide smash, right across the board. Within a few months of its release, the song reached Number One on the Country Songs chart, topping even 'Your Every-thing', making Urban the first Australian act to scale such a lofty peak. The video, meanwhile, was his second CMT chart-topper. 'Grace of God' also topped the other two key American charts, the Gavin Report, a long-established radio 'tip sheet', and the Radio & Records list. 'Your Everything' was the song that defined the 'new' Keith Urban, but 'Grace of God' was his first number one hit – absolute, unassailable proof that Urban was now a star. Duly, he played the song every night he was on the road, although he stripped it right back to voice and guitar. And sales of the *keith urban* album kept ticking over, with predictions that it would reach gold (500,000 copies sold) by Christmas 2000. Even the Coburns might finally start to see some return on their investment.

Urban escaped Nashville again, briefly, in early December, when he flew to New York for another live-to-air acoustic set, this time for station WYNY. Jeff Walker, Urban's number one promo man, remembers the trip vividly, not so much for the 'plugging' of Urban's album, but for the VIP guided tour they received of the World Trade Center twin towers. (Urban's lunchtime show was broadcast from the World Trade Center

Plaza.) 'I believe it was the last time that either of us went into the beautiful buildings,' said Walker, 'which were attacked on September 11, 2001.'

Yet for all this success, Urban seemed more concerned about consolidating his newfound status than enjoying his 15-something minutes. During early December he played his next Capitol Records showcase, essentially an in-house, acoustic night of mutual back-patting for the label's established stars and acts-on-the-rise. Urban flew in his mother, Marienne, while Garth Brooks, Capitol's brightest star and sometimes their biggest firestarter, made a rare appearance. He and Urban shared some time backstage after the gig. (Clearly, the Chris Gaines furore had faded away; they were now labelmates and friends, maybe even friendly rivals – nothing more.) Brooks asked Urban how he felt about his recent success – high-profile live shows, two hit singles, an album that showed no signs of going off the boil, comely women in his crowds stretching back as far as the eye could see. To his surprise, Urban seemed cautious, sombre even. 'I feel responsible,' Urban told him. 'I just feel like I have to justify all this now.'[6] 'Justification' can take many shapes and forms, and in America that often meant reaching one of the seemingly endless 'best of/year-end' lists. But Urban wasn't quite sure what to make of the discovery that he'd hit *People*'s 'Sexiest Men of the Year' list, announced just before Christmas. He was grouped with the usual Oz suspects – actors Russell Crowe and Heath Ledger – and one unlikely winner, Steve 'The Crocodile Hunter' Irwin – in a category awkwardly described as 'Awesome Aussies'. Somehow, in the course of two years, he'd morphed from being one of Music City's best-kept secrets into a legitimate sex symbol, eye candy for the glossies – with his own International Fan Club, no less (his first Fan Club Newsletter appeared in 2000). As Urban's world kept spinning ever faster and faster, an Australian associate of his, closely involved with 'keeping the homefires burning', spoke with Urban on the phone. 'It must feel great, Keith,' they said, 'seeing all your dreams start to come true.' After a short pause, Urban replied: 'This isn't my dream, *it's my destiny*.' Urban may have made some compromises to become successful, but his conviction could not be questioned.

It wasn't clear how Urban could top 2000, the headiest 12 months of his career so far. Yet 2001 kicked off with an almighty bang when he was nominated for an American Country Music award. This was one of the more credible gongs in an industry absolutely raining awards and accolades for their many over-achievers. In an irony that wasn't lost on Urban, he was on the shortlist for Favourite New Country Artist, even though he'd been putting in for the past two decades. But, admittedly, to most of his audience, Urban *was* a new artist, even at the age of 33. He was facing some stiff opposition, namely a 19-year-old Alabama native, Alicia Elliott, and 12-year-old boy wonder Billy Gillman (country's answer to Macaulay Culkin) who had wandered out of Hope Valley, Rhode Island, straight to the top of the country chart with the nauseating 'One Voice'. Thankfully for his own sanity, Urban picked up the award, during an appropriately lavish ceremony held on 8 January. This would be the first of many gongs Urban would collect during 2001 and beyond.

He then set off for yet another Tamworth jaunt, and a glance at his itinerary revealed just how in demand Urban suddenly was. Not so long ago, Nick Erby was arguing that Urban shouldn't be eligible for Golden Guitars, having sold his soul to Nashville – but now Tamworth wanted to eat him up, sound byte by sound byte, autograph by autograph. He arrived in Tamworth on Tuesday 23 January and settled in for a handful of live-to-air interviews and newspaper 'phoners'. The next day he really got to work, playing a show at Wests Leagues

Club, making an appearance at Fan Fest and being interviewed for 4AAA radio station and the *7.30 Report*. On the Thursday he played another set at Wests, hosted a mini press conference, was interviewed for 2GB and radio show the *Outback Club*, attended a sponsor's cocktail party – and then wound down with a CD signing at 10.45pm, with barely enough time to change his sweaty T-shirt after a 90-minute set. This was pretty much the norm for the rest of his stay (he finally left town on Sunday 28 January): a blur of TV and radio 'spots', performances, cocktail parties – oh, and the Golden Guitars themselves, where he picked up yet another Best Instrumentalist statuette. It was a lively few days.

A few months and many shows later, on 9 May, Urban was facing off with precocious pipsqueak Gillman yet again. This time Gillman, along with Kid Rock and others, was presenting the award for the Top New Male Vocalist prize at the Academy of Country Music awards. This, the so-called 'Horizon Award', carried plenty of clout within the industry – past winners included such icons as Garth Brooks and all-round nice guy Vince Gill, while more recent victors, Brad Paisley and Kenny Chesney, were currently fast-tracking their way to significant country music careers. In the rather stodgy words of the event's organisers, the Horizon Award is given to the act that has shown 'the most significant creative growth and development in overall charts and sales activity, live performance professionalism and critical media recognition'. The award was *so very Nashville*, as Bruce Feiler pointed out in his cogent Music City study, *Dreaming Out Loud*. 'Where else,' he pondered, 'is "creative growth" measured in commercial activity, stage professionalism – whatever that means – and media recognition?'[7] With the rare exception, such as Terri Gibbs, who seemingly dropped off the edge of the planet after winning her Horizon Award, the trophy – a hefty crystal candle flame that looked as though it could have once been worn by Madonna during her conical bra phase – was a reliable indicator of future success. Each of the nominated acts got to perform at the awards; Urban tore through an even rockier-than-normal 'Where the Blacktop Ends'.

Duly psyched, Urban had flown in a three-person 'cheer squad': his mother; Allied Artists' Rob Potts; and Rod Laing, from the West Tamworth Leagues Club. Urban ordered a special suit for the occasion, a cream-coloured number trimmed with black, drawstring fly and all, a nod to the legendary creations of 'Nudie' Cohen, who'd somehow made rhinestones cool when outfitting Gram Parsons, Hank Williams, Porter Wagoner and many others. Manuel Cuevas, who was Cohen's head designer, made Urban's outfit; he'd styled the suits worn by the Beatles on the sleeve of the *Sgt Pepper's Lonely Hearts Club Band* LP. Urban requested that the words 'spirit' and 'freedom' were stitched into his garish ensemble, possibly as a nod to the night's over-riding jingoistic theme (there were enough stars and stripes on display to open an America-the-beautiful theme park). Urban pulled the look off, but only just, coming across like a blend of John Travolta circa *Saturday Night Fever* and the Rhinestone Cowboy himself, Glen Campbell. It was certainly hard to ignore him, although Urban wasn't that far out of place alongside Ronnie Dunn's all-leather outfit (leather was especially big that year) and Dwight Yoakam's square-shouldered maroon-with-white-trim suit. The suit and Yoakam's hat were so big that it was hard to find the man underneath it.

Once again Urban came home with the silverware, the first Australian to win an ACM gong since 1974 when a pre-*Grease* Olivia Newton-John claimed Female Vocalist of the Year. Urban adopted an uncharacteristically religious tone with his speech, mentioning that 'I prayed so much for this.' He also acknowledged his mother and Sigler, who was his date on the night. Backstage, Urban gushed:

> All I wanted to do was get accepted in Nashville because you get a lot of buzz about you, but that doesn't mean you've got support or the acceptance of the town. When they visibly show that they're behind you, that's a big deal. That meant a lot to me. Winning the ACM felt like going back to a time before I started going off the rails. It felt like winning my first award in Australia, kind of like the Star Maker award. I felt like I'd finally gotten back on track and picked up where I'd left off. That's how great it felt.[8]

But Music City could just as easily have rejected him, because only weeks before the Nashville awards night, a spectacularly cheesy Urban spread (for want of a much better word) appeared in the April issue of *Playgirl* magazine. Not unlike Urban's post-rehab admissions, this soft-focus, soft-porn feature had all the potential to alienate some of his ultra-conservative fanbase – even if his many female fans snapped up copies as soon as it hit the stands. Urban, to his credit, used the interview as a chance to talk up his music, his recovery, the breakdown of his relationship with Sigler, the support of his family and much more besides. But it was very hard to take anything Urban said too seriously when his confessions were accompanied by snaps of him in a black G-string, reclining in various rooms of a Capitol Records exec's house, sporting a 'come hither' look. In another image, he gazes languorously at his reflection in the mirror, like some sort of country Narcissus. The best he could muster in his defence, when asked about the 'money' shot, in which his trusty Fender is all that separated Urban from a charge of indecent exposure, was this: 'I'm glad I don't play the harmonica.'[9] He may have lost his clothes and a chunk of his credibility, but Urban's sense of humour remained intact.

More red carpets called his name in 2001, including his first Grammy nomination, for Best Country Instrumental for the paint-stripping 'Rollercoaster'. He didn't win, but simply making the shortlist showed how far his star had risen since the album's release. Back home, he claimed an ARIA Outstanding Achievement Award, was named Business Ambassador of the Year and even picked up a Mo Award. His mantelpiece was absolutely sagging under the weight of this collection of pointy statuettes.

Finally, in June, Urban slowed down long enough to toast the gold status of his lower case solo record, at Six Degrees, a flash Nashville restaurant. (Urban had recently been on the road with Brooks & Dunn and hadn't been in any one place long enough to celebrate. Interestingly, his 15-minute opening slot on that tour had been doubled to 30 minutes after just a few dates, a rare concession from such A-league stars.) Among those swigging free drinks and talking shop was Barry Coburn who could now see that his long-ago chance encounter with Kix Brooks in a Nashville carpark had been both fortuitous and profitable. Kelly Brooks, Garth Brooks's brother and co-manager, was also in the house, as was Amy Kurland, the owner of the Bluebird Café, the Nashville songwriters' haunt where Garth Brooks had been spotted many years back. Steve Wariner got up and spoke, reminding Urban of their short, sharp first encounter at the river stage, and then Mike Dungan, the newish Capitol label boss, took the microphone. He launched into a classic 'I don't want to damn my predecessor, but I will' speech, telling the faithful that 'this record was never set up right. It was set up to fail. This record should be platinum.' He didn't mention Pat Quigley by name, but then again he didn't have to. Urban, as ever, toed the party line, giving a shout-out to producer Matt Rollings, his 'right spiritual guide', revealing that they did not argue once during the making of the album. Later on, speaking with some reporters, Urban cut through the crap. While he was overwhelmed by the success, he added that 'there's a part of me that expected this to come sooner'.[10] It was a surprisingly candid revelation from someone who had learned how to say all the right things when a microphone was waved in his face.

Capitol, meanwhile, felt there was sufficient juice left in the *keith urban* album to roll out a fourth single, 'Where the Blacktop Ends', teamed with a video in which Urban briefly ditched his twangy Bon Jovi look in preference for some smart shades and a shaggy moptop; he was a dead-ringer for Bee Gee Robin Gibb (although Urban could claim his hair as his own). 'Blacktop's release coincided with a major shake-up in Keith Urban Inc, when Urban chose to move on from Miles Copeland – and Greg Shaw – and find himself a new manager. It was the endplay in the ostracism of Shaw, the only person who could legitimately say that he 'discovered' Urban (although many would make that claim). Urban, according to Ged Malone, had been 'fed up with Miles for a while', and Malone himself had moved on after his marriage to Jane Wiedlin ended and he returned to the UK to manage Simple Minds (he hasn't spoken with Urban since leaving the USA).

On first glance, Gary Borman seemed the man least likely to take Urban to the top: he was a lean, tallish, urbane kind of guy, quietly handsome in a salt-and-pepper sort of way, whose wire-rimmed specs suggested a college professor rather than a high-profile music manager. But as president of Borman Entertainment he was a serious player in Nashville and beyond. 'Gary Borman was perfect for Keith once he got established,' said Bob Saporiti.

I worked with Gary with Faith Hill, Dwight Yoakam – those kind of acts. He's a great manager and the right place for Keith to end up. He's real smart. But Miles was the perfect interim guy. He had a real worldly view, which was the right link between the Oz guy and the Nashville thing; he wasn't going right into a Nashville situation.

When Borman and Urban joined forces, Borman's roster already included Faith Hill, Lonestar and James Taylor, an early favourite of Urban's, which clearly influenced his decision. Who wouldn't want to be with the same company that looked after the guy who wrote 'Fire and Rain'? And Borman's empire had just expanded significantly when he'd formed an alliance with Tim DuBois who, along with music biz legend Clive Davis, had formed Arista Nashville in 1989 and signed such platinum-plated country stars as Brooks & Dunn, Alan Jackson and Diamond Rio to the label. (DuBois had once taught accounting at Oklahoma State College while writing songs at night, and it was there that he befriended Scott Hendricks, Urban's former boss and champion at Capitol.)

Like Copeland, Borman's international reach offered Urban the chance to 'go global' – he desperately wanted to be more than just a Nashville star. This was one of the reasons he opted to go with Borman and not Brooks & Dunn's management, who had also approached him. Urban was the first signing to the new Borman/DuBois partnership, a nod to both his status and their stone-cold conviction that Urban was the new face of country music. *USA Weekend* magazine had just described Urban as 'a charismatic Australian with spiky, bleached-blond hair, three silver hoops in one ear, skin-tight leather pants and a screaming Fender Telecaster electric guitar' – how could Nashville's kingmakers not respond to that?[11]

But the termination of the relationship between Urban and Shaw was handled poorly. Shaw had promised his son that he would spend his birthday with him, back in Brisbane, and was

Searching for inspiration (and his shirt), Gold Coast, 1992. 'I got a feel that for [Keith, success] was like the *Odyssey*,' said Todd Hunter. 'And when he did it, I thought, "Fuck, incredible, here's a man who lived out the whole thing." He was wearied by it, but he was determined.' *(Photo: John Elliott)*

Urban with wild child Vernon Rust, Tamworth, 1994. Rust contributed most of the songs to The Ranch's only album. But according to one insider, Rust 'definitely smoked the old "herbage" too much'.

At Brisbane's Kangaroo Point. A Nashville neighbour of Urban's admitted, 'Even when he was broke [women] used to throw themselves at him – and he's never been one to turn down a polite offer.' *(Both photos: John Elliott)*

Urban *(right)* with The Ranch bandmates Peter Clarke *(left)* and Jerry Flowers in 1994. They'd planned to call themselves The Farm, but a UK band got there first; then Urban baulked at the idea of Keith Urban's Four Wheel Drive. Naming the band 'caused me so much grief', said Urban.

Slim Dusty jamming in Nashville with *(from left)* Laurie Minson, Peter Clarke, Jerry Flowers and Urban, 1998. When Urban toured with Dusty, he was unsure the audiences would accept him. 'Just go out there and do it your own way,' Dusty wisely told him. *(Both photos: John Elliott)*

Laying it down with Jerry Flowers in Tamworth, 1998. 'He looks like he'd kill you in a heartbeat, but he's such a gentle soul,' one observer said of Flowers, a long-time Urban sidekick. 'And he's one of the best bass players on the planet.'

Urban with his Golden Guitar for the instrumental 'Clutterbilly', 1998. However, the relationship between Urban and the Tamworth establishment has always been shaky at best. John 'True Blue' Williamson disowned Urban for 'selling out' to Nashville. *(Both photos: John Elliott)*

Urban with Charlie Daniels at the country great's base in Lebanon, Tennessee. Urban would sometimes pick Daniels' 'The Devil Went Down to Georgia' while standing atop a bar – blindfolded. *(Photo: John Elliott)*

After winning his first major American industry trophy, the highly prized Horizon Award, in 2001. Urban's suit had the words 'freedom' and 'spirit' sewn into the cloth. 'Winning the [award] felt like going back to a time before I started going off the rails,' Urban said afterwards. *(Photo: Getty Images/Alan L. Mayor)*

When he was named CMA's Male Vocalist and Entertainer of the Year in 2005, at New York's Madison Square Garden, Urban profusely thanked his band. 'Road bands out there,' he said, 'don't get enough appreciation.' *(Photo: John Elliott)*

Urban won the Best Male Country Vocal gong at the 2005 Grammys, and he grabbed the chance to revisit his cover-band past by blasting 'Sweet Home Alabama' with the remaining members of southern rock legends Lynyrd Skynyrd. *(Photo: Getty Images)*

Accepting the CMA International Artist Achievement award at the Australian Consul in New York, 2005, with, among others, Billy Thorpe *(second from left)* and Brian Cadd *(second from right)*. Soon after, Urban tapped Thorpe's 'Most People I Know' for a Gap jeans ad campaign. *(Photo: John Elliott)*

Rocking the free world at Live Earth, July 2007, a few months after checking out of the Betty Ford Clinic. 'I deeply regret the hurt this has caused Nicole and the ones that love and support me,' Urban wrote at the time of his admission. *(Photo: Getty Images/Evan Agostini)*

Urban jamming 'Funky Tonight' with urban hippie John Butler at the ARIA Awards, October 2007. Many insiders are curious which direction Urban will take next. 'I'd love for Keith to do something instrumentally with me,' admitted Tommy Emmanuel. *(Photo: Newspix/Sam Mooy)*

'The Kurbans', as they have been dubbed, and baby bump, 2008. While with Kidman at a gig in Nashville, Urban turned to a friend and whispered, 'She is the love of my life.' Sunday Rose Kidman Urban was born 9 July 2008. *(Photo: Getty Images/Denise Truscello)*

in the middle of the celebrations when Urban called and said that he should return to the States, and quickly. 'Things are really heating up,' Urban said, which was absolutely true. Shaw did his best to make right with his son, and then boarded the next flight out of Brisbane for the USA. When he landed at LAX he put in a call to Urban in Nashville. 'I'll be there soon,' he said. Shaw was then given the biggest shock of his life: after more than a decade with Urban, and having made huge personal and financial sacrifices for him, he was fired – *over the phone*. 'I could not even say goodbye to friends I had met with Keith,' Shaw was quoted as saying soon after. 'I could not get my affairs in order; I was just sacked.'[12]

Still reeling from his dismissal, Shaw headed home and started to make some discreet enquiries about receiving a final payment for his many years of devoted service. But he was contacted by Urban's US lawyers who said that if he went down that road, Shaw would be buying into a lengthy and pricey legal battle and one that he was unlikely to win, given the less-than-formal nature of his relationship with Urban. Certainly they had a contract, but much of their agreement was settled with beers and a handshake. (And the fact that Shaw occasionally imbibed with Urban wasn't the kind of revelation that would help him win a court battle.) They were mates, not just business partners, who'd endured more than their share of hardships. To be treated so shoddily, and with the warning of the lawyers still echoing in his ears – it was enough to convince Shaw that he should simply walk away. He was done with the whole Urban affair.

But having said all that, later in 2001 I witnessed yet another Urban homecoming at City Live, a venue in Sydney's Fox Studios complex. Mid set, Urban made a very noble gesture to Shaw, who was in the crowd; he thanked him warmly, invited him on stage and handed him a framed gold record. Urban spoke about 'the rumours' and made it clear to the many industry types in the room that he remained tight with his erstwhile manager, the man who 'would walk through fire' for him and more. It wasn't a cheque for a million bucks, but it was a very public and 'official' acknowledgement of their joint efforts. Or maybe Urban was simply making peace in an effort to kill off any thoughts Shaw had about suing him. Who's to say? Neither is willing to speak about the train wreck that ended their partnership. Urban's friend and agent, Rob Potts, has his own take on that night.

> That was a public acknowledgement on Keith's part, his way of saying: 'I don't care what all you wankers are thinking over here, Greg and I are still mates.' There was a little bit of showbiz, but it was pretty real.

And it must be said that Shaw should have bought into a co-management agreement, in which he'd do little work and receive handsome financial rewards, well before his eventual sacking. So many well-informed advisers, from Ten Ten's Barry Coburn and Warners' Bob Saporiti down, had told him to 'cut a deal', yet Shaw refused to do so, even though he shared 'co-billing' with Miles Copeland for some time. It's hard not to figure that even today Shaw clings to a somewhat naive belief that Urban will eventually knock on his door and hand over due payment for his efforts and sacrifices. This is a notion supported by many who have gotten close to both Urban and Shaw over the years. But Shaw had served his purpose. Someone in Urban's position – an outsider trying to immerse himself in a closed-off musical community – needed a true believer like the guy who once booked bands at Brisbane's Crest Hotel. But now that Urban had finally 'cracked' the US market, he required heavyweight representation – some real management muscle. As good a supporter and pal as Shaw had been, he simply was not the guy.

As Rob Potts said:

Ultimately, Greg should take from the experience what it really was – he gave Keith his shot in America – and this was also the part of that journey that made Keith a great artist. He was so committed to his own art, and his belief, and he had time to refine it to a point where he became a fucking great song-writer, on the world stage, and that was because of all the hardship, pain and drug abuse. They lived that hard life; they went through that together. I was Keith's guy over here, seeing him whenever he toured, whereas Greg was there all the time; he gave up his family, everything. Totally committed.

Shaw's place as Urban's Australian 'person' was taken by Kerry Roberts, who first met Urban while she was working on the *Midday Show* and he was crooning 'Arms of Mary' while sporting the largest quiff ever seen on that very blue-rinse institution. Roberts had been an entertainment executive at Channel Nine for several years, working first with *Midday* and then across the entire network. Along with presenter Richard Wilkins, she was probably Urban's biggest mainstream media supporter. According to one person I spoke with who knows her very well, Roberts, unlike Shaw, was gifted with dealing with the 'psychology of talent'; she had a clear understanding of how to help someone like Urban express their personality through their music and connect with an audience. 'Kerry was brilliant at that level,' I was told. Naturally, she defended Urban from accusations of any harsh dealings with Shaw. Roberts told a Perth newspaper that an agreement existed between Urban and Shaw, which spelled out that once he was positioned to 'crack the US charts', Shaw could gracefully retire and return to Oz.

'Greg wanted to spend more time with his family here and he even helped Keith find the person to replace himself,' Roberts stated. 'It is now really sad that Greg feels hard-done-by because it is the first we have heard of it.'[13] Shaw has only once been quoted about his expectations, and even then it was in the *Sydney Morning Herald*'s Private Sydney column, hardly the epicentre of serious journalism. 'I have been told I will get something,' he was quoted as saying, 'but who knows when, how or what. But I'm not panicking about it.'[14]

It was a badly stage-managed shit-fight, no doubt about it. One close associate of Shaw's summed it up pretty neatly when they told me: 'How fucking hard would it be for Keith to cut a cheque and thank him? Surely he can afford it.' James Blundell agreed with this.

> There's a lot of issues with Greg. I've watched Greg position [Keith] for 18 years and that gave him the launching pad for the past five years. And there's been nothing forthcoming from Keith to remunerate him.

Shaw even kicked around the idea of writing a book with the assistance of Urban's former girlfriend Angie Marquis, an aspiring writer. It would document Shaw's many years with Urban and give his version of how it all came undone. That book never eventuated, but Marquis is now attempting to write her own tell-all which, as she told me, would ponder, in some length, the story of 'Keith and me'.

It was also strongly suggested to me that Urban's decision to shelve Shaw – and there's no question that he had to sign off on the decision to sack his manager – was prompted, at least in part, by a need to separate himself from anyone who reminded him of his bleak, post-Ranch period. It's a very common part of the 'recovery' program: it's only when you cut yourself free from your past that you can truly move forwards. Urban has also sacked an entire band that played with him when he was using, as well as his long-time Australian publicist, Chrissie Camp, so there's strong evidence that Shaw wasn't the only person to be dumped like a steaming turd as part of Urban's 'recovery'. In a peculiar final twist, Shaw went on to manage the career of Hughie Murray, a Leon Russell-like musician who shared a house in Nashville with Urban during his self-confessed 'dark days'. (And Murray is now working with Mark Moffatt, Urban's former A&R guy at Ten Ten, proving that the circle does indeed remain unbroken.)

Urban, meanwhile, did what any smart artist should do in such a volatile atmosphere, and kept on working. He was back in Brisbane, briefly, during August 2001, for a cameo at the Goodwill Games, and then grabbed his brother Shane and headed to Sydney to collect his Outstanding Achievement Award ARIA from Slim Dusty. Urban, by now quite accustomed to the American way of hugging the award presenter, tried embracing a slightly startled Dusty, who instead stuck out his right paw and hung on tight. Urban gave another heart-felt speech in which he thanked all those who helped his career happen: Brian Harris, Rob Walker, Chrissie Camp and Greg Shaw, among others, even if some of those very people had recently been ostracised. He also gave a shout-out to Kasey Chambers, a homegrown country singer on the ascendancy, someone who shared Urban's fondness for piercings and an 'urban hippie chic' look, even if her musical roots were far more rootsy than Urban's – Chambers was more about Hank Williams than Glen Campbell. (Warners' Bob Saporiti would also become a champion of Chambers, eventually helping her sign a deal via Warners' LA branch. Slim Dusty had plenty of time for Chambers too; as his widow Joy McKean told me, he respected anyone with both a maverick streak and a genuine understanding of country music's roots.)

'Where the Blacktop Ends' had been a rock-solid fourth single from the *keith urban* album, peaking at number three on *Billboard*'s Country Singles list and hanging around various charts for close to six months. But it should be said that Urban's first wave of genuine success had coincided with one of the weaker years in country's recent commercial history: the heady peaks of the Urban Cowboy and Gone Country eras weren't challenged during 2001. Not a single country gig made it to that year's Top 100 Boxscores, a reliable barometer of who (or what) is hot, or not. It didn't help Nashville's year-end numbers that Garth Brooks, that monstrous ego in a Stetson, had retired from the road. As for record sales, something like 9 percent of all music shoppers were buying country albums, a slide back to the dodgy mid-1980s levels. However, to Urban's benefit, trade bible *Billboard* listed him in their 'sophomore class' for 2002 along with Rascal Flatts, Sara Evans and Brad Paisley. He was one of the few acts predicted to survive the slump and actually prosper.

With that very much in mind, Urban and his new team started considering their next move: it was clear that he needed to get back into the studio quickly and consolidate his debut's success – but was Matt Rollings the right producer to move Urban out of the 'sophomore class'? Probably not. What he needed was a studio guy with a track record and some real commercial savvy – and, as Mark Moffatt told me, Urban needed a fellow 'guitar head', an assessment that piano man Rollings told me sits comfortably with him. Dann Huff was very much that guy, and would prove to be Urban's commercial 'touchstone' over the next few years. He was also well connected with Gary Borman through his production work on records by Faith Hill, another move by Urban's manager to keep everything 'in-house'.

But the relationship between producer and artist can be precarious, as Radney Foster, a Texas-born singer/songwriter who has worked with Urban and produced his fair share of records, told me.

> It's an odd thing being a record producer, because the day you finish a record you're fired. If you get hired again, well, that's a good thing, but basically you're done when the record's done.

And Huff and Urban didn't start out so well. On their first scheduled day of working together, Urban came into the studio to find that Huff had begun to lay down guitar tracks – and the one part of Urban's records that he totally controlled was the guitar work: solos, rhythm tracks, overdubs, the lot. Urban hastily and cheekily organised a showcase that night in Nashville and ensured that only one name – Huff's – was on the guest list, in very large letters. The producer turned up to the gig and watched his new charge work his way up and down and around his Fender like a rocked-up Tommy Emmanuel; clearly he didn't know Urban well enough to realise that he was a master blaster on the guitar. The next day, when they returned to the studio, Huff turned to Urban and said: 'I guess you'll be playing the guitar from now on.' That first misstep was never mentioned again.

Urban was initially resistant to a change in producers, figuring that if he hooked up with a fellow guitarist, 'all he's going to do is want me to play the way he does'. (Keep in mind that the producer–artist relationship is at its strongest in Nashville; most successful pairings continue to record together until the hits fade away.) And not every record on Huff's CV could be found in Urban's CD collection, Urban admitting 'he's done a few records I wasn't overly thrilled with'. But

Urban did agree to cut one track with Huff, as an experiment. The song they chose was 'Somebody Like You' and almost as soon as they began recording, Urban was sold on the dark-haired producer with the intense glare, despite their false start. 'It was like [working with] a music teacher,' Urban admitted. 'He came in and took hold of the class. I just stood there and went, "Wow, this guy is awesome."'[15] Not so awesome, mind you, that Huff would get to co-produce the entire LP with Urban. In the final wash-up, Huff worked on six tracks and Urban produced the other half dozen by himself. (Urban cut most of the demos for the album quickly with his band and engineer Justin Niebank, and then Huff came in to add some studio polish.)

Like Rollings, Huff – who once wore a mullet that challenged Urban's in both size and shape – had an impressive CV. Seven years older than Urban, he'd added guitar parts to sessions for Mariah Carey, Madonna, Michael Jackson and big-haired screamer Michael Bolton. And his tastes, like those of so many others who gravitated towards Nashville in the 1980s and 1990s, weren't purely country: when asked to nominate his 'desert island discs', he listed LPs from super-slick ironists Steely Dan, ballsy rockers Bad Company and soul man Bill Withers. And as a player, his key influences were Brit fusionist Jeff Beck, Toto's Steve Lukather and jazz guy David Sanborn. But Huff was probably best known for the tearaway guitar solo heard in Kenny Loggins's 'Danger Zone', the anthem from the *Top Gun* soundtrack. Twangy he most definitely was not, yet he knew a hit when he played on one, without doubt.

Huff came from deeply religious roots, a spiritual attribute that would help him ease into life in the South. He'd shifted from LA in the late 1980s, after some middling success with rockers-for-God Whiteheart, where he played alongside his drumming brother, David. (Their father, Ronn Huff, was a conductor and arranger.) Huff, like Urban, had a finely tuned commercial radar; as early as 1987 he was quoted as saying: 'Producers want to hear the sound they hear on radio every day.' Having now aligned himself with Urban, and having produced records for Faith Hill, Wynonna Judd and LeAnn Rimes, Huff had the chance to forge some hits that radio simply could not resist.

As for Urban, he was juggling dual necessities: playing shows to maintain his profile and trying to write new songs for his next record. In May 2002, during a benefit show in Los Angeles, he previewed a tune entitled 'Song for Dad', a metaphor-free tribute to his eccentric, country music loving father, whose record collection had pointed him in the direction of Nashville and whose short fuse may have led to the burning down of the family home back in Caboolture. 'You tend to just punch your dad in the shoulder to tell him you love him, and it's the same for dads sometimes,' Urban said after the show.

> They're not sure how to tell their sons that they love them.
> The older I get, the more I realise I'm so much like my dad.
> I mean, I say the same things and I do the same things. So it
> just became something I thought a lot of people would get.[16]

This, of course, was the sanitised version of a relationship that was most likely as fraught as that of any other father and son, possibly more so, given Urban's addiction 'issues' and the suggestion that Bob Urban was also known to give substances a nudge. And Urban did hint at something darker in the song's lyric, when he sang: 'There were times when I thought he was bein'' / just a little bit hard on me.' He wasn't going to give too much away, but there were allusions to a family history that wasn't necessarily all rosy. Curiously, Urban premiered the song to an industry crowd before playing it to his father. It seemed as though he still needed the approval of both the music biz *and* his old man.

With this second album under development – he'd cut 10 demos in December, with just the backing of bass and drums – Urban was cementing some key co-songwriting relationships, cooking up tunes with such craftsmen as Monty Powell (who co-wrote 'It's a Love Thing' on his first record); John Shanks, who'd become a key go-to guy for Urban; and the highly regarded Rodney Crowell, who'd spent his fair share of time down at 12th & Porter, watching Urban bust moves out in front of The Ranch. Urban's original plan with the album was to hark back to the same rockier past that Crowell and others had so much admired. He told *Billboard*, prior to the record's completion, that he hoped to showcase 'his very rough, unpolished, raw side', not just his knack as a hunk-cum-balladeer. He nominated one of his key teenage records, John Mellencamp's *Lonesome Jubilee*, as a major reference point, but frankly the finished record leaned more towards the soft-rock of Dan Fogelberg and the melodic West Coast twang of the Eagles.

The lead single, 'Somebody Like You', dropped a good four months before the album, and Urban's expectations weren't massive. He told a reporter in Columbus that he:

> . . . figured the single would mosey on the chart for a few months. I didn't want the single to zoom up the chart and fade. A song can have a short shelf life if it's too popular, like 'Don't Worry, Be Happy'.[17]

Urban was drastically understating his case, because the undeniably catchy 'Somebody' hit like a hurricane, and the release date of the album – now named *Golden Road*, Urban's nod to his new, improved and upwardly mobile life – was pushed up from 5 November to 8 October. This bump in the schedule meant that a few shortcuts had to be taken with the album, and it showed in the final product. Some tracks seemed rushed, a few under-cooked, and the album didn't hang together especially well despite its bumper crop of hit singles and airbrushed, pseudo soft-porn videos.

'Somebody Like You' was a slightly sticky, uptempo valentine, tailor-made for radio, and its video also set in motion a new chapter of Urban's love life. Supermodel Niki Taylor appeared in the clip, a laughable 'live' shoot, with Urban, band and an assortment of comely extras gyrating in the dust, Urban picking at his banjo from the middle of what appeared to be a Californian crop circle. (The shoot, directed by Trey Fanjoy, actually took place in the hills above Malibu in a mansion owned by the son of famous architect Frank Lloyd Wright.) The ultra-photogenic Urban and Taylor struck a variety of provocative poses, and the sparks they generated for the camera continued once the shoot ended.

Twenty-seven years old, Taylor was a native of Fort Lauderdale, Florida; her father was a sheriff's deputy, her mother a photographer. She'd been 'discovered' at the ripe old age of 13 and signed with the Irene Marie Models agency in South Florida. Soon after she won a Fresh Faces contest in New York and pocketed a handy US$500,000 modelling deal. By 17 she'd made the cover of *Vogue*, the second youngest star to do so – Brooke Shields taking that particular honour in 1980 – and in 1991 she reached *People*'s 50 Most Beautiful People list. Taylor married US football star Matt Martinez in 1994, gave birth to twin sons, Jake and Hunter, then duly divorced Martinez in 1996. But she shared more with Urban than a thing for making magazine lists and being 'as single as a dollar bill': after surviving a near-fatal car crash in May 2001 and remaining unconscious for six weeks, she ended up in rehab, dealing with an addiction to the super-strength painkiller Vicodin.

Despite her impressive CV, Taylor desperately wanted to appear in a music video. It just so happened that Urban's hairdresser doubled as Taylor's makeup artist, and before you could say 'it's a love thing', the toothy, golden-haired, all-American Taylor – who was now based in Nashville – was sharing more than an on-set snog with Urban. As 'Somebody Like You' rapidly became his second number one on the Country singles chart, Urban was downplaying their relationship, falling back on some old standards: 'We're good friends,' he said.

> She loves country music. A mutual friend suggested we meet because Niki wanted to be in a video. The video is very earthy and organic. She just fit the bill so well.[18]

Throughout their romance, Urban continued to understate things, sticking with his 'just good friends' line. But he cared enough about Taylor to bring her to Australia to meet his family, as he had done with Laura Sigler. Urban would sometimes attend local school functions with Taylor and her twins. It was even suggested that it was more than a coincidence that his most recent stint in rehab, in late 2006, coincided with Taylor's engagement to NASCAR driver Burney Lamar, even though Urban had just married Nicole Kidman.

Golden Road hit in early October and, unlike its predecessor, was an immediate hit. Helped no end by an appearance on Jay Leno's *Tonight Show*, the album shifted some 66,500 copies in its first week, only being outdone on the country charts by a new album from his buddies the Dixie Chicks, and a sort-of new release from the long-dead Elvis Presley, *30 #1 Hits*. *Golden Road* debuted at number 11 on the *Billboard* Top 200

chart, a massive mainstream accomplishment. Apart from his
Leno spot, Urban also made a key appearance at the 36th
CMA Awards where he'd claimed the Horizon Award the year
before. With the muscle of both Capitol Records and Gary
Borman behind him, Urban was making large-scale cameos
at all the right times and it was paying off at the almighty cash
register. Maybe Mike Dungan had been right when he said
that the *keith urban* album hadn't been 'set up' properly; there
was no way that the label planned to make the same mistake
with *Golden Road*.

As he talked up the album, Urban stuck tight to the notion
that this new set showcased his rockier nature, despite the
overload of strings on 'Song for Dad' and elsewhere. 'I think a
little bit more of my Aussie pub influence has come back into
my playing,' Urban said in the official Capitol propaganda that
accompanied *Golden Road*.

> It has a certain primal rawness to it and I think I'm starting to
> let that come out again. The last record was more about letting
> people get to know me a little bit, and this one is hopefully
> letting out more of myself. It's kind of like the sixth time
> you meet your girlfriend's parents.[19]

Golden Road certainly established a profitable formula for
Urban – his friend Bob Saporiti somewhat disdainfully referred
to it as the 'Nashville pop thing' – but you'd hardly call it loose
and loud. Its commercial high points – 'Somebody Like You',
'Who Wouldn't Wanna Be Me' and the heartstring-tugging
'Raining on Sunday' – consolidated Urban's place as a sensitive country dude with a guitar and excellent hair, the kind
of man who'd rather stay home and canoodle than run wild
at his local honky-tonk. If anything, *Golden Road* set in stone
the marketing strategy that former Capitol boss Pat Quigley

used with his debut LP, when it was declared that Urban was
delivering 'what every woman wants to hear and every man
wants to say'.

Urban's recording of 'Raining on Sunday' was the culmina-
tion of an ongoing relationship with Radney Foster, one of
The Ranch's many muso fans, who co-wrote the song with
Darrell Brown, a gay songwriter/producer (who would also
write with Urban). Foster and Urban had tried out a few song
ideas in the period between *keith urban* and *Golden Road*, but
nothing made it to record (although one song they co-wrote
has now been cut by Fisher Stevenson). Urban, however, virtually from the get-go, told Foster how much he loved his *See
What You Want to See* album, released in 1999, which featured
the original version of 'Raining'. 'One day,' Urban said, 'I want
to cut "Raining on Sunday".' It took a couple of years, but
he was true to his word.

As for the song itself, it originally came to Foster in a
peculiar way, as he told me. 'I was in the middle of a lot of
emotional turmoil,' he said, 'but was also a newlywed.'

I'd been married a couple of years. I don't tend to write on
Sundays but due to logistics I had to write on a Sunday afternoon — a rainy Sunday afternoon. I walked into Darrell's
house, just goofing around, singing: 'Raining on Sunday' and
he went, 'OK, that's what we're doing; here we go.' When
you're in the storms of life, just a day to hide under the covers
with someone is a good thing. An absolute escape.

I thought that no one would record it but me. The entire
second verse is sort of mystical, about God and sex and
Mexico, but not necessarily in that order. It seemed way too
'out there' for anything that Nashville could ever deal with.
But I liked it and put it on my record. And I think it was gutsy
of Keith to record it because of that second verse. He figured
out a way to make it his own.

When Urban decided to cut it for *Golden Road*, he did an unusual thing and called Foster, inviting him down to the studio to listen to the final mix. In a typical Nashville situation, the songwriter is way down the food chain, but not according to Urban, or at least not in this case. 'That's a rare thing; most of the time you hear it after the fact,' Foster confirmed.

> But he called and said that they were mixing the thing and please come by. It was fantastic; the moment I heard it I just went 'Wow!' I pretty much knew at that point that it would be a single, and that's very rare because there's such politics to that. Walking out of there I thought, 'That's a smash.'

'Keith made it his own. It got more anthemic when he did it,' the genial, thoughtful Foster added.

> The solo leading into the final verse is arena rock in the best sense of the word. I can honestly say that there's been plenty of times when I've heard someone cut something I wrote and gone, 'Well, that's gonna make me some money,' but wasn't really thrilled about it. I think the best of what an artist can do is take a song and make it their own, and people now identify that as a Keith Urban song, not a Radney Foster song.

But the finished album did contain some lyrical clunkers, especially during the meditative 'You'll Think of Me'. There, amid various observations of how his ex will one day regret their breakup, he undermines the song's sense of pathos by singing: 'Take your cat and leave my sweater / Cause we have nothing left to weather.' The lines weren't Urban's — it was yet another song written by committee — but you could almost hear him cringe when he reached that particular lyrical lowlight. And for a gifted player who could be breaking new ground for mainstream country, the notion of telling some young lovely how 'you look good in my shirt' wasn't going to win Urban any kudos among serious musos and critics. A remake of one-hit-wonder David Dundas's uber-cheesy 'Jeans On' didn't help his cause much, either. It merely drove home the point that the breakout success of 'Somebody Like You' meant the album was rushed into the shops, and Urban opted to throw every song he had handy into the final mix. It's worth noting that Urban dropped a few things for *Golden Road*, including his lower case obsession, which must have brought a smile to the face of proofreaders everywhere, plus his thing for including a break-neck speed instrumental on all of his long-players to date. He'd also lost the slight gap between his front teeth; Urban now sported a picture-perfect, million-dollar smile. Combined with his ever-present tan, the man positively glowed.

Golden Road was an album more concerned with songs than chops, which was a big letdown. He could have used his success to push things a little further, but instead opted to play it very, very safe. Reviews for the album were varied, but that didn't stop its healthy sales. *The Tennessean*'s Brad Schmitt longed for the Urban of The Ranch, 'the open-shirt bad-boy attitude, the naughty grin and that killer accent'. To Schmitt, with few exceptions, *Golden Road* simply served up 'a collection of tired looks at clichéd topics'. The album typified what Schmitt saw as Urban's 'slide away from passion into vapid, radio-friendly pop-country music'. Other journals, such as *USA Today*, took a more tolerant, upbeat tangent. 'Throughout the album,' wrote Brian Mansfield, 'Urban balances his instrumental chops' – and, admittedly, all the guitar solos were his – 'with his country-pop sense as well as anybody since his idol, Glen Campbell.' Then this, from the *Miami Herald*: '*Golden Road* isn't exceptional, especially original or essential,' noted Howard Cohen, 'but it is entertaining and there's a bit more grit and energy . . . than he offered on his slick 1999 solo debut.' The

Chicago Sun-Times, however, was massively underwhelmed, noting how Urban yelps 'whoo' exactly 13 times over the course of the album's dozen tracks. 'A "Whoo!" yelp typically indicates exciting music,' their critic reasoned, quite rightly. 'That's why it is so incongruous here. For nearly an hour, Urban slogs through a dozen cliché-ridden duds.'

But there was one standout cut on *Golden Road*, a song where Urban tapped into a deeper shade of soul rather than offering up radio-friendly homilies set to a shiny, mid-tempo backdrop. The album closer, 'You're Not My God', was a close relation of 'But for the Grace of God', a few moments of quiet reflection on Urban's part. (For a guy who distanced himself from organised religion, he sure refers to God a lot in his music). Urban, with the help of co-writer Paul Jefferson – a pilot in his spare time, best known for co-writing Aaron Tippin's chart-topping 'That's as Close as I'll Get to Loving You' – cut through the crap as he chewed over the time he wasted while on the crack pipe. 'Little white lies on a mirror', he sang, 'cut neatly in a row / Medicine that kept me from lookin' in my soul / I thought you were the answer / You're not my God.' For a guy doing his best to conform to the expectations of radio and the music biz in general, this was exposition worthy of James Taylor.

Urban may have thought that by writing the song he was finally giving his time in hell one final kiss-off. But while on the road in New York during a typically freezing January, the legacy of his bad habits would return to kick him in the arse yet again.

Seven

THE GOLD-PLATED ROAD

Keith Urban is kind of like contemporary country's Tom Cruise. The kid is just so unjustly talented, likeable and good-looking that it's hard not to hate him.

Bob Allen, www.amazon.com

With *Golden Road* sitting stubbornly at the top of the country albums chart, and with no less than two singles – 'Somebody Like You', which was number one for a crazy six weeks, and its follow-up, the slightly soggy 'Raining on Sunday' – at the business end of the singles chart, life couldn't have been happier in Urbanville come January 2003. Added to that was the neat little bonus that his solo debut was still selling, inching its way towards platinum sales. Commercially speaking, it was the best of times. Urban had also just found out he was being awarded the Centenary Medal for 'Service to Australian Society through Country Music'. The Centenary Medal was a commemorative award designed to 'mark the achievements of a broad cross-section of the Australian community at the commencement of the new century', according to the impressive letter sent to Urban. While Tamworth may have been reluctant to properly acknowledge Urban's climb, it seemed that the Howard Federal Government had no such reservations.

But just before boarding a flight to New York, Urban sensed that his somewhat tender throat was about to pack it in. Ever since his addiction to crack cocaine, Urban's vocal cords had become especially vulnerable – and given the toxic garbage that's added to crack in backstreet drug labs, the damage can be long lasting. Urban had some high-profile Manhattan media in place, including spots on *Good Morning America*, the *Caroline Rhea Show* and the *WB Morning Show*, and planned to drop in to Nashville's Vanderbilt Voice Clinic on his way to the airport, purely for a check-up. He'd had a polyp on his right vocal cord for about 12 months, and knew it wasn't getting any smaller. As he recalled later, 'I went to Vanderbilt thinking they'd give me a little shot and I'd be on my way.' Urban's physician, Dr C. Gaelyn Garrett, poked around the star's throat and gave him some bad news. New York was definitely off the schedule, as was talking in any way, for at least a week. 'You're not going anywhere,' he told Urban.[1]

With the obligatory press release announcing that Urban was suffering from a 'persistent and serious vocal cord ailment', the TV spots and a few shows were blown out. But when he returned to the clinic, Urban was given an even worse prognosis: complete vocal rest was required for no less than six weeks. Out the window went a proposed Canadian tour with Carolyn Dawn Johnson, plus prominent Nashville showcases during the Country Radio Seminar and a performance at the downright salubrious Houston Livestock Show & Rodeo. Dr Garrett launched into print, stressing the fragility of Urban's throat. 'Although Keith is improving,' he said at the end of January, 'he is still very much at risk. Should he return prematurely to normal voice use, including singing and speaking, he could risk damage of a potentially permanent nature.' Urban resorted to a written statement – what option did he have? – that packed an unintentionally witty punch. 'There are no words to express my disappointment,' he wrote, 'but I know that I need to abide by my doctor's instructions.'[2]

Indeed there were no available words to express Urban's dismay – he now resorted to using a whiteboard and magic marker to let his people know of his needs. Later on, Urban could see the funnier side of his predicament. To minimise the need to try to express himself, he only kept the company of 'people who knew me best, and they sort of knew what I was talking about. Or not talking about, actually.'[3] During his enforced downtime, Urban went skiing. He was riding in a ski lift when he spotted some of his group down on the slopes. Urban's skiing instructor was seated alongside him, and when Urban pointed out his friends, he told him: 'Just yell out to them.' Urban was about to do just that when he realised the damage that yelling could inflict on his already damaged throat. As he recalled, 'Something inside said: "Don't."' For a guy who spent most of his time in front of a screaming amplifier in a world of electricity and noise, silence was one alien concept.

When Urban was ready to get back to work in early April, he targeted the rushed turnaround of the *Golden Road* album – brought on by the hit-and-run success of 'Somebody Like You' – as the key trigger for his vocal relapse. 'I found myself doing maybe two or three times the amount of work that we had planned in a very short space of time,' he (finally) said, 'and it really took its toll on me.' Urban admitted that he 'wasn't necessarily taking the best care of myself at the time,' but was basically referring to being overworked and under-rested, nothing more.[4] Every time his voice packed it in, though – and this was neither the first nor final time it happened – it served as a reminder of the worst period of his life.

Urban summed up the first few months of 2003 as 'a weird time', but the upside was that his absence didn't raise a murmur of discontent in either the singles or the album chart. 'Somebody Like You' was the song that refused to die, while 'Raining on Sunday', teamed with yet another moody, hormonally charged video, was on its way to a chart peak of number three. And speaking of threes, *Golden Road* was barnstorming its way to triple platinum sales, a whopping all-time high for the new king of Capitol (and country). On a personal level, it was the weirdest of times for Urban, a flat spot where he was 'reminded of the vulnerability of your livelihood' – he feared, for a while, that his voice may never return. But the sales momentum that he'd established over the previous couple of years, and the goodwill he'd built up with punters and media, was enough to keep the numbers ticking over.

And if the company you keep is any measure of a person's own stardom, Urban had definitely made the A-list: at the CMA Awards, he was mixing it up with country greats George Jones and Dolly Parton, as well as 21st century stars the Dixie Chicks, Alan Jackson, Brooks & Dunn, George Strait and Shania Twain. And when Urban put in a Farm Aid cameo, before his voice packed it in, he shared the spotlight with Willie Nelson, Neil Young and Mr *Lonesome Jubilee* himself, John Mellencamp. Once upon a time, Urban dreamed of maybe meeting such big names – *now he was one of them*. He even bought into the right-minded spirit of Farm Aid, stating, simply enough: 'Supporting American farmers is something we all need to do, especially if we want to eat.' Heaven knows what the conservative denizens of Tamworth made of that particular 'sell-out'.[5]

Urban knew he'd escaped a potential disaster during his time off the road; after all, in America, a high public profile can sell more records than actual good music. Yet Urban was an unstoppable force. And it helped his cause immeasurably when his music publisher, Ten Ten, managed to place 'Somebody Like You' on the soundtrack of the hit flick *How to Lose a Guy in 10 Days*, which did some serious business during February and March. To make the soundtrack of a box office burner like this Kate Hudson vehicle ensured an even longer life for the song – and also helped Urban 'cross over', meaning that he wasn't simply a country star. 'Crossing over' was not just the biggest goal for most Nashville acts, it was also their largest hurdle – audiences beyond the Mason–Dixon Line often found it hard to relate to big hats, bigger voices and the cloying jingoism that was commonplace in Music City. Wisely, Urban avoided most of those country clichés.

The *How to Lose a Guy* soundtrack was all over the musical shop – it included cuts from soul great Al Green, second division rockers the Gin Blossoms, pop siren Carly Simon and the very twee Sixpence None the Richer, with Urban's 'Somebody Like You' the opening track. As www.amazon. com's reviewer shrewdly noted:

> If you came anywhere within earshot of country radio in 2002, you'll immediately recognise the lead cut on this sound-track, Keith Urban's chart-topping 'Somebody Like You', presented here in a pop remix that doesn't diminish the original's catchiness. The rest of this set is routine but well-selected romantic comedy fare.

Clearly, Urban had made the smartest commercial move of his career by hooking up with Gary Borman; this guy knew how to make shit happen, even when his star was out of commission. Tastemakers such as Bill Gubbins, the editor of *Country Weekly* mag, were watching Urban's evolution with some interest. 'Where some people might see, "Oh, Keith is crossing over," it's not a case of the artist crossing over, *it's a case of the artist pulling the audience over.*' Even Sheryl Crow jumped on the bandwagon, stammering: 'The whole thing about him is attractive, the fact that he can play, and *he is attractive.* He's . . . he's downright cute.'[6]

Interestingly, early concert numbers for the *Golden Road* tour weren't that great. At a House of Blues gig in South Carolina in late 2002, Urban only drew 593 'payers' in a room that could comfortably hold 2200, grossing a paltry US$17,000, which would barely have covered production costs and his backstage rider. Yet by April 2003 Urban was locked into a lengthy tour of America's concrete bunkers and super-domes with Kenny Chesney, so it was highly unlikely that he'd walk on-stage and face the ego-sapping sight of an empty room. Chesney, a 'good time all the time' kind of act, had a knack for filling the stadia of Middle America, and Urban happily came along for the ride. This was the tour – going by the name of 'Margaritas and Senoritas', which said plenty about the prevailing attitude – where Chesney christened Urban 'the Australian stud'; clearly, the on-stage good times rolled on long after the gigs had ended. Urban responded by changing the lyrics of his version of Tom Petty's 'Free Fallin'' to read: 'She's a good girl / Crazy about Kenny Chesney.' Every night, seemingly on cue, the crowd went nuts.

Urban would play a tight, polished 50-minute set – a mixture of easy-rolling banter (his 'Your Everything' wedding story was given a good airing) and crowd favourites such as 'Raining on Sunday', 'Where the Blacktop Ends' and 'Some-body Like You', now a standard set closer. His early shows, admittedly, were a little scratchy; Urban complained of how the tips of his fingers hurt because he hadn't come near a guitar during his convalescence, and his voice had a new, nasally edge to it, which he blamed on the abundance of pollen in the Nashville air, saying it messed with his allergies. But these bite-sized warm-up slots with Chesney were the ideal way to ease him back into both the spotlight and the grind of touring. 'It's all good,' Urban insisted backstage. 'The crowds were very sympathetic and compassionate so I was very grateful.' It wasn't just BBQ that you could smell in the air during the Margaritas roadshow – there was also the strong, heady whiff of goodwill, most of it heading Urban's way.[7]

Musically speaking, once his fingers stopped aching these gigs were very satisfying for Urban, as Tamworth's Nick Erby told me. 'You'd find that the things he likes best in the world are like the time he first went out with Chesney, [when] he was on his own,' said Erby.

> We've talked about that a couple of times. It was just Keith and the guitar and he loved that. He would come on and watch this crowd of 15, maybe 20,000 who'd come there to party with Chesney – and Chesney's music is all party music – and his biggest buzz was that he could shut them up and have them listen to him. He did the same thing with Brooks & Dunn, the first time he went out with them.

Chesney, who would later marry and then just as swiftly divorce Hollywood darling Renée Zellweger, was full of praise for Urban. 'He wasn't somebody that came to Nashville with a karaoke tape looking for a record deal,' he told NBC *News Today*. 'He's honest, and his music is honest,' Chesney said of his opening act and running buddy.[8]

But it was as a headliner that Urban made the biggest impact, as the summer of 2003 kicked into high gear. Playing on the key Saturday night showcase at Fan Fair, Urban shared stage time with crowd-pleasers Trace Adkins, Jo Dee Messina, Neal McCoy and Tracy Lawrence, but he rocked harder than the lot of them combined. With barely a 'hello', he strolled out on-stage and unleashed what one reviewer described as a 'guitar cannonade', lasting a full five minutes, as he and his band transformed the easy-going 'Who Wouldn't Wanna Be Me' into a far more dynamic slab of stadium rock. His set might have been short – nowhere were Nashville infomercials more concise than at Fan Fair – but having ripped through 'Where the Blacktop Ends', 'Somebody Like You' and the more restrained 'But for the Grace of God', Urban had left his mark on the full house. Admittedly, though, even this shining star couldn't compete with Neal McCoy's cheesy, pseudo-rap parodies of 'The Ballad of Jed Clampett' and 'The Banana Boat Song', which actually featured costume changes. Only in Nashville would someone consider mixing up the Beverly Hillbillies with Harry Belafonte.

Back on the Chesney tour, Urban found himself defending his commercial inclinations. Speaking with *The Boston Herald*, he delivered a bizarre analogy, harking back to his time with Laura Sigler, as an explanation for his approach to music and songwriting. He related how Sigler would feed heartworm medicine to dogs by hiding it inside a block of cheese. She told Urban, 'The dog won't eat the tablet but he'll eat the cheese, so I gave him the whole thing.' According to Urban, 'To some extent that's what a lot of really great pop songs can be. If you just sneak one little nugget of substance in there and dress it up in this great little hooky melody, it's a good thing.' The heartworm tablet/pop song nexus had never been explained in such curious detail, but there was the slight hint of defensiveness to Urban's tone. A couple of years later, in an on-the-set rap with another of his heroes, Creedence's John

Fogerty, Urban would touch on this again, insisting that he loved to hear his songs on the radio: surely that wasn't a bad thing? Fogerty nodded in agreement; there was no crime in wanting to get your music to the masses. Mind you, Fogerty also fell into a dissertation about getting to a 'happy place' for songwriting, and advised Urban to stick with egg-white omelettes and spinach for breakfast in order to keep the hits coming – so it was hard to take either of them too seriously. And Urban definitely looked uncomfortable when he and Fogerty jammed songs such as 'You'll Think of Me', coming as they did in the wake of 'Bad Moon Rising' and other Creedence classic rock standards. Who was he to say that his songs stacked up with those of a solid-gold legend?

The sex symbol tag was another subject that began to follow Urban like a hungry old dog. He agreed to make touchy-feely videos where the camera would linger on his frame, his face, his hair and smile, so in many ways he bought into that side of the dream. But when asked if his looks could actually be an obstacle to serious regard as a musician, once again he sounded just a touch wary. 'We live in an age that is often so visually driven,' Urban shrugged.

> And if that's a card that you can play you're kind of foolish not to do it. But you have to balance that with not letting it get in the way of the music.[9]

Even with *Golden Road* working its way to a remarkable 111 weeks on the *Billboard* album chart, and 'Who Wouldn't Wanna Be Me' perched at the top of the singles chart – his third number one – Urban still seemed to be suffering a credibility crisis.

And the other thing that Urban was lacking was a home. A tidy sum of money was starting to accumulate in his bank account but because he spent so much time on the road, he simply didn't have the time to sniff out a decent Nashville spread. He'd moved out of his last rental and hadn't found anywhere else to live; virtually everything he owned was either stashed away at the homes of friends, in the corner of his hotel room or somewhere on the tour bus. 'There isn't anywhere I've settled yet,' he said at the time. 'But the bus is *tremendous*.'[10]

Back in Australia in October 2003, Urban swiftly learned that his US success hadn't necessarily translated to the country he considered home. For this latest lap of Oz, he was second on the bill to former teen queen LeAnn Rimes, and his entire Australian experience was summed up by an encounter he had at the US Consulate in Sydney. One of the guards approached him, stars in his eyes, asking for his autograph. He said to Urban, point blank: 'I'm sorry that your success hasn't trans-lated here.' Urban smiled a little uncomfortably and replied: 'Well, that's what I'm back here working on.'[11] Another ARIA, this time for Best Country Album, helped ease the pain a little, but the crowd numbers for the Rimes tour were inconsistent at best. They nearly filled the 5000-seat Brisbane Entertain-ment Centre but fell well short of full houses in rural centres Newcastle and Wollongong, both traditionally solid earners for country acts. They pulled 4500 punters to a modified Sydney Entertainment Centre (the so-called 'Intimate Mode'), and almost 4000 in Melbourne, but ended the run in front of a half-empty Adelaide Entertainment Centre. The flipside was that chunky ticket prices ensured the tour grossed around A$1.4 million from six dates. Still, there were musical highs on most nights, mostly in the manner Urban chose to mourn the passing of his friend and mentor, Slim Dusty, who'd died in September 2003. Each night Urban would sneak in a chorus of Dusty's 'Pub with No Beer' and then quietly say, 'God bless, Slim,' before segueing into 'But for the Grace of God'. The Slim-savvy crowd loved it.

Keith Urban is not a man without his personal flaws, as he would admit to those close to him. According to Rob Potts, 'Keith once said, "Fuck, yeah, I've got some issues. I spend night after night standing in front of people saying: Look at me! Look at me! What does that tell you?"' Nevertheless, while he may have had his share of demons, Urban closed 2003 in a style befitting a platinum-plated artist. Urban and entourage took over BB King's Blues Bar in downtown Nashville, on Monday 8 December, ostensibly to raise a Coopers or ten in honour of his latest number one, 'Who Wouldn't Wanna Be Me'. Monty Powell, the song's co-writer, came along for the party, as did Urban's music publishers, Barry and Jewel Coburn. The Ten Ten bosses had a gift for their charge: a black leather chair, reading lamp and a journal. Powell gave Urban a red electric six-string featuring the same motif that Urban had tattooed on his wrist, a Latin phrase that equated to: 'Love conquers all'.

But there was more than another hit song being marked on that one night in Nashville. Urban's collected album sales were now zeroing in on the six million mark, and it was clear that he was in the middle of a near-peerless commercial run. A solitary number one – 'Achy Breaky Heart', anyone? – could denote a one-hit wonder, but three chart-toppers in such a short time meant that he was the real deal. Urban knew this, too, when he stepped on-stage to make this speech:

> I'm humbled by everyone's support, and I just really want to thank everybody that goes to bat for me. Because this is an industry where people pick and choose and change sides so fast.[12]

The serious business of the evening over, Urban kicked back with a few drinks and started to map out 2004.

A *Billboard* wrap-up of events in country 2003 showed the previous year's slide may have been just a blip, and Urban had played his part in this upswing. In fact, the year had set new records for country touring in America, with the genre's leading nine acts generating some US$266 million in grosses at the turnstiles. Urban had been a drawcard on the monstrous Kenny Chesney tour, which grossed US$36.7 million in 2003; these were huge numbers. *Billboard* ranked Urban among the 'breakthrough acts [that] are moving up', along with the likes of Chris Cagle and Montgomery Gentry, 'breaking' acts that were muscling in on the territory of such established singers as Dwight Yoakam, Vince Gill and Trisha Yearwood. Urban was perfectly positioned to quickly move up to the lucrative casino circuit, and his next step would be straight into the arenas. And this time, unlike on the Chesney tour, he could bring along the band.

Despite the obvious compromises he'd made to reach this new high, there's no doubt Urban was enjoying the ride. He was living in the bus, on the road, with his only reminders of the 'real world' being Christmas, New Year and other holidays when the family guys in his crew would head home to share some time with their kids and partners. 'When you're touring, it's wonderful,' Urban said, in transit yet again, 'because you're always on the move.'

> I would love to be married. I would love to have children. But you have to make sacrifices in a relationship, and I feel that one would suffer – my relationship or my career. And this is my home, out here, in the middle of nowhere. [I wouldn't want] to give it up for anybody, or anything.[13]

Urban was true to his word, at least for the time: his romance with supermodel Taylor was stop–start at best, and he hadn't yet met up with a certain Aussie golden girl.

★

Knoxville, Tennessee hell–raiser Kenny Chesney was proving to be a useful touchstone for Urban, both on–stage and off. Commitment-free for a few days in early January 2004, and just back from Christmas in Australia with his folks, Urban didn't quite know what to do with himself so he called his big-hatted buddy Chesney and headed down to the Caribbean. Drinking and hanging out was all well and good, but the pair couldn't resist an impromptu jam session, much to the surprise of the holiday-makers kicking back at the same hotel. The pair stepped up to the pokey stage and howled their way through AC/DC's 'Ride On' and Aerosmith's 'Sweet Emotion', as well as belting out 'Act Naturally', the Buck Owens song once crooned by Beatles drummer Ringo Starr. Urban wouldn't let on, but maybe he related to the lyrics:

> We'll make the scene about a man that's sad and lonely
> And beggin' down upon his bended knee
> I'll play the part but I won't need rehearsin'
> All I have to do is act naturally.

The best way to avoid such self-analysis, of course, was to keep moving and Urban did just that, heading back out with Chesney on his 'Guitars, Tiki Bars & a Whole Lotta Love' tour, which kicked off mid March in Houston and generated yet another spike in *Golden Road* sales. But Urban did make one concession to the real world, finally buying a house in Nashville, the first home that this serial-renter-cum-gypsy ever owned. Workaholic that he was, Urban's first consideration was this: 'Can I make music here?' He definitely could; the spacious and sparsely furnished spread had the perfect spot for a home studio and Urban set to work designing the ultimate music room. 'That [studio] will come before anything gets furnished,' he promised, and stayed true to his word.[14]

Already, Urban Inc was mapping out another album. In modern-day Nashville it was all about seizing the moment, riding the zeitgeist – the five years or more that elapsed between LPs from such rock acts as U2 was an act of madness in Music City, a sure-fire one-way trip to the bargain bins. Urban was right when he said that he was now knee-deep in a business where tastemakers – and fans – 'change sides so fast'. There was no better way to keep people listening than by continuing to tour and pump out new records over a roughly 18-month cycle. Urban, with Dann Huff once again signed on as producer, headed back to the studio in February before yet more road-tripping with Chesney in March and April.

There were any number of reasons why someone in Urban's position returned to the studio so quickly, as Nashville commentator Dan Daley told me:

> Historically, country records take little time to make compared to rock records, the Ramones excepted. From the late 1960s – the beginning of the 'modern' era – through the 1980s, it was common to see entire albums done in a week, maybe two. This was driven by money, of course. The A-Team musicians – the so-called 'Nashville cats' – had developed a workflow that had them doing three three-hour sessions a day, and they expected to knock out three songs per session.
>
> In the 1990s, with the rise of country as more of a pop proposition, records became slicker, in part because production values increased. That required more time, of course, but not as much as it might take in other genres. The fact that country artists generally still 'track' records with live ensemble playing means that the workflow is inherently faster. If the creative decisions are limited to the artist and the producer – who is still likely to be a label exec, like Tony Brown, for instance – the decisions are made faster and there's no waiting for input from the label. And country has always had a conventional wisdom of heavy touring to promote

records and build a fanbase that would last them for decades –
it's country's Social Security, so to speak. As long as you're out
[on the road], sell as many records as you can make.

Firstly, though, there was a key event for Urban to celebrate,
namely his debut headlining show at Nashville's Ryman Auditorium. This historic venue first threw open its doors in 1892
when it was known as the Union Gospel Tabernacle. Urban,
admittedly, played and filled the 'new' Ryman, located just
outside the Opryland USA Theme Park, which was opened in
the early 1990s, but the venue's pews served as a reminder
that this was once a house of worship. It was now used to
'worship' country music, Nashville's second-biggest industry
outside of God. To regulars, the Ryman was known as 'The
Mother Church of Country Music', one of the reasons Neil
Young chose the stately venue for his 2006 concert film *Heart
of Gold*. And a little of the old Ryman lived on in the new
venue, quite literally: a one and a half-metre chunk of the stage
had been removed from the original venue and inlaid into
the new stage floor. As country music institutions go, there was
none more venerable than the Ryman, and it was the ideal
place for Urban to wind down the frenetic year and a half since
Golden Road dropped. The sense of history wasn't lost on
Urban who, despite his bump up to the A-list, remained a
country music fan at heart.

Be Here, which reached the stores in September 2004, could
well have been titled *Golden Road Revisited*. The album was a
textbook case of treading water creatively and offering up
more of the same commercially; the key philosophy appeared
to be: 'Why fuck with the formula?' (Or, more harshly put:
'Same crap, different wrapper.') Urban and producer Huff had

locked into a hugely profitable country-pop formula with *Golden Road* and decided to not stray from that platinum-plated path, providing another steady balance of shiny rockers, weepy ballads and hand-on-heart emotions, heavy on the clichés and light on true revelation. Even the album titles: the Zen-like *Be Here*, the 12-Step-ish *Golden Road*, had a similarly upbeat, we-can-make-it-if-we-try kind of feel. At the top of Urban's reading list at the time was *The Power of Now: A Guide to Spiritual Enlightenment*, Eckhart Tolle's runaway bestseller, a work of pop psychology that was reflected in Urban's choice of album titles. Tolle implores the seeker to 'feel the power of this moment and the fullness of Being. [Author's caps.] Feel your presence.'[15] Depending on whom you believe, the Deepak Chopra-endorsed tome is either an essential guide to spiritual enlightenment or a long-winded ramble, top-loaded with 'New Age mumbo jumbo' that 'did not live up to its hype . . . 191 pages full of the same idea phrased with different words,' according to one heretic at www.amazon.com. Urban leaned towards the former, although it's uncertain whether he was ready to shell out the requisite five bucks to buy a photo of Tolle from his website.

Sometimes it seemed as though even the tracks on both albums were interchangeable. For tunes, Urban had turned to a lot of the same writers and co-writers from his previous long-players, including Rodney Crowell, Monty Powell and John Shanks. On first listen many of the songs already seemed strangely familiar: 'Days Go By', one of numerous hits from the record, seemed like an upgrade of 'Somebody Like You', while 'Making Memories of Us' – the song Urban would croon to Nicole Kidman at their wedding – was basically 'Your Everything' (Redux). (It wasn't lost on Urban that the two ballads recognised as his signature tunes – 'Your Everything' and 'Making Memories' – were written by others.) 'God's Been

Good to Me' was effectively a variation on 'Who Wouldn't Wanna Be Me', both in subject matter and mood. Even the selection of studied Urban portraits that dotted *Be Here*'s CD sleeve seemed like out-takes from *Golden Road*: the modern country artist as sensitive beefcake. Urban's ubiquitous designer stubble and a shot of him astride his Harley suggested a hint of danger, but nothing that would scare off his more conservative fans. Urban and his label Capitol used the same art director, hair and makeup person – even the same 'digital imager' – on the album artwork sleeve for both *Golden Road* and *Be Here*. And numerous musicians, including drummer Chris McHugh, bassist Jimmie Lee Sloas and keyboardist Tim Akers, also played on both records. It felt as if one super-sized LP had been split neatly into two pieces.

Admittedly, there were a couple of new creative twists with solo record number three. Urban had become friends with Richard Marx, a one-time big-haired pop wailer, best known for the 1989 hit 'Right Here Waiting'. But what wasn't so well known about the Chicago-born Marx was that prior to his MTV makeover he'd been a tunesmith-for-hire, pumping out hits for Kenny Rogers and Chicago. Marx could also be heard providing backup vocals on Lionel Richie's 'All Night Long' and 'Running with the Night'. He even contributed a song to the soundtrack of *Staying Alive*, the not-so-successful sequel to *Saturday Night Fever*. While on the set he met, and later married, Cynthia Rhodes, John Travolta's female lead in the film. Like many of the singer/strummers with whom Urban worked, Marx was a journeyman – a 'pop-rock pro', according to one critic – albeit with his share of gold and platinum records. And just like Urban, Marx was hardly the critic's choice; *Rolling Stone* used the words 'glib', 'sappy' and 'hard to take', all within the one review of his 1989 long-player *Repeat Offender*.

Marx and Urban had tried co-writing earlier on in Nashville, but no sparks flew. Then Marx invited Urban 'out to the house' – Marx had a sizeable spread on the outskirts of Chicago – and this time some serviceable melodies were forthcoming. The ever-superstitious Urban brought with him his banjo, 'which seems to be a good luck charm for me'. Once settled in Marx's music room, Urban began to pick and pluck over the top of a drum loop and the song 'Better Life' gradually emerged. Urban was so smitten with the tune that, for a time, it was the working title of the album. 'I thought of calling the album "Better Life" because everybody wants one,' Urban figured, reasonably enough.[16]

On *Golden Road*, Urban had written with Rodney Crowell, his admirer from back in The Ranch days. They didn't get the chance to co-write for its follow-up, but Larry Willoughby, an exec at Capitol, gave Urban a heads-up about a Crowell song called 'Making Memories of Us' which Crowell had written as a Valentine gift for his wife Claudia. Urban was wary – he knew that cutting a Crowell song was walking on what he called 'sacred ground' – but he fell for this starkly romantic ballad in the same way he'd gone gaga over 'Your Everything'. (For 13 years, Crowell was married to Johnny Cash's daughter Roseanne, which made him American music royalty by association.) But according to Urban, there was 'something gritty and sexually romantic about the song' that he could not resist – and he knew that the many gushing females in his audience would eat it up, too. Urban and Huff struggled with it in the studio, making several passes at it without much luck. Then Crowell came into a session and sat through Urban's latest attempt. From the other side of the glass, Crowell liked what he heard and gave it his seal of approval: the two thumbs up. 'I was very grateful for that,' Urban understated afterwards.[17]

Some of the other tracks on *Be Here* came from peculiar situations. The melody for 'She's Gotta Be' hit Urban while he was waiting in a green room to do a promotional double-header, appearing on both the *Sharon Osbourne Show* and *The Tonight Show*. He liked the melody enough to put a call through to his answering machine at home and play it down the line, just for safe storage. He plucked 'Tonight I Wanna Cry' from the file marked 'old tunes' – he and Monty Powell had written it a few years earlier. It was one of two tracks on *Be Here* that hinted at a certain battle with the bottle, as Urban sang how he was 'drunk enough to cry'. '[That] is perhaps not something my sponsor would endorse,' Urban accepted, 'but that's where I was when I wrote the song.'[18]

The second boozing song on the album, however, was more interesting. Matraca Berg and Jim Collins wrote 'Nobody Drinks Alone', but they just might have penned it with Urban in mind. At least he seemed to think so. Urban freely admitted to 'being that guy in the song . . . being in that place'. Urban felt 'Nobody' spoke to those who needed to be:

> . . . accountable for your actions in this life. The point is that no matter where you are, and what you are doing, there's always another presence. Call it your conscience, call it God, whatever you will, but it can be what you need to turn to when you're doing less than healthy things.[19]

Using the mix of songs and subjects on *Be Here* as an indicator of Keith Urban circa 2004, he may have been packing rooms and shifting shitloads of product, but he was unlucky in love and boozing too much. That could have been right on the money, too, judging by the manner in which he cradled a bottle of Coopers on the tour bus when talking with Australia's *60 Minutes* for a spot called 'Urban Cowboy', which had been filmed as *Golden Road* climbed the charts. At one point the camera zoomed in on Urban's beer bottle, not so subtly suggesting that *something* was happening here. In another interview from that time, he insisted he'd 'long kicked' using coke, but his addiction still lingered. 'I've had no desire for the longest time for any of that,' he said. 'Any addict will tell you that you never beat it. [But] I know where I'm at. God knows where I'm at.'[20] Drinking, however, wasn't mentioned. And a meltdown was in the wind, although it was still a little while off.

Another interesting inclusion on *Be Here*, and yet another suggestion that this record, too, was rushed out the studio door, was his cover of Elton John's 'Country Comfort', a highly hummable slice of faux-country that dated way back to 1971. But Urban came to the song from a peculiar direction: he first heard it on Juice Newton's 1981 LP *Juice*, which the teenage Urban had grabbed specifically for her hit cover of the uber-weepie 'Angel of the Morning'. 'My version is probably a combination of Juice's and Elton's,' said Urban. 'Purists will freak out, but that's just the way it is.'[21] Its inclusion on *Be Here* made a strange kind of sense: it was a sweet tune about 'country comfort and a truck that's goin' back home', with a cast of preachers and grandmas, first recorded by an Englishman hung up on America and now covered by a Nashville obsessive from Caboolture. Why not? The paths of Urban and Elton would cross soon enough, too.

There were deeply felt emotions throughout *Be Here* – Urban was in an especially humble mood, deferring to his 'better half', owning up to a tendency to drink his troubles away, confessing that 'tonight I wanna cry', and more. But it seemed as though he stored his gushiest outpourings for his co-producer Dann Huff (and studio go-to guy, engineer Justin Niebank, whom Urban nominated as 'my right-hand man').

Coming clean in the album liner notes, Urban offered this fulsome shout-out: 'You have both inspired me constantly throughout the making of this album, not just as musicians, but as husbands, fathers, friends and brothers' – technically, Urban was only two of those – '[and] I've learned so much from you and feel so blessed that God saw fit for this time of our lives to intersect.' To which Huff replied: 'Thank you from the bottom of my heart for including me in your life and on your musical journey. I am honoured to be your co-producer and a brother.'[22] Their love-in read more like an Oscars acceptance speech than the usual checklist of thank-yous found on most LPs. Urban and Huff were a winning combination, and both seemed especially grateful to have hooked up. There's no doubt that their respective financial advisers thought so, too.

As flawed as *Be Here* was, the 'larger' music media were now starting to pay attention. Even *Rolling Stone*, who'd ignored everything that came before, were now reviewing Urban. 'Urban's "You'll Think of Me" was the best breakup song of the year in any genre, a carefully detailed evisceration of a petulant ex,' wrote Jon Caramanica in their 25 November 2004 edition.

> He turns the cruel lens on himself with 'The Hard Way', the starkest track on *Be Here*. His fifth album's main fault: most of it is saddled by stubbornly traditional country-rock arrangements ('Days Go By', 'Better Life') that worked for, say, John Mellencamp, but that Urban doesn't quite have the gravel pipes to roughen up.

This three-star review didn't praise the Urban Cowboy to the heavens and back but, as any savvy manager would tell you, better to be noticed and slammed than completely overlooked.

Others were more generous. Writing for www.amazon.com, Bob Allen drew an interesting parallel:

Keith Urban, hot off the double-platinum success of his 2002 sophomore album, *Golden Road*, is kind of like contemporary country's Tom Cruise. The kid is just so unjustly talented, likeable and good-looking that it's hard not to hate him. But such jealousy is apt to melt into begrudging admiration and affection after a quick listen to this third album.

Sue Keogh reviewed the album for www.BBC.co.uk, and she took a more Anglophilic approach, calling Urban 'the David Beckham of country music'.

As far as the record's commercial potential was concerned, www.allmusic.com's William Ruhlmann summed it up pretty neatly in his review:

> Keith Urban has been a consistent presence in the Top Ten of the country singles charts since 2000, scoring eight consecutive entries as of the release of his third US solo album, *Be Here*, the eighth being the disc's lead-off track, 'Days Go By'. And there's plenty more where that came from. The album has a distinct storytelling arc, beginning with the carpe diem sentiments of 'Days Go By' and continuing into a series of songs that celebrate life and love, notably Rodney Crowell's unabashedly romantic 'Making Memories of Us', which finds Urban doing his best Crowell imitation.

While many of his country contemporaries were ripping each other off – Aussie Lee Kernaghan seemed to specialise in making localised versions of hit American records, virtually song-for-song – Urban, to his credit, was copying the masters, as he'd been doing for years.

Promotionally speaking, all the pieces once again fell into place for Urban during the lead-up to *Be Here*'s due date. During June 2004 he fulfilled a life-long dream by sharing the stage with Glen Campbell at the CMA Music Festival. This wasn't long after his introduction to Campbell, arranged by

Barry Coburn, and their subsequent songwriting session, the results of which are yet to be heard by the public. (Coburn also helped get Urban into the studio with Campbell's song-writing touchstone, Jimmy Webb, upon Urban's request. When they met, Webb asked Urban: 'You're from New Zealand? I love New Zealand.' It turns out that he headed south every time the America's Cup was staged there. The song they wrote while gathered around a rented grand piano was duly recorded by none other than Glen Campbell, and awaits release.) Soon after, Urban hosted his annual Fan Club party, at the Ryman Auditorium, a well-meaning fundraiser for his charity of choice, Nashville's St Jude Children's Research Hospital. It was also a chance for a dozen lucky Urban nuts – active members of his on-line community 'Monkeyville' – to get in on the action. Their ticket numbers were drawn, which meant they got to hang out on stage, wailing backup vocals as Urban smiled his way through an hour-long set.

But it was in September that the serious business of Keith Urban Inc was cranked up a notch. 'Days Go By', the album's lead single, hit the charts with the same velocity as 'Somebody Like You', generating yet another country number one, his fourth. It was in its fourth week at the top when *Be Here* reached the stores; the LP shifted 148,000 copies in its first week – huge sales – and topped the country album chart as well as leaping into the third position on the all-important *Billboard* Top 200 chart. Its race to the top was only halted by Green Day's *American Idiot* and Nelly's *Suit*. Who wouldn't wanna be him, indeed.

It was as natural as big hats worn with jeans for Urban to now headline his own tour, known imaginatively as Keith Urban Be Here '04, and sponsored by massively influential cable network CMT. In the wonderfully wacky world of cross-promotion, the tour featured something named CMT Cross Country, a 'star-studded red carpet' where fans could pose with their favourite stars – or at least life-sized cardboard cut-outs of same. Loving Urban's nose was one thing, but mugging for a snapshot with his cardboard facsimile indicated how high his star had risen.

And unlike some of his dates from 2002 and 2003, these shows filled houses. Wisely, the tour concentrated on smallish theatres; Be Here '04 opened in the 3280-seat Emens Auditorium in Muncie, Indiana and then stuck with similar-sized venues. Muncie was a sell-out, while subsequent gigs in Austin, Houston, Birmingham, Savannah, Atlanta, Pittsburgh and elsewhere either drew full, or near-full houses in venues that ranged from 2500 to 4500 capacity. Only in Cincinnati, Ohio, where Urban pulled just 2812 payers to a venue that held just over 6500, did he fail to connect at the box office. After another full house, this time at New York's wonderfully crusty Beacon Theater, the tour rolled through Milwaukee, Detroit, Cleveland and Louisville before winding down just prior to Christmas with two near-full houses at LA's Wiltern Theater, shows that were filmed for the *Livin' Right Now* DVD. Urban was now a very bankable live proposition: the nightly gross takings for each of these shows ranged from US$100,000 to a very healthy US$215,000 for a one-off at the E Center in West Valley City, Utah. He was on a roll.

Reporting from the road in Cincinnati, www.cmt.com stated pretty clearly what made Urban stand out from the pack – for one thing, his audience was roughly 80 percent female. But there was something else, something more substantial, at work here. 'Though it sounds ridiculous to say so, few country stars are as focused on their music as Urban,' wrote Craig Shelburne.

Most of the time, the entertaining comes down to a few yells of 'how y'all doin'?' and some eye-popping video clips in the background. But Urban relies on rhythm, crowd energy and a band that enhances his performance, rather than simply accompanies it.

While his crowds may have gone home happy, not everyone was convinced that Urban was 'delivering'. Two members of his Aussie contingent, Rob Potts and Kerry Roberts, joined the tour in Detroit and were less than impressed by what they witnessed. As Potts recalled, 'Kerry and I stood there going: "Hello?" He phoned it in.' They both knew that an uneasy encounter loomed with Urban as they joined him on the bus after the show, headed for Columbus, Ohio. Potts brought along a couple of bottles of top-shelf wine, which he figured would be necessary in order to make his point.

'I have this thing with Keith where I'll never bullshit him, *if he confronts me*,' Potts admitted. 'So my position that night was to talk about anything but the show.' But Urban knew something was up.

> We're on the bus, an hour and a half into the ride, we're drinking some wine and he leaned to me and said: '*OK, cunt, what didn't you fucking like about the show?*' I stumbled: 'Oh, erm, the crowd went nuts,' but he persevered. 'What the fuck was wrong with it?' He knew I'd tell him what I thought; Kerry too.
>
> I said, 'Well, what was special about your show tonight? What would I have gotten from that that I didn't get from the record? You played great, the sound was good, but you were closed off. Why aren't you giving these people the experience of being at a Keith Urban show?'

Urban didn't reply straight away, so Potts tried another tangent.

I asked him who his favourite front man was, and he said: 'Freddie Mercury'. I knew he had the *Queen Live at Wembley* tape with him; he always does. So we pulled it out and we watched it, and I said to him: 'Geez, you did a lot of that tonight mate, standing up on the foldback, conducting the crowd. *You're obviously paying attention to Freddie.*' And he sat there, going 'OK, OK.' He took it.

Then Kerry asked why didn't he talk to them. 'You're from Australia, find an anecdote that you can play with and change every night and tell every night. Connect.' The next night in Columbus, I fucking teared up; he blew me away. His performance went: 'BOOM!' From that point on he started putting his guitar down or slinging it behind his back, and started talking and pulling people out of the audience. A year later the difference was extraordinary; the shows got better, the reaction got better. The whole thing is that by surrounding yourself with 'yes' people, there's not that many people that have much impact or input. Gary [Borman] wouldn't be game to have that conversation with him. No way. What's 15 percent of $30 million a year? That's what he's got coming his way.

Freddie Mercury may have played his part in Keith Urban's live resurrection, as another hugely successful year wound down with a rousing gig in San Jose, California. But a totally different kind of superstar was about to enter Urban's life when he agreed to front at G'Day LA, a celebration of all things Australian, held in Los Angeles a few weeks later. Keith Urban was about to fall in love.

Eight

THE KURBANS

He whispered to me, 'She is the love of my life.'

Jeff Walker

The press release was appropriately grand. It read:

Urban Joins Gibson and Kidman to Celebrate Australia.

Keith Urban, actor Mel Gibson and actress Nicole Kidman will be honoured January 15 during a gala highlighting the second annual 'G'Day LA: Australia Week' in Los Angeles. The event at the Century Plaza Hotel honours Australians who have made significant international contributions. Set for January 15–23, Australia Week will showcase Australian food and wine, travel, film, arts, culture, fashion and business. It is produced through a partnership of the Australian Consulate in Los Angeles, the Department of Foreign Affairs and Trade, Tourism Australia, AusTrade and Qantas Airways.

This annual celebration of all things 'Aussie' was to be attended by the honourees and such expats as Cameron Daddo, with whom Urban had recorded way back when, plus Tommy Emmanuel, actors Geoffrey Rush and Cate Blanchett, ageless songbird Olivia Newton-John and the then Foreign Affairs Minister Alexander Downer (who claimed credit for introducing Urban and Kidman, but that simply wasn't the case). Julian McMahon was there, too, posing for photos with his mother, Sonia, Australia's erstwhile first lady.

As always, there was a back-story to this orgy of back-patting. The original idea had been to 'honour' Australians Mel Gibson, Nicole Kidman and Delta Goodrem. The former two honourees made perfect sense – they were now Oscar-winning members of Hollywood royalty – but Goodrem was way out of her league. She may have sold records in Farnham-like numbers back home, but she'd made no impression whatsoever in the far tougher US market. And what chance did she have? There was a conga line of Delta-like belters there already, most of whom packed big hair and even bigger voices, so why would they need an Australian over-emoter?

Urban supporter Kerry Roberts, a woman with a lot of pull at Channel Nine (which was involved with the event), realised that Urban was a far worthier recipient. Some intense lobbying by Roberts got her charge's name on the honourees' list at the last moment, at the expense of Goodrem, and justifiably so. *Be Here*, his latest record, was selling by the warehouse-load – it's currently at four million and counting – and had generated another three number one hits in 'Days Go By', 'Making Memories of Us' and 'Better Life'. He'd also recently claimed the Country Music Association award for Male Vocalist of the Year; Urban was the first non-American to be crowned country music's top dude. The mantelpiece of his Nashville spread, a home that set him back a handy US$1.7 million, was positively bulging under the weight of so many trophies and framed albums.

Walking the red carpet on the day of G'Day LA, Urban and Kidman were a study in contrasts: Urban 'styled up' for the occasion in a black velvet sports jacket and collared shirt, his ubiquitous three-day growth in place. Kidman, as ever, was coolly elegant in a strappy, glittery black dress cut just above the knee, her hair coloured a golden blonde. The event itself was a massive schmoozefest, conducted amid a strange collection of yellow-and-black road signs warning of kangaroos ahead, and posters depicting red sandy deserts; it was Hollywood via Ken Done with just a hint of Mambo.

Then the formalities began. Kidman was the first honouree to claim her gong, which was handed over by fellow thespian Cate Blanchett. Geoffrey Rush then 'honoured' Mel Gibson and, finally, Olivia Newton-John called Urban to the podium. He brushed his shaggy hair out of his eyes, thanked all and sundry, then headed for the safety of the bar. 'I did have a chat with him,' laughed Cameron Daddo, 'though I had nothing to do with their introduction.' In fact it was Kerry Roberts who introduced Urban to Kidman, and quite innocently set in motion a very public affair, although it took its own sweet time to develop.

The introduction Roberts made was brief; Kidman admitted that in the wake of her very public and hostile split from Tom Cruise she attended the event in a 'very wary, very damaged' state of mind, and was hardly responsive to a potential new suitor. In a recent interview she'd admitted that after the breakup with Cruise there was a period, as unlikely as it seemed, when she lived in her pyjamas for several months. 'I'd just like to meet a normal guy,' she said, somewhat presciently.[1] Kidman's date at G'Day LA was her ever-supportive sister Antonia. After their introduction, both Urban and Kidman were swept up in the 1000-plus crowd that filled the Century Plaza's ballroom; they spent very little time together on that first meeting. Urban then returned to the road – he had a run of shows in Florida at the end of the month, an episode of CMT's *Crossroads* to shoot with one of his idols, John Fogerty, and an all-star Grammys jam of 'Sweet Home Alabama' to participate in – but their paths would cross again before too long.

At first, Urban seemed a bit reluctant to 'hook up' with Kidman, despite the connection that existed between the two. He was consumed by a heavy touring and promo schedule; the gypsy world was still very much the only lifestyle to which he seemed suited. And Urban's wariness was understandable: surely he was asking himself, *why me?* Like so many in his profession, he was hardly the most self-assured of people. Now here he was daydreaming about a woman who'd been married to a Hollywood prince and who, it had been rumoured, had been involved with such heavyweight stars as Robbie Williams and Lenny Kravitz. She was a UNICEF ambassador, recently named Australia's richest young celebrity: her worth was valued at around US$120 million. (Chanel had recently forked over more than US$3 million for Kidman to star in a four-minute ad.) And Kidman came from good stock, literally; she was a descendant of Sir Sidney Kidman, who'd held vast land and livestock holdings in rural Australia. She was also an Oscar winner, for her portrayal of doomed author Virginia Woolf in the film *The Hours*, and was the mother of two children that she and Cruise had adopted. What could she see in a scruffy country-rocker from Caboolture, whose dad used to work at the local tip? (There are hard-to-prove rumours, incidentally, that it was Kidman who did much of the chasing, too.)

On paper they were one odd couple; with his three-day growth, shaggy hair and slight stoop, Urban looked like he'd just wandered in from the direction of an all-nighter at the Gympie Muster. The frail, pale, ice-cool Kidman – a well-educated, urbane woman raised on Sydney's North Shore –

looked so fragile that you feared she might snap at any minute. She was almost like a porcelain doll brought to life. One Urban colleague, who met 'the Kurbans' after a screening of the Rolling Stones movie *Shine a Light* – outside the Fox Studios toilets, oddly enough – backed that up. 'She's so pristine; she's like glass,' he told me. 'You're almost afraid to shake her hand for fear it might break.' But the more cynical could see why Urban appealed to Kidman: he was down to earth and rootsy, the poster boy for blue-collar folk; his working-class audience loved him for his 'realness'. He was the manifestation of that 'ordinary guy' Kidman was dreaming about, despite the interesting assortment of demons in his psychological closet. Meanwhile, Kidman's ex-husband had been jumping up and down on Oprah Winfrey's couch, shouting the name of his new love, Katie Holmes, like a mantra and talking up the 'wonders' of Scientology, all the while taking the air out of his stalled Hollywood career.

It was as if Urban and Cruise came from different planets. And, frankly, what better person was there to help Kidman (and her career) move on from Cruise, whom she'd divorced in February 2001, than a humble bloke who loved his guitar, his mum and his Harley? (*Be Here*'s liner notes featured a snap of Urban astride his hog, which he'd bring along and ride while touring.) And as a career move for Urban, marrying a princess would surely help him shake off his bad-boy reputation. Clearly there were benefits for both of them. Those close to Kidman began to call Urban the 'anti-Tom'. Darlene Montgomery, a family friend who lived in LA, was one of many who thought this. 'Keith lives by a different set of rules,' she said in late 2006.

> Tom is very conservative and very concerned about appearances. When Nic was with him, she was often on edge. It

was a pressure-cooker situation . . . even the attention she received back then was different.[2]

That's not to downplay the fact that it was, at least in part, a love match. When they decided to make their relationship public, Urban and Kidman were spotted at a Nashville concert of Tommy Emmanuel, Urban's hero and one of his brotherhood of recovering addicts. Jeff Walker, another long-time 'booster', caught up with Urban backstage. He introduced his new lady friend, and then Urban pulled Walker aside. He had a confession to make. 'He whispered to me, "She is the love of my life,"' Walker told me.

> I was really happy for him and them both. I think Keith has found what he was looking for in the days when I was working closely with him. I think many industry insiders want it to work for him.

This Nashville show was one of many 'sightings' in the second half of 2005 of the couple dubbed the 'Kurbans', who referred to each other in private as 'Hank' and 'Evie', a tag they'd later use for their own fashion line of shoes, boxers, belt buckles, pyjamas and the like. In July there was a report of the unlikely sight of Kidman on the back of Urban's chopper, as they pulled out of a health food restaurant near Woodstock in upstate New York. (The idea of Kidman as a 'motorcycle mama' simply didn't equate with her poised persona; you could imagine her riding a horse perhaps, but not a hog.) Soon after, Urban and Kidman were spotted in Connecticut, the green and sleepy New England state that was called home by everyone from David Letterman to Keith Richards and Paul Newman, a wellheeled place that seemed more on Kidman's radar than that of her new beau.

This New England outing wasn't long after their first 'formal' date. In the spring, Kidman was in New York playing the role of photographer Diane Arbus in the film *Fur*, and got in touch with Urban, who was also in town. (This was a rare occasion when they were in the same place at the same time.) There was nothing especially outrageous about their date; they simply took a walk through Central Park. But a connection was very clearly made, especially for Kidman. Allegedly, she told a friend that Urban was 'hot, hot, hot', and asked someone to track down the nearly nude shots of him in *Playgirl*.

A few months later, Urban was forced off the road yet again when a blood vessel burst on his right vocal cord. But this time, rather than lock himself away with a whiteboard and marker pen for company, he and Kidman made some very public appearances in Nashville. They hung out at the Country Boy Restaurant in Leiper's Fork and then, closer to town, shared snowcones at Maggie Moo's Ice Cream Parlour. It was simply too cute for words, and evidence that they'd chosen Nashville (and, later on, Sydney) as their 'safe havens'. To attempt such a public wooing in Hollywood would have led to a paparazzi stampede, something Kidman was very happy to avoid. (She'd quite famously spoken of how she 'feared for her life' while being 'stalked' by celebrity photographer Jamie Fawcett. Urban would come off his Harley, on his way to an AA meeting, while being pursued by an Aussie paparazzo.)

Jewel Coburn, Urban's former employer at Ten Ten, was one of many Nashville insiders who sometimes bumped into them around town. They were just another country couple doing their shopping. Well, sort of. 'Here you can see them in coffee shops and bakeries in their baseball caps,' she told me.

> They're very down to earth. I think they feel comfortable here in Nashville. It's a big country town, really, in many ways. The

countryside is beautiful and the people are pretty normal. It's not like LA or New York.

'Raining on Sunday' co-writer Radney Foster, who laughingly called them Australia's 'Elvis and Priscilla', sensed that there is 'loads of goodwill' for the couple from Nashville's music biz elite. 'The nice part about Nashville and country music in general is that you run into people in the grocery store all the time,' Foster said.

> These are people who can afford to have someone else buy their groceries for them, or buy their coffee, but these guys walk into the Starbucks and buy their own. So far so good for them in this town, paparazzi wise. The culture of the people here is that they leave you alone. LA is filled with guys trying to work out how to make 500 bucks selling a photo. Nashville isn't filled with people like that. Part of it is demand, too: do people really want to see Martina McBride buying her groceries?

'They're together for all the right reasons and that's a great thing,' said Tommy Emmanuel, who has spent some lazy Sunday afternoons at Urban's home with the couple. 'The last time I saw them we had a BBQ at their house, and that was a lovely day.'

Despite numerous spottings, Urban and Kidman continued to play the PR game in the early stage of their romance, referring to each other as 'good friends', even when it was clear that what was brewing between them was 'a love thing'. When asked upfront by one reporter, 'What's with you and Nicole, anyway?', Urban coolly replied: 'Keeping your private life private is definitely a challenge, but it's one I'm maintaining as best as I can,' before smoothly changing subjects. Having spent the past five or so years churning out interview after interview, Urban had mastered the art of deflection.[3] 'I don't get caught up in the hoopla,' he said in another one-on-one, again steering the conversation elsewhere, politely but firmly.[4] Still, it should be said that a woman like Kidman was unlike any partner he'd previously been with; the differences between Kidman and Angie Marquis couldn't be expressed in words. Urban simply didn't know how to talk about their relationship.

James Blundell was one of many people to spot that, but he also knew that Urban could cope with the pressure. Since coming clean about his addictive ways, pretty much anything else would be easy. 'Without that I don't think Keith would have been in a position to cope with a relationship with the public visibility that he now has with Nicole,' he told me.

> After a time you really develop the skin of a rhino, but it can fuck people up. But I think he's coping brilliantly. And he does have a good sense of fuck you about him, so I was never expecting him to be the handbag. I think it's really balanced.

Tamworth tastemaker Nick Erby had another read on the relationship; he sensed that their casual public attitude was one of the reasons the Kurbans had been well treated by the press (although the media intensity would increase by many degrees pretty swiftly). 'It's their demeanour that says a lot,' he figured. 'There's no aggression; there's a polite "take your picture then please go away" attitude and for that reason we admire them and do our best to leave them alone.'

By late 2005, some very strong rumours began circulating in the usual media outlets that Urban had popped the question. The event took place while the pair dined at the upscale 1789 restaurant in Washington DC where they were toasting his 38th birthday and enjoying some rare Kidman downtime – she was in DC filming *The Visiting*. (The maitre d' had handed the resolutely down-market Urban a sports jacket to comply with the eatery's dress code.) Those in search of a bitchy angle noted that the pair might have been in a hurry to beat Cruise and Katie Holmes to the altar, but it didn't play out that way.

They were now, however, being far more open with their relationship. When the Urban *Be Here* roadshow reached Boston, Kidman breezed into town and they shared a fancy suite at the chic Fifteen Beacon Hotel, and were snapped strolling through the city, hand in hand. When the tour hit New York, a giddy Kidman was seen blowing her guy kisses from the front row. She also began sporting a hefty rock on her left hand; when asked from whence it came, she simply replied: 'My fiancé gave it to me.' All the deflections and denials in the world couldn't conceal that they were fast-tracking their way straight to the chapel of love.

The flipside of this, of course, was the emergence of the occasional carpetbagger seeking to cash in, especially those who'd been involved in Urban's seedy past. The lowest of all was a *Daily Mail* piece, delicately titled 'Nicole and the crack addict cowboy', which quoted various 'friends' whose grabs helped drive home the story's very defined angle: this wasn't a relationship built to last, and what the hell was such an angel doing with this sleazebag? 'Keith is still wild and always will be,' said one 'source'. 'He has looked into hell.' A 'musician friend' of Urban's (some friend) spilled on the singer's skirt-chasing ways. 'He's never been one to turn down a polite offer.' The same friend predicted that the Kurbans would last six months, tops. A less-than-subtle comparison was drawn between the couple and the recent failed marriage of Urban's big-hatted buddy, Kenny Chesney and Kidman's peer, actress Renée Zellweger, which came undone after only a few months. (There had been some successful Nashville/Holly-wood couplings – the marriage of Clint Black and Lisa

Hartman being one – but it was deemed best not to mention that.) 'Surely a girly heart–heart with Renée,' the piece concluded, 'might persuade Nicole that a home on the range might be more than she bargained for.'[5] And Zellweger did just that, albeit indirectly, advising Kidman to 'beware of cowboys' during an interview with an American newspaper. Kidman smiled and said nothing in response.

While all this speculation was going on, many overlooked the fact that Urban the music star was in the midst of probably his finest run yet. *Be Here*'s sales breezed past the two million mark while in late September, *Livin' Right Now*, the film of Urban's two-night stand at LA's Wiltern Theater, was granted a limited cinema release, quite an achievement in a time of straight-to-DVD releases. He also appeared at the Live8 show in Philadelphia, jamming the Rolling Stones' 'Gimme Shelter' with R&B princess Alicia Keys, a most unlikely musical pairing. Urban also turned up in a Gap ad campaign, belting out Billy Thorpe's Oz-rock staple 'Most People I Know Think That I'm Crazy', a song that would have drawn a blank with most American listeners. It said something about Urban's respect for Thorpe and Oz music that he insisted that the song be used. Urban was also on the bill of a Kenny Chesney concert in Pittsburgh that drew a massive audience of 54,133, the largest ever crowd for a strictly country show. It's fair to say that Urban helped place a few of those bums on seats.

Urban was also racking up yet more awards: a CMT Video of the Year gong for 'Days Go By'; ACM Album of the Year for *Be Here*; Top Male Vocalist at the Country Music Association awards. Soon after, he was handed the CMA's International Artist Achievement award during a ceremony at the Australian Consulate General's office in New York. It was a nod to those who helped spread the word of country beyond the city limits of Nashville; previous recipients included Dolly

Parton, Shania Twain and the Dixie Chicks. Most of the 100-odd people in attendance were Australians, and a beaming Billy Thorpe handed over the award to Urban. It was the best homecoming Urban could have without actually going home. 'It was a very special occasion for him,' said Jeff Walker.

While in New York, Urban attended the annual CMAs, held at the bunker-like Madison Square Gardens, smack dab in midtown Manhattan. Walker was also there, and acknowledges that it marked a significant week for country music, and Urban in particular. 'It was a big deal for the Nashville music industry,' he told me.

> It was really special and important for Keith as it showcased him in front of Madison Avenue, the advertising hub of the US, as well as the country music industry.

A few months earlier, Urban had signed a development deal with a film company called Melee Entertainment whose founder, Bryan Turner, had first found success with the hardcore rap act NWA. Although a script hadn't yet been written with Urban in mind, exposure to a larger audience couldn't harm his nascent acting career. He was a well-known, good-looking guy who was no stranger to the camera: of course he could become a movie star. At this point in Urban's unlikely rise, anything was possible.

Early in the night at the CMAs, Urban collected his second straight Male Vocalist of the Year award, but the capper on both a big night and a banner year for Urban was when he was crowned Entertainer of the Year, the CMA's equivalent of an Oscar. He nudged out big-hitters Alan Jackson, Toby Keith, Brad Paisley and his pal Kenny Chesney. Duly humbled, Urban said: 'I want to thank Kenny for being so good to us and for teaching me so much about entertaining.' Soon after, when asked yet again about his blossoming love affair, he shut down any conjecture, even though it was clear by now that Urban and Kidman were coupled. 'Well,' he said, 'I'm very grateful for this award and I'd hate to use up such valuable time discussing my personal life.' Conversation was over, as was Urban's most successful year to date.

When Urban was a kid, he'd belted out a Dolly Parton song during one of his appearances on the down-market talent show, *Pot of Gold* while Bernard King scoffed and looked on. Early in 2006, the larger-than-life Parton repaid the favour, in her own quirky way. Urban was hosting the annual Music City Jam, an invite-only event that kicked off the Country Radio Seminar. Midway through his set, Urban strummed an acoustic guitar as his band locked into an oddly familiar riff. 'It sounds like a Rolling Stones song,' Urban bluffed, and then said: 'All we need is a chick singer.' With that, Parton stormed the stage and powered her way through 'Jolene'. She and Urban then held their own on 'Two Doors Down', another Parton tune.

Afterwards, Parton was in a typically chatty mood, joking about her upcoming 40th wedding anniversary and how she maintained the heat in her boudoir. 'I make out with my husband and pretend it's Keith Urban,' she chuckled, before adding this snappy little bookend, directed at the man himself: 'And there's nothing you or your leggy girlfriend can do about it.'

During the early months of 2006 Urban was juggling yet again, doing his best to see Kidman whenever their schedules allowed, as well as touring and getting back into the studio. Nashville waits for no man, hatless or otherwise, and Urban was struggling to keep it all together. Leaving the studio one night, someone asked him what kind of record he was making. 'A polka album,' was his strange reply. He added:

The odd part is, when you're making a new record, you're going out on tour and doing all these old songs. And your head is very much in the new record. So that very side of it is very discombobulating.[6]

The working title of his fourth solo record for Capitol was *Love, Pain & the Whole Damned Thing*, a perfect commentary on his life, which was currently being lived in fast-forward.

In mid May, briefly in New York with Kidman for a UN gala – Urban was just back from New Orleans, where he inspected the carnage inflicted by Hurricane Katrina, a nod to his expanding social conscience – the couple finally revealed the entertainment world's worst-kept secret. When Kidman was asked about her 'boyfriend', Kidman corrected the interviewer: 'He's actually my fiancé,' she smiled. 'I wouldn't be bringing my boyfriend.' This particular cat was now well and truly out of the bag. Urban celebrated a few days later by screaming through the desert on a motorbike as part of an Academy of Country Music motorcycle ride. This time around Kidman declined the offer of a double.

Greg Shaw, the man ruthlessly cast aside by Urban a few years earlier, briefly re-entered his former charge's life in the days leading up to the Kurban nuptials on 25 June. Virtually every daily and gossip rag was sniffing out a cover story, and a writer from Perth's *Sunday Times* tracked down Shaw. Clearly, the resentment Shaw felt towards Urban was still pretty fresh, because he spoke frankly of how Urban would play shows while wasted ('He hated letting people down'), and referred to his sacking as being 'cast aside'. Curiously, despite evidence to the contrary, Shaw said that he 'was not the one taking drugs . . . or buying [Urban] drugs. I was the guy telling him to treat people nicely and be responsible for his behaviour.'[7] A number of sources interviewed for this book claimed they did in fact see Shaw taking coke with Urban.

Urban (and most likely Kidman, too) felt betrayed by Shaw. His name may have been on their wedding invite list before he spoke to the press, but he was duly bumped. I was told that at the time it's possible Urban was even considering 'making right' with Shaw and cutting him his long-overdue 'thank-you' cheque. That act of reconciliation was promptly removed from the schedule. The Catholic priest who was to conduct the ceremony, Father Paul Coleman, was also instructed to 'cool it' by the Kurbans when he quite innocently told a reporter that they were 'very much in love' and that the service would be short, sweet and simple. Kidman's heavy-hitting publicist, Wendy Day, was running the show with her usual assertiveness. Even a priest could be told (politely, of course) to put a sock in it.

Not since the Coffs Harbour wedding of Russell Crowe and Danielle Spencer has the Australia media gone into quite the frenzy that ensued when Urban and Kidman finally tied the knot. Three days before the wedding, Kidman's children, 13-year-old Isabella and Connor, 11, arrived from Tokyo by private jet, while such celebrity invitees as Hugh Jackman, Naomi Watts, Kylie Minogue, Russell Crowe and Baz Luhrmann were seen in and around the harbour city, dusting off tuxes and trying on gowns. Urban's parents flew into Sydney, as did Capitol label head, Mike Dungan; Urban's attorney, Ansel Davis; and his financial adviser, Mary Ann McCready. His manager Gary Borman also arrived, likewise Anastasia Pruitt, his co-manager from the days of The Ranch, plus producer Dann Huff, Urban's 'right-hand man', engineer Justin Niebank, drummer Chris McHugh and co-writers Darrell Brown and Monty Powell. Urban's bassist from way back, Marlon Holden, who was a groomsman, came down from Queensland; he was one of the few guests on either side who was neither a celebrity nor someone from the entertainment 'biz', which begged the question: 'Don't they have normal friends?' Urban's brother Shane was set to be his best man. Antonia Kidman was to be her sister's maid of honour; daughter Isabella was a bridesmaid and Kidman's niece, Lucia, a flowergirl.

The ceremony took place on the Sunday night, at the Cardinal Cerretti Memorial Chapel near Manly's St Patrick's College. Slightly uncomfortable in his black tux with a white vest, Urban, who'd spent his buck's night at a soccer international at the Sydney Football Stadium, arrived in a silver Beemer with his brother and strolled in a side door, barely noticed by the sizeable crowd that had gathered outside. Dozens of police officers and security guards patrolled the area but the crowd was curious, not threatening. Some local volunteers who helped with traffic control, braved the chill in order to show off their 'Nicole and Keith' T-shirts. The bride rocked up in a cream Rolls Royce limo with a fleet of media helicopters swooping in their wake, like a scene straight out of *Apocalypse Now*. Kidman, in a white Balenciaga gown, was her usual sleek, stylish self, clutching a bouquet of white roses and working the crowd as she would a red carpet, oblivious to the choppers. 'You are beautiful,' screamed one onlooker to Kidman. 'You are all beautiful,' she replied, before heading inside the chapel, which was decorated with thousands of lit candles, white lilies and white orchids.

Father Coleman was right on the money; the ceremony itself seemed to end in a heartbeat. Urban's vows included the quite touching declaration: 'You make me feel like I'm becoming the man I was always meant to be,' which sounded as though it was lifted directly from one of his lyrics. (It wasn't.) At 6.25pm the chapel bells tolled for five minutes and everyone within earshot knew that the knot had been tied. The Hollywood princess and the 'Aussie stud' were now the Kurbans. (Later on, Hugh Jackman described it as a 'natural, loving, real Aussie wedding'.) At the reception, held in a huge marquee near the church, Neil Finn serenaded the newlyweds, while Urban couldn't resist the opportunity to belt out a tune himself, singing 'Making Memories of Us' directly to his bride, briefly forgetting about their 230 guests. There were no gifts on display; instead, the newlyweds asked their guests to fork over cash to their charity of choice.

Despite their ever-present smiles, and a few tears shed by both, the couple was very wary about giving too much away to the hungry press. They issued a simple statement: 'We just want to thank everyone in Australia and around the world who have sent us their warm wishes.' Rob Potts and Kerry Roberts, who were both wedding guests, thought it reasonable to say something to the assembled media and both provided 30-second grabs on the day, revealing little more than how wonderful Urban and Kidman looked, and how some people chose the chicken, others the fish. However, this unauthorised move didn't sit well with the Kurbans; when the newlyweds returned to Nashville after their Pacific Island honeymoon, both Roberts and Potts were chastised and neither remains on his payroll.

Gary Borman emailed Potts some time later, simply asking: 'Can you please take my artist off your website,' thereby severing another long, close and fruitful relationship. Potts, who has said elsewhere in this book that Urban would remove people 'in a heartbeat' if they were impeding the forward momentum of his career, now has no ill feelings towards Urban, although that wasn't always the case. 'I intrinsically believe that Keith is a lovely person,' he told me in mid 2008.

The entire Kurban affair had an interesting effect on Urban's career. Leading up to their high-profile romance, he was known locally as 'that country singer', a slightly scruffy-looking guy who was doing OK in the States but wasn't heard much on Australian radio. ('Isn't he big in Tamworth?' seemed to be the standard question.) Yet suddenly he was the partner of 'our Nic' – a celebrity by association. While Urban had a reasonable grasp on fame – and he was a solid-gold star in the USA – becoming a 'celebrity' was an entirely different trip. Now his life would be judged not so much by what new record he had in the stores or his next show, but by where he was last photographed with his new wife, what they were wearing, doing, drinking, whatever. It was nothing new for Kidman, who'd had her own close encounters with the paparazzi, especially after her run-in with lensman Jamie Fawcett and the ensuing court case, but until now Urban had been able to live his off-stage life in relative privacy. That just wasn't the case anymore. As someone who knew him reasonably well told me, 'Keith now looks like a rabbit trapped in the headlights.' Magazines that typically wouldn't touch a country musician now saw him as worthy of the front page. It was pretty insulting, really; the underlying message was that marrying Kidman was the only newsworthy achievement of Urban's life.

It'd be fair to describe Kidman and Urban as workaholics, and neither could stay away from their respective careers too long. Within two weeks of their wedding, Urban put in a cameo with Kenny Chesney at a stadium show at LP Field in Nashville. Duly warmed up, by 13 July he was back on the road, playing to a full house in Ontario, Canada, with Kidman watching from side-stage. A few nights later, back in the USA, Urban began his set by playing 'Days Go By' as he ran down a 23-metre-long catwalk, which led him deep into the crowd. Even the pouring rain – Urban dropped in a few bars of Creedence's 'Who'll Stop the Rain' as a nod to the unkind weather gods – didn't prevent the 30,000 crowd from going apeshit.

Within a few weeks Urban was well and truly back on the rollercoaster. He had more dates to play, but was also talking up his new album – whose title had been modified to *Love, Pain & the Whole Crazy Thing*, in order not to offend his conservative fanbase – at the same time. 'Once in a Lifetime', the lead single, was an instant smash, becoming the highest-charting country single in Billboard's 62-year history, reaching number 17 during its week of release.

In early October, Urban played a show at the Fox Theater in Atlanta. It was a typically rock-solid set, but Urban seemed physically drained; there was a faraway look in his eyes that suggested he was running on a tank that was pretty close to empty. A couple of weeks later, Kidman was in Europe, filming *The Golden Compass*, when Urban finally came undone, losing himself one night on a major bender. (And only once, incidentally; he'd been straight since he got involved with Kidman.) When Kidman was advised of what happened, it was pretty clear what needed to be done. Kidman called her publicist Wendy Day and put it to her straight. 'Wendy,' she said, 'I'm standing by Keith and that's all I have to say [publicly].'[8] Kidman returned to the USA as Urban checked into the Betty Ford Clinic in California on 19 October – a place with 'a really good, solid program', according to Tommy Emmanuel. 'I deeply regret the hurt this has caused Nicole and the ones that love and support me,' said Urban in a hastily arranged press release.

> One can never let one's guard down on recovery, and I'm afraid that I have. With the strength and unwavering support I am blessed to have from my wife, family and friends, I am determined and resolved to a positive outcome.

Urban's timing was appalling – a new album was set to drop, his single was climbing the charts, he was due back in Oz for an ARIAs cameo – on so many levels, Urban's fuck-up couldn't have been more poorly arranged. But it may well have been his gridlocked schedule and life on the straight and narrow that brought him undone. Rob Potts backed this up:

> Look at it in sequence: the album is set to come out, he's just gotten married to Nicole, he goes out, gets fucked up, has a night that's denied by all and sundry. He got told very early in that relationship that being out of it wouldn't make that relationship work. You only have to let your guard down once or twice and it can come back and bite you bigtime. [There were rumours of a hefty pre-nup, which basically hinged on Urban's ability to stay on the wagon. Wags dubbed it the 'no fuck-ups' clause.]
>
> He made the record before he went to rehab, but he made it while adjusting his lifestyle to go forward and fit with that relationship. Look at that record and it hasn't performed as well as some of the others and his on-stage persona has changed.

In an interview close to the time of his relapse, Urban hinted at some difficulty adapting to his new, clean life. As he said:

> It's a struggle for me, because I hate the straight road. I find it monotonous and boring. I like to dip my toe in the water – but not too far. That is where the trouble begins.[9]

And all the public scrutiny of his marriage clearly would have messed with Urban's peace of mind. When *Interview* magazine arranged a sit-down with 'celebrity interviewer' Elton John, just prior to the album appearing, John's first question was hardly the softball Urban was hoping for. 'Some of [your new songs] seem to be specifically about Nicole,' John mused.

Urban spun his way through the heart-to-heart with the former Reggie Dwight – he was a big fan, for starters – but he must have been thinking: Couldn't one person ask me about my songs, rather than my wife?

Potts was absolutely right about *Love, Pain & the Whole Crazy Thing*. *Be There* may have felt like *Golden Road Revisited*, but *Love, Pain* was a poor relation to both albums. The songs were solid, the playing was slick, the production slicker still. But the entire album failed to leave any kind of emotional mark, maybe with the exception of the thunderous power ballad 'I Can't Stop Loving You', which included some arena-sized soloing from Urban. Urban and the ubiquitous Dann Huff had truly 'phoned it in'.

Potts summed up the attitude of a lot of people who know Urban when he told me this: the straight life might be good for Urban's sobriety and his marriage, but it has dulled his creative edge. 'I'm very sceptical about enforced rehab on creative talent,' he said.

> The path out of addiction is to maintain the lifestyle in this flat spot, and to remove the highs and lows from the creative spirit. All that remains is a rhythm track. Why do you enjoy it? is the next question. What drives you to get fucked up? There's a whole bunch of issues with every person but what you have to look at it with a really creative guy like Keith, and Tommy [Emmanuel], is that you start fucking with what makes them unique at any level. Ultimately you fuck with the creative juice and we're seeing that with Keith right now.

Kidman definitely exerted a heavy influence over Urban. It's clear that she was extremely supportive of his decision to go back into rehab after just one slide; certainly she wanted her husband to dry out, but the damage that a second dud marriage could inflict on her career didn't bear thinking about. There have also been strong suggestions that she 'encouraged' her husband to sever ties with some of his Australian friends and colleagues in order to distance himself from those who knew him during his notorious 'fucked-up' past. In an unfortunate coincidence, Angus Hawley, Kidman's brother-in-law, also entered rehab soon after Urban, spending several weeks at the Sydney Clinic, which specialised in drug addiction and mood disorders. (He and Antonia Kidman separated soon after.)

It didn't help that another carpetbagger soon emerged, claiming that she'd partied hard and long with Urban as recently as May 2006, just a month before his wedding. Amanda Wyatt was a 23-year-old Nashville good-time girl whose story was swallowed whole by UK paper *The Mail on Sunday*, based on a few flimsy 'facts': Wyatt had a backstage snap of herself and Urban; she knew the security code for his house; and was familiar with his cologne and body wash. 'Keith was always high on something,' she said. '[He told me] I have this huge gaping hole inside of me I just can't fill.' She talked of his sometimes 'sexual' text messages and Urban's longing for a child. 'Maybe he came to Nashville and partied with me,' Wyatt figured, 'because he could do things with me he couldn't do with Nicole.'[10] As dodgy as her story seemed, it still scored plenty of damaging column space. It read like a sordid, X-rated companion piece to the 'Nicole and the crack addict cowboy' article that had surfaced before they wed. Urban's shady past appeared to be always lingering in the background, ready to be dusted off whenever he messed up.

The original plan was for Urban to undergo the standard 30-day spell in rehab, just as he'd done back in 1998. While it would delay the promotion of his new record, it wouldn't overly harm its inevitable success; in fact, the mainstream attention he was now receiving while detoxing might actually increase interest in the record. Urban walked through the gates of the Betty Ford Clinic without his guitar, quite deliberately, in an effort, as he later revealed, 'to focus on the inward journey'. In the same way that his friend Tommy Emmanuel gave himself over to God during his recovery, Urban totally embraced the 12 Steps program. 'The night I went in,' he said, 'it was total surrender. I just thought: "Let's do it, and let's do it right this time."' As Urban's people hastily rejigged his promo and touring schedule, his wife holed up in LA with her girl pal and fellow Aussie Naomi Watts.[11]

Capitol and Gary Borman must have gone into a spin, however, when mid November rolled around and Urban told them he was extending his stay at the clinic by another 30 days. Capitol boss Mike Dungan made the dignified comment that 'we just want him to get healthy,' but Urban's album had been one of the label's key pre-Christmas releases and now they didn't have a star to promote the whole crazy thing. Reluctantly, they decided to release the LP sans Urban – and it debuted at number three in the USA and number one in Australia. (Although, admittedly, it wouldn't have the staying power of *Golden Road* and *Be Here*.) Urban, seemingly, was so chuffed that he added a further 30 days to his 'residency' at the Betty Ford Clinic.

Bob and Marienne Urban may have maintained their 'no comment at any time' policy, but that didn't extend to other members of the Urbahn family, who spoke quite freely when asked about their famous nephew's misadventures. Paul Urbahn heard on the radio about Keith's relapse and confessed that 'it was a bloody shock'. His brother Brian was more blunt. 'Well, he's done it before, hasn't he? It didn't fix him. Why should it work the second time?'[12] At a time when the support of his family was essential, this wasn't quite the vote of confidence Urban needed.

Urban's physical absence, however, didn't seem that much of a hindrance to his career. On 6 November, he had been sched- uled to appear at the CMAs but was, of course, 'indisposed'.

Nonetheless, he was awarded his third straight Male Vocalist of the Year gong. Ronnie Dunn, who'd duetted with Urban on *Love, Pain*'s frenetic bonus track, 'Raise the Barn', stepped forward and read a statement prepared by Urban. 'I'm pained not being here with you all tonight,' he read, as a silence descended over the Gaylord Entertainment Center in downtown Nashville.

> My deepest appreciation and thanks goes to the Country Music Association, country radio, country music TV for this award. To my wife Nicole, I love you. And to my friends and family and to all of the Monkeyville community, for your love and faith, I thank you from the bottom of my heart, and I'm looking forward to coming home and seeing you all soon. God bless you.

Then Dunn grabbed the trophy and walked off-stage. The sales of *Love, Pain* spiked accordingly, shifting 270,000 copies during the week of 16 November.

Urban was allowed 'day leave' from Betty Ford, and there were occasional sightings in the latter months of 2006: he lunched with Kidman at the Polo Lounge in Beverly Hills and they both headed to Australia for Christmas, the couple's first homecoming since their June wedding. But upon returning to the US he disappeared once again behind the clinic's gates, finally re-emerging in mid January. Rather than sitting through a series of uncomfortable interviews, Urban cut a video that was posted on www.keithurban.net on 22 January. Looking far fresher than he did a few months earlier, Urban seemed by turns contrite, humbled, frank and positive during a lengthy address that had all the intimacy of a confession, despite the occasional lapse into recovery-speak.

'I just wanted to take a moment today to talk a bit about the last three months,' Urban said, looking straight down the barrel of the camera.

On 19 October, I checked into the Betty Ford Center in Palm Springs, California, with the support of my wife and family and friends, for what I thought was going to be a 30-day stay at Betty Ford.

Now, there was no big, cataclysmic event that happened right before I went in. But, what it was, was a lot of small things that were happening in my life, and a lot of small moments that were starting to accumulate that were telling me very loud and clear that I was a long way from my program of recovery, and they were making my life unmanageable.

I got to a point where I wanted to go into treatment, so I went in on that date. It was far from an ideal time to go into treatment. I want to say that much, too. While I was in there, of course, I had my birthday on 26 October, my record was released, I missed Thanksgiving and all the holidays. So, it was a time that had a lot of consequences, that particular three months.

The reason why it was so long, too, was just what I was learning as I stayed in there. That first 30 days, I learned what they say in there: abstinence is the ticket into the movie. It's not the movie. So, learning about abstinence was one thing, but then there was all this other area of my life to start learning about. So, 30 days became 60, 60 days became 90, and with each week that passed, I found myself really learning to surrender – especially with my career, with playing music – because it's what I've always done. I love playing guitar, I love touring and I was going to be doing a lot of that right when I went in.

But I had amazing support from everybody while I was in there that helped. I can't even tell you guys how much that helped me. I felt very, very, loved, and I felt very supported, and [it] made the time go by. I never felt alone. And, as I say, during that time, I started to learn a lot about myself and how I got to be in this position that I'm in right now.

And it's hard to quantify what I learned in 90 days, but suffice to say, it's been one of the most impactful times of my whole life. And I wanted to take this opportunity to thank everybody out there that's watching this right now for your support. I got cards, I got letters, I got emails when I finally got to my laptop and I could retrieve them all. There were hundreds of emails, and I just didn't expect that kind of support. I truly didn't, and it helped so much. Especially through a lot of the lonely days which there was plenty of those in there.

But my wife stayed extraordinarily strong and loving, and my friends and family were there, and, man, it's just been really overwhelming. I feel so much gratitude, and it feels really good to have gone through it and be where I am right now. Because where I am right now is starting on that road to getting back to doing what I love – which is playing music. And I'm looking forward to coming to your town to see all you guys and thank you personally for the support I've gotten. And I know I keep harping on that, but it's meant so much to me, and I wanted you guys to hear that from me personally. I look forward to seeing you guys very soon. And from the bottom of my heart, thank you, and God bless every one of you.

His statement read that it was now to be business as usual, and the Urban camp swiftly announced an international tour to begin in April, after a run of US shows commencing in Chicago on 8 February, which was another fundraiser for St Jude. (He'd make his 'proper' return to the road in June, playing a run of 36 dates in 33 US cities.) But a few days before a high-profile *Saturday Night Live* spot on 10 February, Urban became embroiled in a peculiar legal action that briefly took his mind off both his recovery and his upcoming publicity onslaught. A New Jersey painter, also known as Keith Urban, had registered the domain name www.keithurban.com, much to the chagrin of those who represented the far better known country-pop heartthrob. The bitterest pill, at least according to the suit that was filed in the US District Court in Nashville, was that Keith Urban of New Jersey had failed to mention on his site that he wasn't the Nashville-based musician of renown. The suit requested that the site be shut down, that the domain name be returned to its 'rightful' owner and that unspecified monetary damages be paid to the singer. At the time of writing, however, Urban is still using the domain www.keithurban.net.

But this lawsuit was no less ridiculous than an alleged outburst Urban made a few months earlier, prior to his admission to the Betty Ford Clinic. While playing a show in Minot, North Dakota, Urban allegedly asked all the Canadian members of his audience to leave the gig because of that country's refusal to support the American-led invasion of Iraq. There were no reports of disgruntled Canucks asking for refunds, nor was anyone sharp enough to record Urban's diatribe, if indeed it did happen. These were strange days, indeed. Unusual times lay ahead for Urban, too; later in the year, while on a Qantas flight between Sydney and Adelaide, a flight attendant quite innocently offered him a glass of wine. One of Urban's entourage snapped back: *'He doesn't drink.'* Qantas felt the need to issue a press release, stressing the point that the attendant 'genuinely did not realise who the passenger was'. It appeared that at least one person in Australia didn't read *New Idea*.

As Urban's public return picked up pace, certain conditions were attached to interviews with the star: there was to be no talk of rehab, his famous wife or country music ('Keith has moved on,' a publicist archly informed one journalist). But what he did reveal was the Kurbans' plans to spend more time in Australia, which must have disappointed the baristas and star-spotters of Nashville no end. Urban also dared to whisper the dreaded 'b' word (as in babies, not bourbon). 'I'm really looking forward to fatherhood,' he freely admitted. Soon after, he and Kidman put their Nashville home on the market, seemingly backing up his comments about a gradual relocation to

Australia, although they then bought a larger Nashville estate as well as a home in Los Angeles. In 2008, they bought a sizeable spread in NSW's Southern Highlands.

Meanwhile, Capitol prepared a best-of set, clumsily entitled *Keith Urban's Greatest Hits: 18 Kids*. This confirmed two things: *Love, Pain & the Whole Crazy Thing* didn't have the commercial oomph of its predecessors; and Urban had reached the end of his existing deal with Capitol. A greatest hits record (and, just as often, a live album) are sure-fire indicators that an artist is in some haste to deliver their contractually agreed number of LPs, and is keen either to stitch up a handsome new arrangement or shop around for another recording home.

By mid 2008, there was no definite word on either, not that Urban was in such a great position to negotiate. The previous year had been a dud 12 months for country music – record sales had slipped from 75 to 63 million units in the States during 2007, even though seven country stars, including Urban, were among the Top 10 most played acts at radio. It appeared that Nashville was entering another of its periodic downturns, which might explain Urban's gradual move away from the genre. His feisty jamming of 'Funky Tonight' with be-dreaded urban hippie John Butler, at the 2007 ARIAs, surprised those who'd written Urban off as a true cowboy, while a high-profile billing at the 2008 East Coast Bluesfest was another statement of intent: Keith Urban was tiring of twang. With his movie production deal still lingering in the background, he seemed to be setting himself up to explore quite different creative outlets.

Many of those who know Urban well are hoping that he'll use his status to push the creative boundaries a little more; frankly, he has enough fans that'll stick with him to do whatever he wants. And no one I spoke with seemed excited by the idea of Urban doing more of the same. 'I'd love for

Keith to do something instrumentally with me, that'd be great,' said Tommy Emmanuel. 'There's a piece of mine called "The Shaker" which I recorded with my brother [guitarist Phil] many years ago. We could really get around that.' 'I'd love to hear him think about that Glen Campbell side of what he's capable of,' said Radney Foster.

> He rocks so hard, and that's really cool, but I'd love to hear him really break something down and do something in the style of the Dixie Chicks' 'Home'. I think the world is the man's oyster; he can do what the hell he wants. I think he tells Capitol what he wants to do now.

According to Rob Potts, Urban would be keen to tap into his rockier past.

> Keith would say that he wants to get closer to where The Ranch was. You can never go back, so that in its own way, to me, having known this guy for so long, is an indication that he's seeking out somewhere new and different: *how can I grow?* His creativity is being squashed out of him; back there was where he was feeling true to himself as an artist.

'I'd love to see him play with Mark Knopfler and Levon Helm,' said Bob Saporiti. 'If The Band was still around he'd be great with them.' It remains unclear, of course, whether Urban is willing to take that jump into the creative unknown, especially while a million or so cashed-up Americans hope he'll keep churning out more listener-friendly 'saddle-pop'.

Biggest news of all, of course, was an announcement in early January 2008: the Kurbans were expecting. Little Hank or Evie was due in July. Rumours had been doing the rounds for a few months – both had spoken openly and hopefully of having children – even though Kidman's pregnancy was barely noticeable; she had more of a baby lump than a bump, even six months or more into her term. Still, it's unlikely that so many lenses have been directed at one part of a star's anatomy since the halcyon days of Jennifer Lopez's billion-dollar booty. When Urban and Kidman fronted for a day of tennis-watching at the 2008 Australian Open, the TV cameras spent more time monitoring their movements than the on-court action. Compare-and-contrast shots of Kidman's stomach, taken days apart, became a common sight in even the more credible dailies, as Australia's latest royal couple prepared themselves for parenthood. Water cooler discussions focused, somewhat cruelly, on the big question: 'Is she really pregnant?' It seemed hard for people to swallow that someone who appeared as icy – *and Hollywood-thin* – as Kidman could actually conceive a child. And if so, would the kid be born with stubble?

On 5 July 2008, while standing on stage at Nashville's LP Field, sharing yet another bill with his big-hatted pal Kenny Chesney, Keith Urban couldn't resist himself. 'This song,' he announced, 'is for my very, very, very, very, *very* pregnant wife.' Then he and the band eased into 'Better Half', as the full house of 50,000 yelled with knowing delight. Backstage, a fit-to-burst Kidman smiled along, cradling her not-inconsiderable baby bump. Before heading home after his 60-minute set, the couple climbed into a golf buggy, waving at fans and well-wishers before disappearing into a waiting limo. A few days earlier, Kidman's mother, Janelle, had arrived in Music City, getting ready for the birth of her latest grandchild. Kidman's sister, Antonia, herself a mother of four, travelled with her mother. All was in place.

Although they were spotted in a Borders bookstore the next afternoon stocking up on glossies, this was the Kurbans' last public appearance before the appearance of Sunday Rose Kidman Urban, who was born in Nashville on 7 July, weighing in at just a notch under three kilos. (The inclusion of the

Kidman surname, apparently, was an attempt to ensure that the family name continues, just in case there were to be no male offspring.) Their firstborn emerged on a Monday, so the child's name had nothing to do with the timing of her birth. Instead, it was a nod to Kidman's faith, Sunday being the holiest of all days for Catholics, as well as a tribute to Sunday Reed, the muse of Australian artist Sidney Nolan. Her middle name was chosen in honour of Urban's late grandmother Rose. To ease her through the birth, Kidman chose a soundtrack that consisted primarily of Urban songs and the easy listening of Sir James Galway, the sexagenarian flautist and the stubbly cowboy making for the most unlikely of mix tapes.

'We want to thank everybody that has kept us in their thoughts and prayers,' reported Urban, who was by Kidman's side during the birth, on his website. 'We feel very blessed and grateful that we can share this joy with you.' Soon after, Kidman revealed that their daughter bore a strong resemblance to Urban, which he shyly played down. 'She's a bit of a mix, I reckon. She's just awesome; we're just stoked.' Kidman, however, did admit that the little hair their daughter had showed a 'reddish tinge'. She was a hungry child, feeding every three hours, as Kidman reported to a Sydney radio station soon after her daughter's birth.

Not too long before the birth, the Kurbans had added a sizeable hacienda in LA's Brentwood, just a few blocks from Kidman's gal pal Naomi Watts, to their ever-expanding real estate holdings. But it seemed likely that the couple would spend most of their early days with baby Sunday Rose at their seven-bedroom Nashville base, alternating between there and their recently acquired estate in the NSW Southern Highlands, near Sutton Forest.

Father Paul Coleman, who united the pair back in 2006, was given the nod to baptise the child as soon as the newborn was deemed OK to travel to Sydney. But to the parents' eternal credit, they resisted the temptation to flog baby snaps to the highest tabloid bidder, even though it was estimated that the pics could easily pull $5 million. Urban confirmed this when he and Kidman put in an unexpected call to Sydney morning radio duo Kyle and Jackie O, during August 2008. He also asked for just a little respect from the local media while they were introducing their daughter to their second home, Sydney. 'I get the media interest,' an upbeat Urban said, 'but at the same time it's our little girl. Any parent would understand that they don't want someone getting up in their baby's face.' Kidman backed this up when she spoke: 'Keith and I are appealing to the press and stuff to give us a little space, so we can show her our town.'

In typical Urban fashion, he was back on the road by 19 July, within two weeks of Sunday Rose's birth, playing in Philadelphia, with shows booked right through to the middle of September 2008. He also showed up on Brad Paisley's instrumental album, *Play*, released in early September, picking a tune called 'Start a Band'. This was followed by a new Urban single called 'Sweet Thing' in early November and then, a few weeks later, a live DVD called – surprisingly enough – *Love, Pain and the Whole Crazy World Tour*. The single hinted strongly that Urban wasn't straying from the formula – it was co-written by Monty Powell and co-produced, once again, by Dann Huff. Kidman, too, returned to work, shooting the musical *Nine*, alongside hip-hopper Fergie and fellow Oscar-winner Daniel Day-Lewis.

While it's impossible to predict what lasting changes baby Sunday Rose would bring to Keith Urban's life, there was one thing that was undeniable. As long as there were punters keen to part with their hard-earned to see him perform, Urban would be out there, smiling, pleasing the masses, doing the one thing that came naturally to him: playing music.

DISCOGRAPHY

Keith Urban
EMI, 1991
Only You / Got It Bad / Without You / Arms of Mary / Yesterday / Don't Go / Hold on to Your Dreams / Lovin' on the Side / Future Plans / Love We Got Goin' / Clutterbilly / The River / What Love Is That Way / I Never Work on a Sunday

The Ranch
WEA, 1997
Walkin' in the Country / Homespun Love / Just Some Love / Some Days You Gotta Dance / My Last Name / Desiree / Freedom's Finally Mine / Hank Don't Fail Me Now / Tangled Up in Love / Clutterbilly / Man of the House / Ghost in This Guitar

keith urban
Capitol, October 1999
It's a Love Thing / Where the Blacktop Ends / But for the Grace of God / Your Everything / I Wanna Be Your Man (Forever) / A Little Luck of Our Own / You're the Only One

/ If You Wanna Stay / Don't Shut Me Out / Out on My Own
/ Rollercoaster / I Thought You Knew

Golden Road
Capitol, October 2002
Somebody Like You / Who Wouldn't Wanna Be Me /
Whenever I Run / What About Me / You'll Think of Me /
Jeans On / You Look Good in My Shirt / You're Not Alone
Tonight / You Won / Song for Dad / Raining on Sunday /
You're Not My God

Be Here
Capitol, October 2004
Days Go By / Better Life / Making Memories of Us / God's
Been Good to Me / The Hard Way / You're My Better Half
/ Could Fly / Tonight I Wanna Cry / She's Gotta Be /
Nobody Drinks Alone / Country Comfort / Live to Love
Another Day / These Are the Days

Livin' Right Now (DVD)
Capitol, 2005
These Are the Days / Days Go By / Better Life / Raining on
Sunday / You Won / You're My Better Half / Where the
Blacktop Ends / But for the Grace of God / The Hard Way
/ Making Memories of Us / Jeans On / You'll Think of Me
/ She's Gotta Be / You Look Good in My Shirt / Free Fallin'
/ Somebody Like You / Tonight I Wanna Cry / Who Wouldn't
Wanna Be Me / These Are the Days

Love, Pain & the Whole Crazy Thing
Capitol, November 2006
Once in a Lifetime / Shine / I Told You So / I Can't Stop
Loving You / Won't Let You Down / Faster Car / Stupid Boy

/ Used to the Pain / Raise the Barn / God Made Woman /
Tu Compañia / Everybody / Got It Right This Time

Greatest Hits: 18 Kids
Capitol, November 2007
Romeo's Tune / Got It Right This Time / I Told You So /
Stupid Boy / Better Life / Making Memories of Us / Once
in a Lifetime / Tonight I Wanna Cry / You're My Better Half
/ Days Go By / But for the Grace of God / You'll Think of
Me / Who Wouldn't Wanna Be Me / Raining on Sunday /
Where the Blacktop Ends / Your Everything / Somebody Like
You / Everybody

Keith Urban also appears on the following albums:
1991
INXS, *Live Baby Live*
Anne Kirkpatrick, *Hand It Down*

1992
Cameron Daddo, *A Long Goodbye*

1996
Paul Jefferson, *Paul Jefferson*

1998
Garth Brooks, *Double Live*
Fiddle Fire: 25 Years of the Charlie Daniels Band
John Mohead, *Mary's Porch*
Various Artists, *Not So Dusty*
Tim Wilson, *Gettin' My Mind Right*

1999
Dixie Chicks, *Fly*
Charlie Daniels Band, *Tailgate Party*

2000
Sons of the Desert, *Change*

2002
Olivia Newton-John, *2*

2003
Glen Campbell, *Legacy 1961–2002*
Neal McCoy, *Luckiest Man in the World*

2004
Carolyn Dawn Johnson, *Dress Rehearsal*
Katrina Elam, *Katrina Elam*
Richard Marx, *My Own Best Enemy*

2005
Olivia Newton-John, *Doubleplays*
LeAnn Rimes, *This Woman*

2007
Cledus T. Judd, *Boogity, Boogity: A Tribute to the Comedic Genius of Ray Stevens*
John Anderson, *Easy Money*
Trisha Yearwood, *Heaven, Heartache and the Power of Love*
Various Artists, *Kneel at the Cross*
Martina McBride, *Waking Up Laughing*

2008
Rhonda Vincent, *Good Thing Going*

Note: For a complete list see www.allmusic.com

Studio albums

Year	Album	Chart Positions								Certifications	
		US Country	US	CAN Country	CAN	AUS Country	AUS	UK	World	US	CAN
1991	*Keith Urban*										
1999	*keith urban*	17	145	27							
2002	*Golden Road*★	2	11				29			3× Multi-Platinum	2× Platinum
2004	*Be Here*^	1	3			3	11		8	4× Multi-Platinum	2× Platinum
2006	*Love, Pain & the Whole Crazy Thing*+	1	3	1	2	1	5	73	2	2×Multi-Platinum	Platinum

★ 3× platinum USA   ^ 4× platinum USA   + 2× platinum USA

Compilation albums

Year	Album	Chart Positions								Certifications	
		US Country	US	CAN Country	CAN	AUS Country	AUS	UK	World	US	CAN
2007	*Greatest Hits: 18 Kids*	4	11	2	10	2	7		13	Gold	Gold

Singles

Year	Album	Chart Positions									Album
		US Country	US Hot 100	US Pop 100	US Digital	US AC	CAN Country	CAN Hot 100	AUS Country	AUS	
1990	'Only You'								1		*Keith Urban*
	'I Never Work on a Sunday'								1		
1991	'Arms of Mary'								1		
	'The River' **(All Oz No 1s)**								1		

Year	Single								Album
1999	'It's a Love Thing'	18	105				25		*keith urban*
2000	'Your Everything'	4	51				22		
2001	'But for the Grace of God'	1	37						
	'Where the Blacktop Ends'	3	35						
2002	'Somebody Like You'	1	23						*Golden Road*
2003	'Raining on Sunday'	3	38						
	'Who Wouldn't Wanna Be Me'	1	30						
2004	'You'll Think of Me'	1	24	41	48	2			
	'Days Go By'	1	31				1		*Be Here*
2005	'You're My Better Half'	2	33				2	34	
	'Making Memories of Us'	1	34	60	47	5	1		
	'Better Life'	1	44	92			1		

(continues)

Year	Album	Chart Positions									Album
		US Country	US Hot 100	US Pop 100	US Digital	US AC	CAN Country	CAN Hot 100	AUS Country	AUS	
	'Tonight I Wanna Cry'	2	36	49	36		2				
2006	'Once in a Lifetime'	6	31	48	33	26	1			18	*Love, Pain & the Whole Crazy Thing*
2007	'Stupid Boy'	3	43	60	51		1				
	'I Told You So'	2	48	81			1	56			
	'Everybody'	5	64				2	71			
2008	'You Look Good in My Shirt'	6	53		67		4	54			*Greatest Hits: 18 Kids*

NOTES

Chapter One: The Lost H

1: Cooper, Peter, 'Rosanne Cash shares her pain', *The Tennessean*, 16 April 2006.

2, 13, 33: Toombs, Mikel, 'Manchild in the Promised Land', *The San Diego Union-Tribune*, 8 December 2005.

3: Rodley, Aidan, 'I won't get an invite to Kidman wedding', *Waikato Times*, 5 May 2006.

4: Sams, Christine, 'ARIA award will add to Urban myth', *Sun-Herald*, 23 September 2001.

5: Tucker, Ken, 'Keith Urban keeps it real at radio', *Billboard Radio Monitor*, 10 February 2006.

6: Watson, Chad, 'Urban sprawl', *Newcastle Herald*, 28 October 2000.

7, 9, 16: Nicholson, Sarah, 'Urbane country', *Courier-Mail*, 11 September 2004.

8: McCabe, Kathy, 'Country's new king is no Urban myth', *Daily Telegraph*, 12 November 2004.

10: www.cmt.com Keith Urban biography.

11, 20, 23: McMahon, Bruce, 'Lone star', *Courier-Mail*, 15 October 2005.

12, 32: Torpy, Kathryn, 'Learning guitar never child's play for Urban', *Courier-Mail*, 26 October 2002.

14, 15: Taylor, Andrew, 'Country's troubadour', *Sun-Herald*, 27 January 2008.

17: Jameson, Julietta, 'Urban living', *Daily Telegraph*, 23 October 2003.

18, 19: Anon, *Capital News*, January 2006.

21: Overington, Caroline, 'Country battler who won the girl', *The Australian*, 24 June 2006.

22: Best, Sophie, 'Urbane cowboy', *Sunday Age*, 19 October 2003.

24, 25, 27, 28: Woods, Erika, 'When I was 10', *Sunday Life*, 9 September 2007.

26, 35, 37, 38, 39: Saurine, Angela, 'Urban affairs', *Daily Telegraph*, 20 May 2006.

29: McWhirter, Erin and Moran, Jonathon, 'Once wild Keith Urban sets sights on quieter life', AAP, 22 June 2006.

30: McLean, Sandra, 'Caboolture remembers its young musician', *Courier-Mail*, 17 June 2006.

31: Anon, *Capital News*, January 2006.

34: Anon, *Playgirl*, April 2001.

36: Anon, 'Star rises above an early failure', *Caboolture Shire Herald*, 14 February 2006 (plus excerpt from Urban's entry in Caboolture High School commemorative yearbook).

40: Sung, Ellen, 'Crossover crooner', *The News & Observer*, 17 February 2006.

Chapter Two: Sticky Carpets

1, 2: www.cmt.com, October 2004.

3, 4, 5: McMahon, Bruce, 'Lone star', *Courier-Mail*, 15 October 2005.

6: Stewart, Paul and McWhirter, Erin, 'Urban myth, ex-girlfriend doubts Urban will settle', *Sunday Times*, 25 June 2006.

7: www.cmt.com/artists/news/1563200/20070622/urban_ keith.jhtml, June 2007.

8: Lester, Libby, 'The young country', *Sunday Age*, 16 January 1994.

9: Toombs, Mikel, 'Manchild in the Promised Land', *The San Diego Union-Tribune*, 8 December 2005.

10, 11: Daley, Dan, *Nashville's Unwritten Rules*, The Overlook Press, 1998.

12: Anon, 'Sex symbol new images of the 90s', *Sun-Herald*, 28 January 1990.

13: Cooper, Peter, 'The resurrection of Keith Urban', *The Tennessean*, 15 May 2005.

Chapter Three: Saddle-pop

1: Kent, Simon, 'Going country', *Sun-Herald*, 20 January 1991.

2: Elder, Bruce, 'Urban tops the country in Nashville', *Sydney Morning Herald*, 2 October 2000.

Chapter Four: Global Peace Through Country Music

1, 2, 19, 20a, 21, 21a: CMT *Loaded*.

3: Nick Erby, *Capital News*, January 2006.

4, 5: Cooper, Peter, 'The resurrection of Keith Urban', *The Tennessean*, 15 May 2005.

6: Elder, Bruce, 'Just the twang', *Sydney Morning Herald*, 27 May 1993.

7: Scott, Paul, 'Nicole and the crack addict cowboy', *Daily Mail*, 26 November 2005.

8: Rollings, Grant, 'Don't marry Keith . . . It will not last long', *The Sun*, 27 December 2005.

9, 10, 11: Anon, *Playgirl*, April 2001.

12: Waddell, Ray, 'Country touring rebuilds in 2002', *Billboard*, 6 April 2002.

12a: Jarvis, Susan, 'Keith's far from your average Urban artist', *Sun-Herald*, 8 October 1995.

13, 14: Rodman, Sarah, 'Urban update: Life is good', *Boston Herald*, 18 July 2003.

15: Quill, Greg, 'A bit of Outback country', *Toronto Star*, 27 September 2004.

16: McCabe, Kathy, 'Singing praises of a true Mr Nice Guy', *Daily Telegraph*, 22 June 2006.

17, 23: Stooksbury Guier, Cindy, 'Meet country's new talent', *Amusement Business*, 29 September 1997.

18: Lomax, John, 'Another country', *The Australian*, 11 January 1997.

20: Rocca, Jane, 'An Urban charm', *Townsville Bulletin*, 24 September 2004.

22: Capitol Nashville, The Ranch Interview Disc, 1997.

Chapter Five: Friends in Low Places

1: Feiler, Bruce, *Dreaming Out Loud*, Avon Books, Inc, 1998.

2: WEA press release, 8 May 1998.

3, 9: Rollings, Grant, 'Don't marry Keith . . . It will not last long', *The Sun*, 27 December 2005.

4: Goos, Aileen, 'Keith Urban discovers there is no escape from suffering', *Winnipeg Free Press*, 15 April 2000.

5: Best, Sophie, 'Urbane cowboy on the golden road', *Sunday Age*, 19 October 2003.

6: Anon, 'Womack, Paisley top CMA nominees tonight', Associated Press, 16 November 2005.

7: McCabe, Kathy, 'Aussie set to wow Nashville', *Sunday Telegraph*, 22 August 1999.

8: Smith, Michael, 'Fresh out of the Ranch', *Drum Media*, 24 August 1999.

10: Kent, Simon, 'Going country', *Sun-Herald*, 20 January 1991.

11: Lalor, Peter, 'Creating the Urban legend', *Daily Telegraph*, 29 August 1999.

12: Yorke, Ritchie, 'Creating the Urban legend', *Sunday Mail*, 10 December 2000.

13: Graff, Gary, 'With awards and success, Urban's having the time of his life', *The Plain Dealer*, 28 October 2005.

14, 21: Jansen, Ara, 'Australian Urban legend', *The West Australian*, 7 January 2000.

15, 17: Thomas, Sarah, 'Exploding another Urban myth', *Adelaide Advertiser*, 30 December 1999.

16: Apter, Jeff, 'Keith Urban album review', *Rolling Stone*, December 1999.

18, 19, 20: Anon, *Playgirl*, April 2001.

22: Netherland, Tom, 'Urban development singer on the rise to superstardom', *The Richmond Times-Dispatch*, 17 November 2005.

23, 26: WEA press release, 17 November 1998.

24: Cooper, Peter, 'The resurrection of Keith Urban', *The Tennessean*, 15 May 2005.

25, 26a: Hitts, Roger, 'Angry rocker: I'm the real Chris Gaines', *The Star*, 16 November 1999.

27: Capazzoli Jr, Michael A., 'Keith Urban on Chris Gaines', *Entertainment News Wire*, 29 October 1999.

28: Burch, Cathalena E., 'Urban renewal yields a hot country career in US', *Arizona Daily Star*, 28 April 2000.

29: Dawson, David, 'Our Urban success story', *Sunday Advertiser*, 7 January 2001.

30: Capitol Records press release, August 1999.

31: Price, Deborah Evans, 'Aussie Keith Urban debuts on Capitol', *Billboard*, 25 September 1999.

Chapter Six: Toeing the Line

1: Capitol Records, press release *keith urban* album, October 1999.

2: www.cmt.com, 2 March 2004.

3: McCabe, Kathy, 'Success in US charts country music career', *Sunday Telegraph*, 22 October 2000.

4: Elder, Bruce, 'Urban tops the country in Nashville', *Sydney Morning Herald*, 2 October 2000.

5: Watson, Chad, 'Urban sprawl', *Newcastle Herald*, 28 October 2000.

6: Yorke, Ritchie, 'Creating the Urban legend', *Sunday Mail*, 10 December 2000.

7: Feiler, Bruce, *Dreaming Out Loud*, Avon Books, Inc, 1998.

8: www.cmt.com, 14 November 2005.

9: Anon, *Playgirl*, April 2001.

10: www.cmt.com, 13 July 2001.

11: Mansfield, Stephanie, 'Up from Down Under', *USA Weekend*, 4 November 2001.

12, 13: Stewart, Paul and McWhirter, Erin, 'Urban myth: ex-girlfriend doubts Urban will settle', *Sunday Times*, 25 June 2006.

14: Hornery, Andrew, 'PS – Private Sydney', *Sydney Morning Herald*, 17 June 2006.

15: Aly, Chuck, *Music Row*, 1 October 2002.

16: www.cmt.com, 29 May 2002.

17: Carlton, William, 'Down Under Wonder', *Columbus Republic*, 19 September 2002.

18: http://saltyt.antville.org, 11 April 2002.

19: Capitol Records press release, December 2001.

Chapter Seven: The Gold-plated Road

1, 2, 3, 4: www.cmt.com, 31 January and 8 April 2003.

5: www.cmt.com, 29 August 2002.

6, 8: Couric, Katie, 'Country star Keith Urban discusses his career and performs', *NBC News Today*, 14 April 2005 (transcript).

7: www.cmt.com, 8 April 2003.

9: Nankervis, David, 'Country's perfect match', *Sunday Mail*, 24 August 2003.

10, 11, 20: Jameson, Julietta, 'Urban living', *Daily Telegraph*, 23 October 2003.

12: www.cmt.com, 8 December 2003.

13: Best, Sophie, 'Urbane cowboy on the golden road', *Sunday Age*, 19 October 2003.

14: Edward Morris, www.cmt.com, 5 January 2004.

15: Tolle, Eckhart, *The Power of Now: A Guide to Spiritual Enlightenment*, New World Library, September 2004.

16, 17, 18, 19, 21: Capitol Records *Be Here* press release track-by-track, October 2004.

22: Capitol Records *Be Here* album liner notes.

Chapter Eight: The Kurbans

1, 5: Scott, Paul, 'Nicole and the crack addict cowboy', *Daily Mail*, 26 November 2005.

2, 9: Taraborrelli, J. Randy, 'Keith Urban's fall from grace', *Australian Women's Weekly*, 18 December 2006.

3, 12: Rockingham, Graham, 'Keith's about more than Nicole', *The Hamilton Spectator*, 7 November 2005.

4: Netherland, Tom, 'Urban development', *The Richmond Times-Dispatch*, 17 November 2005.

6: www.cmt.com Keith Urban biography.

7: Stewart, Paul and McWhirter, Erin, 'Urban myth', *Sunday Times*, 25 June 2006.

8: Grant, Sarah and Cummings, Larissa, 'Tragic Nicole pledges to stand by her man', *Hobart Mercury*, 23 October 2006.

10: Graham, Caroline, 'How Nicole's new husband cheated on her with the girl from the Tin Roof Bar', *The Mail on Sunday*, 24 December 2006.

11: Shedden, Iain, 'Demons bottled up', *The Australian*, 22 March 2007.

INDEX

ABOUT THE AUTHOR

In a writing career spanning more than 20 years, Jeff Apter has written eight commercially and critically acclaimed biographies, and has contributed to *Rolling Stone* (where he spent five years as Music Editor), *The Sydney Morning Herald*, *Vogue*, *GQ*, *The Bulletin*, *Australian Hi-Fi* and the renowned Rock's Backpages website.

His first book was the 2003 Silverchair biography *Tomorrow Never Knows*, which was given a four-star review by *Rolling Stone*, who described it as 'a riveting rockography'. It was later updated and released by Random House Australia as *A New Tomorrow*. The bestselling Fornication: *The Red Hot Chili Peppers Story* followed in July 2004, while *Never Enough: The Story of the Cure* was published in 2005, a book *Spin* described as 'a wry portrait whose edge is as sharp as any Charles Addams cartoon.' Both books have since been published in German, Italian, French and numerous other languages. *The Dave Grohl Story* appeared in 2006, followed by *A Simple Kind of Life: Gwen Stefani & No Doubt* in 2007 (Omnibus Press). *A Pure Drop: The Jeff Buckley Story* was released in September 2008. Jeff co-wrote the 2005 sporting bestseller, *Slats: The Michael Slater Story* (Random House Australia) and 2008's *In Harm's Way*.

Jeff's views on popular culture have been aired on numerous TV and radio programs, while he contributed to SBS's Great Australian Album series and has also worked on DVDs for leading Australian bands Silverchair, You Am I and Powderfinger.

Jeff lives on the New South Wales south coast with his wife, Diana; his children, Elizabeth Asha and Christian Jai; and a wall-to-wall collection of books and records. He is represented throughout the world by the literary agency Curtis Brown.

www.jeffapter.com.au

Gift
MAR 1 7 2015